Pragmatism and Realism

D1224693

Studies in Epistemology and Cognitive Theory
General Editor: *Paul K. Moser, Loyola University of Chicago*

A Useful Inheritance: Evolutionary Aspects of the Theory of Knowledge
    by Nicholas Rescher, University of Pittsburgh
*Practical Reasoning: Goal-Driven, Knowledge-Based, Action-Guiding
    Argumentation*
    by Douglas N. Walton, University of Winnipeg
Epistemology's Paradox: Is a Theory of Knowledge Possible?
    by Stephen Cade Hetherington, University of New South Wales
*The Intellectual Virtues and the Life of the Mind: On the Place of the Virtues in
    Contemporary Epistemology*
    by Jonathan L. Kvanvig, Texas A & M University
Blind Realism: An Essay on Human Knowledge and Natural Science
    by Robert Almeder, Georgia State University
Epistemic Virtue and Doxastic Responsibility
    by James A. Montmarquet, Tennessee State University
Rationality, Morality, and Self-Interest: Essays Honoring Mark Carl Overvold
    edited by John Heil, Davidson College
Metaepistemology and Skepticism
    by Richard Fumerton, University of Iowa
*Warrant in Contemporary Epistemology: Essays in Honor of Plantinga's
    Theory of Knowledge*
    edited by Jonathan L. Kvanvig, Texas A & M University
A Defense of the Given
    by Evan Fales, University of Iowa
Pragmatism and Realism
    by Frederick L. Will; edited by Kenneth R. Westphal, University of New
    Hampshire

Pragmatism and Realism

FREDERICK L. WILL

Edited by
Kenneth R. Westphal

With a Foreword by
Alasdair MacIntyre

ROWMAN & LITTLEFIELD PUBLISHERS, INC.
Lanham • Boulder • New York • London

ROWMAN & LITTLEFIELD PUBLISHERS, INC.

Published in the United States of America
by Rowman & Littlefield Publishers, Inc.
4720 Boston Way, Lanham, Maryland 20706

3 Henrietta Street
London WC2E 8LU, England

British Cataloging in Publication Information Available

Library of Congress Cataloging-in-Publication Data

Will, Frederick L.
    Pragmatism & realism / Frederick L. Will ; edited by Kenneth R. Westphal ; with a
foreword by Alasdair MacIntyre.
        p. cm. — (Studies in epistemology and cognitive theory)
    Includes bibliographical references and index.
    ISBN 0–8476–8349–4 (cloth : alk. paper). — ISBN 0–8476–8350–8 (pbk. : alk.
paper)
    1. Knowledge, Theory of. 2. Pragmatism. 3. Realism. 4. Truth. I. Westphal,
Kenneth R.   II. Title. III. Series.
B945.W553P73   1997
191—dc20   96–32048
                                                                       CIP

ISBN 0–8476–8349–4 (cloth : alk. paper)
ISBN 0–8476–8350–8 (pbk. : alk. paper)

Printed in the United States of America

♾ ™ The paper used in this publication meets the minimum requirements of American
National Standard for Information Sciences—Permanence of Paper for Printed Library
Materials, ANSI Z39.48–1984.

To my family,
Louise Hendrickson Will
Katherine Will Jorgensen
George Frederick Will

CONTENTS

Foreword, *Alasdair MacIntyre*   ix

Editor's Introduction   xiii

Sources and Acknowledgments   lxiii

1. Thoughts and Things   1

2. Truth and Correspondence   21

3. The Concern About Truth   39

4. The Rational Governance of Practice   63

5. Reason, Social Practice, and Scientific Realism   85

6. Reason and Tradition   105

7. Rules and Subsumption: Mutative Aspects of Logical Processes   121

8. Pragmatic Rationality   137

9. Philosophic Governance of Norms   159

Bibliography   193

Index   200

About the Author   207

Foreword

This is a time when the sheer quantity of philosophical production makes it more likely than ever before that even work of the highest quality and of lasting significance will not receive the degree and kind of attention that it deserves. It is therefore all the more necessary to try to remedy this by insistently and persistently drawing attention to such work. That is why I am privileged to write this foreword to the later essays of Frederick L. Will, a philosopher whose books and articles taken together constitute one of the more remarkable achievements of twentieth-century North American philosophy. I say "taken together," because although all his articles and books are each of them by themselves philosophically of a very high order, the whole is in fact greater than the parts. For that reason we are all deeply indebted to Kenneth R. Westphal for collecting these later essays and so making it easier to understand just how much it is that Will has achieved.

Will's progress from his articles in the 1940s through his first but never published book, completed in 1964, his second, but first published book, *Induction and Justification*, which appeared in 1974, the essays between 1969 and 1985 which are reprinted in this book, his third, but second published book of 1988, *Beyond Deduction*, and finally his essay on "Philosophic Governance of Norms," also reprinted here, is emblematic of the progress of American philosophy in the same period. And it is progress! Those who are skeptical about whether real progress is ever achieved in philosophy could do no better than to make their way carefully through Will's writings in chronological order. Those who do so will find themselves moving through three stages, at the second and third of which explanations become available of the inadequacies and limitations of their predecessors.

All philosophers since Socrates have had to begin from the theses affirmed and the problems debated among those from whom they first learned their trade. Will was no exception. He began as an analytical philosopher, distinguishing different uses of language with the aim of showing that certain traditional philosophical problems need no longer trouble us, once we have understood how to make the relevant linguistic distinctions. The enemies were two: the philosophical skeptic who poses these false problems and the philosopher who thinks that the skeptic needs to be answered. So in "Is there a Problem of Induction?" (*Journal of Philosophy*, 1942) it is two senses of "know" that are to be distinguished: "All the uneasiness, the pseudo-skepticism and the pseudo-problem of induction, would never appear if it were possible to keep clear that 'know' in the statement that we do not know statements about the future is employed in a very special sense, not at all its ordinary one." And in "Will the Future be like the Past?" (*Mind*, 1947) it is asserted that two senses of "future" can be distinguished, one in which what is now future will in time become first present and then past and one in which what is future can never become present or past. The skeptical argument that past experience affords no grounds for conclusions about future occurrences is plausible only when "future" is used in the second sense, but has no implications for the validity of inductive inferences which are concerned with the future only in the first sense of "future."

Will's dissatisfaction with this mode of argument was the result of his developing those arguments into a book-length manuscript and then recognizing, when he confronted them fully spelled out, that he had in a way missed the point. His conclusions carried weight, if and only if the standards and forms of rational justification employed or presupposed by those philosophers whose accounts of inference had generated the Humean problem of induction were not in fact rationally defensible. But *this* his earlier arguments had done little or nothing to show. Will therefore left unpublished the manuscript which he had completed in 1964, an act of philosophical integrity of a kind all too rare.

Will then proceeded to set himself the tasks of expounding and putting to the question the relevant standards and forms of justification in what he called "An Investigation of Cartesian Procedure in the Philosophy of Knowledge," the subtitle of *Induction and Justification*. If the rest of us had only paid sufficient attention to this book, it would have rendered a good deal of more recent anti-Cartesian writing unnecessary. Indeed it would have guided us towards a more constructive and fruitful rejection of Cartesianism than most of those which have become fashionable. Like almost all other anti-Cartesians, Will rejected the notion that the justification of statements or arguments is a matter of grounding them on "first cognitions." And like some other recent anti-Cartesians, Will recognized that the rules which are to provide the justification of statements asserted and inferences drawn within our practice are not to be discovered beyond or outside that practice, but within it. But, unlike some of the most influential of those fellow anti-Cartesians, Will recognized that this confronted us with the task of radically reconceiving the nature both of the relevant type of rule and of the procedures of justification.

This task he had already begun to undertake in *Induction and Justification*, but it was only with the later papers and *Beyond Deduction* that the full interest of his inquiries became clear. The central contrast of *Beyond Deduction* is that between deductive processes and ampliative processes. Where deduction is concerned, a norm, specifiable in advance, is applied to particular cases with the aim of solving a puzzle, also specifiable in advance, by subsuming the particular under some universal rule. In ampliation the norm itself may be transformed through its applications to particular cases so as "in deriving results to mold and accredit the norms, and, of course, sometimes to discredit them" (p. 34). Moreover it may be only after the application of some norm—or, more likely, set of norms—has provided a solution to a problem, that the problem itself can be correctly characterized. Deductive aspects of procedures are embodied in the conscious and intentional activities of individuals. The ampliative aspects are social, embedded in practices, and they may sometimes be recognized as having been employed only after the event.

The philosophical interest of this contrast lies of course very largely in the detail in which it is developed by Will. It enabled him to put in perspective theses advanced by other critics of earlier views of scientific reasoning, such as Toulmin and Kuhn, integrating their insights into his own larger view, while avoiding the limitations of their work. One feature of Will's position is especially important. Those who have rejected Cartesian, Lockean, or Humean accounts of perception and knowledge—most famously Richard Rorty—have often supposed that they are thereby committed to a rejection of any version of the correspondence theory of truth. Will's position enables us to show why they are mistaken. Correspondence between our beliefs and what they are about is a goal that inquiry cannot discard: "there is something fundamentally sound and of absolutely first importance to philosophy in the intuitive idea of truth as a congruity to be sought, tested, or achieved" ("Truth and Correspondence," ¶40).

Both in his continuing allegiance to a conception of truth as correspondence and in his use of the notion of ampliation Will has been continuing, correcting, and extending the philosophical enterprise of the greatest of all

American philosophers, C. S. Peirce. He cites Peirce only occasionally and he certainly goes beyond Peirce—what he has made of the notion of ampliation is after all very much his own. And he draws on a wide range of philosophers, pragmatic and nonpragmatic—Dewey, James, and Wittgenstein are cited as often as Peirce—but yet I know of no contemporary philosophical writing which is more in the spirit of Peirce. And as with Peirce, Will's philosophizing is self-referential. His own practice of inquiry exemplifies the principles of inquiry about which he writes.

Reading through Will's writings from beginning to end reveals how much of his earlier work is taken up and put to new uses later on. Will has often presented himself as a critic of the limitations of his earlier writings. But because he is a constructive rather than a merely negative critic of himself as well as of others, his later thoughts often turn out to be more indebted to his earlier ones than perhaps he himself has always recognized. It is indeed, as we should expect from his own principles, only in the light afforded by his later positions that we are able to characterize adequately, let alone to evaluate, his earlier positions. So in yet another way it is philosophically rewarding to read his work as a whole. I have no doubt at all, that if philosophy is to prosper in the coming decades, it will have to treat with great seriousness that splendid body of philosophical writing of which the essays in this volume constitute one major part.

Alasdair MacIntyre

Notre Dame, Indiana
September 1994

Frederick L. Will's Pragmatic Realism: An Introduction

Juxtaposing "pragmatism" and "realism" may seem paradoxical. Both terms have developed protean meanings. "Realism" as here understood means simply that there is a way the world is, which is not generated by our cognition, and we can know much about the world. "Pragmatism" is a designation for a cluster of philosophical views which stress the centrality of our interactions with each other and with our environment, of our practices, for understanding human knowledge and value.[1] The root idea of the pragmatic attempt to avoid both the skepticism typically resulting from foundationalist epistemology and the relativism typically resulting from coherentism is nicely put by Sellars:

> *Above all*, the [foundationalist] picture is misleading because of its static character. One seems forced to choose between the picture of an elephant which rests on a tortoise (What supports the tortoise?) and the picture of a great Hegelian serpent of knowledge with its tail in its mouth (Where does it begin?). Neither will do. For empirical knowledge, like its sophisticated extension, science, is rational, not because it has a foundation but because it

---

[1] For a very useful brief survey of pragmatism, see Susan Haack's entry on it in *A Companion to Epistemology*, E. Sosa and J. Dancy, eds. (Oxford: Blackwell, 1992). For an excellent extended critical survey of the classical American Pragmatists (Peirce, James, Dewey, and Mead), see Arthur E. Murphy, "Pragmatism and the Context of Rationality," *Transactions of the Charles S. Peirce Society* 29, nos. 2–4 (1993): 123–78, 331–68, 687–722. (Anyone wishing glosses on terms used in this Introduction will find excellent entries in Sosa and Dancy.)

is a self-correcting enterprise which can put any claim in jeopardy, though not *all* at once.[1]

A wide variety of claims have been made recently to inherit the mantle of pragmatism.[2] Frederick Will's recent work represents one legitimate, important, and timely development of some basic pragmatist ideas, because (among much else) he shows how to combine a socially grounded theory of knowledge with realism, in the sense just specified. Will's recent work (the essays collected here appeared from 1969 to 1993) represents a significant departure from his earlier, more widely known work on the problem of induction. A brief look at Will's development provides useful background for the innovations developed in the present volume.

1. Reassessing Induction

Will is generally known for his widely anthologized articles which attempted to dissolve the problem of induction by ordinary language analysis.[3] Among specialists in induction he is also known for a substantial series of articles on various aspects of the problem of evidence, confirmation, and induction.[4] His first book, which was to solve the problem of induction, was awaited with high expectations. In 1974 he published a book titled *Induction and Justification* (Cornell University Press). The main title appeared to offer the promised solution. Instead, the book's subtitle, "An Investigation of Cartesian Procedure in the Philosophy of Knowledge," announced an extended critical assault on the very formulation of the problem of induction and on the foundationalist assumptions about knowledge which undergird that formulation. What had happened?

---

[1] Wilfrid Sellars, "Empiricism & the Philosophy of Mind," in *Science, Perception and Reality* (London: Routledge, 1963), 127–96, p. 170.

[2] For a critical review of the extent to which some of the more familiar recent forms of "pragmatism" descend from the classical American Pragmatists, see Susan Haack, "'We Pragmatists ...'; Peirce and Rorty in Conversation" (*Synthese*, 1996). Richard Rorty has admitted recently that his reading of Dewey is selective ("Just One More Species Doing its Best," *London Review of Books* 25 [July 1991: 3–7], pp. 5–6).

[3] In particular, "Is there a Problem of Induction?," *The Journal of Philosophy* 39, no. 19 (1942): 503–13, and "Will the Future be Like the Past?," *Mind* 56, no. 224 (1947): 332–47.

[4] A complete bibliography of Will's publications appears below, 193f.

Will had in fact completed the originally proposed manuscript, titled "The Problem of Induction," in 1964. His proposed solution relied on what he called "principles of factual reasoning." Like Ryle's "inference tickets," such principles formulate supposed factual relations among events or objects, such that the occurrence or observation of one would reliably warrant inferring the occurrence or observation of the other. In the manuscript Will contended that such principles are constantly generated, assessed, and revised in the course of our ordinary and specialized (technical or scientific) affairs, always in conjunction with other such principles. During final revisions he realized that his proposed solution was inadequate on two main counts. First, the inductive skeptic could grant those contentions while denying that they had anything to do with genuine, philosophically legitimate justification. Given the essentially Cartesian terms in which the problem of induction is formulated, the only admissible premises must not be justified on the basis of other "principles of factual reasoning," and they must be "analytic" or necessary truths, because the justification of synthetic principles is precisely what is challenged by Hume's problem.[1] Second, thinking about inferential reasoning in terms of "principles of factual reasoning" inherits the basic foundationalist model of knowledge as charting our inferential way from one basic experience to another.

Hume's problem of induction and its foundationalist presuppositions required instead radical critique and replacement. This involved going far beyond the point Will argued in 1959, that Hume's problem of induction is incoherent: it is incoherent because eliminating all unjustified synthetic principles from the solution to the problem also eliminates all "the considerations necessary for understanding what the inference is about, and thus for grasping not only the scope and significance but, therewith, the very meaning of the inductive conclusion that is supposed to be in question."[2] To take only one example, if one were to strip Newton's famous inductive generalization which ascribed mass and gravity to all planets of every "synthetic" proposition (*The Mathematical Principles of Natural Philosophy*, Rule 3), one would be bereft of any principles for understanding Newton's problem as part of an astronomi-

[1] Will discusses Goodman's "riddle" of induction in *Beyond Deduction* (London: Routledge, 1988), 117–18.

[2] "Justification and Induction," *Philosophical Review* 68, no. 3 (1959): 359–72, p. 371.

cal investigation of planetary motions relying on data collected with a variety of observational instruments.

Will's critique of foundationalism and the problems of induction which it generates was delivered in *Induction and Justification*. Part One of that book placed the problem of induction in the context of foundationalist models of knowledge. Part Two examined the main root of foundationalist models of justification, the regress argument, and argued that neither the alleged sensory foundations of human knowledge nor the various analytic, postulational, or inductive principles for justifying nonfoundational beliefs met the requirements of the skeptical model of knowledge underlying the regress argument.

Induction and Justification criticized a fairly strong form of foundationalism, one according to which basic beliefs or experiences are self-justifying. Weaker forms of foundationalism have proliferated recently, in part in order to avoid the kinds of objections Will raised. At the time, Will's critique of foundationalism was most sharply criticized by William Alston, who contended that "simple foundationalism," according to which basic beliefs or experiences need only *be* justified, was much more defensible than the stronger "iterative" foundationalism which requires self-justifying basic beliefs or experiences.[1] Alston was right that simple foundationalism avoids much of Will's critique. Will's response was that simple foundationalism eviscerates, rather than preserves, foundationalism, and it cannot do what a theory of justification needs to do. One thing it does not do is provide any insight into how we might justify our beliefs to one another. This is a major shortcoming, since foundationalist epistemologies originally had been developed to do precisely that; that is the challenge hyperbolically expressed by radical skepticism.[2] At the time, Alston claimed that "simple foundationalism" was worth refuting in order to be rid of foundationalism and to develop a different kind

---

[1] "Two Types of Foundationalism," *Journal of Philosophy* 72, no. 7 (1976): 163–85 and "Has Foundationalism Been Refuted?," *Philosophical Studies* 29 (1976): 287–305, rpt. in *Essays in Epistemic Justification* (Ithaca: Cornell University Press, 1989), 19–56.

[2] Alston is right that the contrast between first- and second-person perspectives is fundamental to the distinction between simply being justified and showing that one is justified in some belief. However, in those essays he treats it as some kind of inadvertent error or confusion that philosophers mistakenly concentrated on the more demanding issue of showing one's justification to another party (e.g., *Essays in Epistemic Justification*, 23, 28 note 12, 29, 32).

of epistemology, perhaps a kind of contextualism.[1] Very recently, Alston has taken a pragmatic turn with his "Doxastic Practice Approach to Epistemology."[2] There he admits he had hoped that something more objective could be found than this kind of contextualism.[3] After holding out such hopes so steadfastly, Alston's shift in a pragmatic direction is striking corroboration of Will's pragmatic turn twenty-five years earlier.[4]

2. Thoughts and Things

Although Part Three of *Induction and Justification* sketched some elements of an alternative, social account of human knowledge, the real substance of Will's pragmatic realist alternative to foundationalism was begun in his 1968 Presidential Address to the Western (now Central) Division of the American Philosophical Association. That address, titled "Thoughts and Things," is the first chapter in the present volume, and each of its successors steadily work out further elements of a pragmatic account of rationality and of the justification of cognitive and practical norms. I shall sketch some of the main issues and points in each of these chapters in order to highlight their great integrity as a unified set of analyses, and to relate Will's issues to some current discussions in order to show how timely his analyses remain.

To appreciate Will's analyses one must bear in mind the point of their general level of discussion. Analytic philosophy in particular has benefited greatly from maximizing the specificity and detail of philosophical inquiry. Focus on detail can, however, lead to recalcitrant difficulties if philosophers

---

[1] I was an undergraduate at Illinois at the time, and I clearly recall Alston's making this remark to me when I was a student in his undergraduate epistemology course. Alston's comment to me then accords with his opening and closing remarks in "Has Foundationalism Been Refuted?," *Essays in Epistemic Justification*, 39, 56. Similarly, my report just above of Will's general response to Alston's critique is from remarks Will made to me then.

[2] In *Knowledge and Skepticism*, M. Clay and K. Lehrer, eds. (Boulder: Westview, 1989), 1–29. He has extended his views in "Belief-forming Practices and the Social," in *Socializing Epistemology*, F. Schmitt, ed. (Lanham, Md.: Rowman & Littlefield, 1994), 29–51.

[3] "Doxastic Practice," 21. Also see the disappointment expressed about his objectivist hopes being dashed in his review of Frederick Dretske's *Knowledge and the Flow of Information*, *Philosophical Review* 92, no. 3 (1983): 452–54.

[4] For a detailed examination of Alston's views on these matters, see ch. 5 of my book, *Hegel's Epistemological Realism* (Dordrecht: Kluwer, 1989).

implicitly assume misleading or unwarranted models or ideas when formulating problems and their resolution. Will shows that this has happened in the interminable struggle between foundationalism and coherentism cum relativism, and that such assumptions have prevented most philosophers from recognizing that a pragmatic, social account of knowledge and justification is consistent with realism.

It is difficult to probe problems which underlie the apparently obvious assumptions philosophers make. Because these assumptions underlie many specific formulations of and proposed solutions to a given problem, it requires discussing the problem and its associated assumptions at a general level, a level which can capture the common tendencies among closely related but nevertheless distinct formulations. However, to address and resolve the perplexities caused by such assumptions requires formulating those general assumptions and their problems clearly and precisely. Will fulfills this dual demand admirably. However, appreciating the full character and significance of his analyses requires one, as Nietzsche said about his own works, "to read slowly, deeply, ... cautiously, [and] with doors left open."[1] We must, that is, be prepared to reflect on the character of our own philosophical assumptions and methods—and in particular on the history and current state of the philosophical debates which inform our assumptions and methods. This is where, I believe, analytically trained philosophers have had most difficulty appreciating Will's writings. The strong emphasis placed on detail and precision within analytic philosophy has not encouraged philosophical reflection. Indeed, this kind of reflection was precluded by Mill, who identified reflection with introspection. He thereby replaced broad reflection on one's philosophical position and method with a specific and restricted psychological method. Reflection has begun to wax again recently with the demise of confidence in various philosophical schools and programs.[2] Philosophical reflection has been much more central to the post-Kantian European philosophical traditions.[3] However, in those traditions it has often not been properly guided by careful attention to detail. To permute Kant's famous dictum once again: Reflection without

---

[1] F. Nietzsche, *Daybreak*, R. J. Hollingdale, tran. (Cambridge: Cambridge University Press, 1982), Preface §5.

[2] For an excellent discussion of the fate of reflection in Anglo-American philosophy, from classical positivism to its recent resurgence, see Robert Scharff, *Compte After Positivism* (Cambridge: Cambridge University Press, 1995).

[3] For discussion, see Herbert Schnädelbach, *Reflexion und Diskurs: Fragen einer Logik der Philosophie* (Frankfurt am Main: Suhrkamp, 1977).

detail is empty, detail without reflection is blind. Will is acutely aware of the need for both, and his philosophical reflections are the fruit of long involvement with the details of philosophical puzzles and proposals about induction and about knowledge and practical reason more generally, both in recent Analytic philosophy and in the history of philosophy.

The kind of reflection Will engages in bears brief comparison with Dewey's. In the first chapter of *Experience and Nature* Dewey comments on the apparently oxymoronic apposition of "experience" and "nature" in his title:

> I know no route by which dialectical arguments can answer such objections. They arise from associations with words and cannot be dealt with argumentatively. One can only hope in the course of the whole discussion to disclose the meanings which are attached to "experience" and "nature," and thus insensibly produce, if one is fortunate, a change in the significations previously attached to them.[1]

The attempt to alter the associated meanings of words is central to classical American Pragmatism, and it is an important source of Dewey's prolixity. Will focuses not on meanings, but on implicit assumptions, and he gets right to the point. However, the points to which he draws attention are very basic, very general ones. Consequently, one can miss his points if one takes seriously only the tightly argued, narrowly focused analysis of arguments that has become canonical in analytic philosophy. That kind of detailed focus is possible only on the basis of broader, usually implicit assumptions about the subject analyzed. Thus it is very important to consider the broader concerns Will addresses in order not to thwart in advance a detailed analysis by mak-

---

[1] *Experience and Nature* (2d ed., rpt. New York: Dover, 1958), 1a–2a. The supposed tension between "experience" and "nature" stems from regarding "experience" as something subjective, and "nature" as something objective, where never the twain shall meet. Dewey later thought that he should have titled his book "Nature and Culture" (see *Dewey and his Critics* S. Morgenbesser, ed. [New York: Journal of Philosophy, 1977], "Introduction," xxviii; and J. H. Randall, "John Dewey, 1859-1952" [ibid., 1–9], 6). However, the point of present concern is not this substantive issue, but rather what Dewey here reveals about his philosophical method and style. Dewey further states: "Selective emphasis, choice, is inevitable whenever reflection occurs. This is not an evil. Deception comes only when the presence and operation of choice is concealed, disguised, denied. ... The purport of thinking, scientific and philosophic, is not to eliminate choice but to render it less arbitrary and more significant" (*Experience and Nature*, 29–30).

ing misleading assumptions. For example, Will argues that philosophers have made misleadingly narrow assumptions about reason. While not aiming to change the "meaning" of the term, Will does seek to broaden our understanding of rationality. In my overview of Will's main issues I shall sketch the bearing of his analyses on a number of recent or current debates, in the hope of encouraging the reader to discern more such connections on his or her own.

One primary strategy of skeptics about empirical knowledge is to exploit a common distinction between how things actually are and how they appear to be, to contend that nothing among those appearances indicates that any particular appearance (or set thereof) is intrinsically more trustworthy than any others, and to generalize this point by contending that none of the appearances of an object can be known to be cognitively trustworthy.[1] The skeptical nightmare is that all of our thoughts and sensory experience could be exactly as they seem to us to be, even though none of the supposed objects of our thought or experience are as they seem to be, if they exist at all. This skeptical threat assumes that thought and sensory experience are or at least can be radically independent of their supposed objects. Skeptical qualms can indeed be raised about any particular thought or alleged experience. Kant was the first philosopher to recognize, however, that such piecemeal doubt cannot be extrapolated without further ado into wholesale skepticism. The main point of Kant's infamous "Refutation of Idealism" is that for human beings, inner experience in general is only possible through outer experience in general. If this is true, then the mere ability to pose the radical skeptical hypothesis suffices to refute that hypothesis.[2] Once this skeptical generalization is blocked, then we are entitled to rely on our common sense ways of distinguishing veridical from unreliable perceptions. Setting aside concerns about the soundness of Kant's idealism, the problem with Kant's argument that it relies on theses (theses about the conditions required to determine the apparent

---

[1] See, e.g., Sextus Empiricus, *Outlines of Pyrrhonism*, R. Bury, tran. (Cambridge, Ma.: Harvard University Press, 1933), I §210, II §§77–78; Descartes, *Meditations on First Philosophy*, in *Philosophical Writings of Descartes*, J. Cottingham, R. Stoothoff, and D. Murdoch, trans. (Cambridge: Cambridge University Press, 1985), Meditation 1 (AT 18); Kant, *Critique of Pure Reason*, N. K. Smith, tran. (New York: St. Martin's, 1929), A197/B242; Russell, *The Problems of Philosophy* (Oxford: Clarendon, 1912), 9–11.

[2] *Critique of Pure Reason*, B274–77.

order of our experiences) which have remained controversial, if not obscure, to the present day.

In "Thoughts and Things" (ch. 1) Will takes issue with the basically Cartesian notion that human thought and experience can or might be radically divorced from its putative objects. Will blocks the skeptical generalization, from occasional perceptual error to universal ignorance, with resources found in ordinary language analysis. Drawing on the notion of the "open texture" of concepts and such "bizarre fictions" as Austin's exploding goldfinch, Will shows how without the general and recognizable stability of the things around us, we would not be able to think or speak at all. Will's basic pragmatic point is that human thought is based in and depends on the structure and regularity of the environment, of the world itself in which we live.

This dependence of thought on things was touched on by Wittgenstein, Waismann, Austin, and before them by Leibniz. Wittgenstein touched on this dependence in connection with our not having complete rules for the use of empirical terms, Waismann in connection with the "open texture" of empirical concepts. All four of them consider it in connection with what Leibniz called "bizarre fictions": Wittgenstein's chair that disappears and reappears (or at least seems to); Waismann's friend who does the same, and his cat which grows gigantic or revives in circumstances where cats surely die; Austin's goldfinch which explodes, or quotes Virginia Woolf, or "does something outrageous"; Leibniz's angels or inhabitants of the moon who display rational thought, speech, and action like humans, but who have extraordinary powers or machines.[1] The most important point about these bizarre fictions is not simply that there are always borderline cases for applying empirical terms, or that we don't have fully explicit or explicable rules for using empirical terms. The fundamental point is touched on by Austin's negative remark that in such cases "we don't know what to say" because "words literally fail us," and by Leibniz's positive remark that "we are spared these perplexities by the nature of things." While these philosophers noticed these puzzling kinds of cases, and concluded that they show something important about human understanding, they did not develop their analyses beyond a criticism of verificationist or rule-following theories of meaning.

Will uses these examples to reconsider thought and its objects and to criticize both the broad Cartesian tradition and the conventionalism found in many recent theories of meaning or of knowledge, inspired if not directly

---

[1] References are provided in ch. 1.

espoused by logical empiricism, by the later Wittgenstein, or by Derrida. The foundationalist cum skeptical project of establishing the link between thoughts and things is gratuitous because were there no such link, as the examples of "bizarre fictions" show, we would be incapable of thinking. Skeptics and traditionalists (closet Cartesians all) may retort that Will begs the question by insisting that thought depends upon things, the stability and identifiability of which transcend our experience; they may retort that such alleged stability and identifiability cannot be assumed or demonstrated precisely because it transcends our experience.

This retort rests upon the very supposition that Will, in keeping with the pragmatic tradition, challenges, namely, that thought can be identified with those supposedly mental episodes which we can explicitly identify and describe. The point of the examples of "bizarre fictions" is to show that this identification is unwarranted. These examples concern not simply the extent of our evidence, but the fact that what "content" of thought we can explicitly formulate and identify by means of descriptions, classifications, and demonstratives, is only part of the content of our thought, and this explicit aspect of our thought is neither sui generis nor self-sufficient. The portion of our thought which we can explicitly articulate is always outstripped by the specificity, and sometimes by the unexpected characteristics or capacities, of the things we engage with by thinking about them and doing things with them. The most important point about "open texture" is that our thought occurs and proceeds only on the basis of and in conjunction with the relatively stable and identifiable things with which we interact and about which we think and speak.[1] Will puts his point this way:

> Thinking is an activity which we engage in not only in the world of things, but by means of things in this world, supported and sustained by them. And when these things fail us in certain ways, as they sometimes do, then, to extend Austin's pronouncement, words do literally fail us, because our thoughts fail us.[2]

---

[1] G. P. Baker and P. M. S. Hacker seriously underestimate the philosophical significance of the "open texture" of the meanings of ordinary descriptive terms. See *Wittgenstein: Understanding and Meaning* (Chicago: University of Chicago Press, 1980) vol. I, 433.

[2] "Thoughts and Things," below p. 14.

Our cognitive predicament is not one of establishing a link between our thoughts and their supposed objects, it is instead one of exploiting the links our thinking does and must have with things in order to discriminate the genuine characteristics of things. This may sound like a minor reformulation of the problem, but it is not. It blocks the skeptic's generalization and it provides a major philosophical reorientation, away from both Cartesian skepticism and conventionalism toward recognizing the natural conditions of the possibility of human thought and experience. Will develops this prospect throughout the subsequent chapters.[1]

3. Questions about Truth

"Truth and Correspondence" and "The Concern About Truth" (chs. 2 and 3) are closely related in their aim to preserve the good sense found in the idea of truth as correspondence, as expressed, for example, in Austin's classic paper "Truth," against the unfortunate influence of persuasive but ultimately inapt views on closely related matters.[2]

In "Truth and Correspondence" Will argues that the correspondence analysis of truth is independent of the issue of semantic atomism, and that

---

[1] Will thus argues for a qualified form of what later was dubbed an "externalist" account of the content of mental states, according to which the content of mental states depends in part on distinct, usually environmental, states of affairs. There remains intense debate between "internalist" and "externalists" about mental content. Will's analysis contributes to this debate both directly and indirectly, by reflecting on the context and motives of "internalism." In "Affinity, Idealism, and Naturalism: The Stability of Cinnabar and the Possibility of Experience," *Kant-Studien* (1997), I analyze the Humean and Kantian background to Will's insight.

Michael Williams proposes to respond to skepticism by shifting the burden onto the skeptic by revealing the skeptic's implicit theoretical assumptions (*Unnatural Doubts* [Oxford: Blackwell, 1992/Princeton: Princeton University Press, 1996], 31–32). Williams nevertheless agrees with skeptics that Descartes's Evil Deceiver and Putnam's brain in a vat "seem to show that I could have all the ... knowledge [of the apparent content of my experiences] I presently have even if I knew nothing whatever about the external world" (53; cf. 43). Will's reflections show that this "seeming" is a mere appearance and a major theoretical assumption, and a false one at that. Williams's contextualism is not the only way out of skeptical problems. Indeed, Will's point provides the "definitive refutation" of skepticism Williams thinks is impossible, and does so without recourse to high-flown theoretical arguments which lack the intuitive appeal of skeptical considerations (ibid., ch. 1).

[2] J. L. Austin, "Truth," *Proceedings of the Aristotelian Society*, Supplement 24 (1950): 111–28.

the recognition of the holistic character of judgment, verification, or empirical justification is compatible with truth as correspondence. A correspondence analysis of truth would be incompatible with semantic or evidential holism only if thoughts or concepts were independent of the things they are about; and that supposition, Will contends, in line with "Thoughts and Things," is false. Similarly, the standard objection to coherence theories of truth, that there may easily be equally comprehensive, internally consistent, but mutually inconsistent systems of propositions, also supposes that thoughts are or can be radically independent of their objects. While some coherence theorists have shared this fatal assumption, acute coherence theorists, like the pragmatists, held that propositions are inextricably embedded in the cognitive and practical contexts in which we state and evaluate them, where those contexts intimately involve the objects about which those statements are made.[1]

Will notes that the supposed independence of thoughts or concepts and things has been supported recently by the attempt to analyze truth in natural languages on the model of truth in formalized languages. The independence of thoughts and things this view involves, and the problems it generates, are nicely brought out in Putnam's original argument for internal realism.[2] "Internal realism" holds that truth is relative to linguistic framework. It counts as a "realism" because sentences within that framework are true only if they refer to objects; it is "internal" realism because truth is internal to a linguistic or conceptual framework. Putnam stated:

[1] For example, Brand Blanshard rightly recognized that thought and its objects cannot be related merely accidentally if knowledge is to be anything other than sheer luck (*The Nature of Thought*, vol. 2, ch. 26 §2, p. 145), and he clearly recognized that the cognitive system whose coherence is sought must include much more than beliefs or propositions because it must include our sensations and our experience of "everything real and possible" (ch. 26 §§8, 13, 16; pp. 147, 148, 150). However, he regarded the "medium" of our ideas as a "veil" (ch. 26 §8, pp. 147–48), and held that the facts about which we make judgments are affected by their incorporation into judgments about them (ch. 25 §21, p. 143). These two views produce a rift between our thought or experience and its supposed objects. Blanshard's view is thus unstable and ultimately infected by the "Coherence Illusion," on which see ch. 5 below. (References are to B. Blanshard, *The Nature of Thought* [London: George Allen & Unwin, 1940] vol. 2; excerpted in *Meaning and Knowledge* E. Nagel and R. Brandt, eds. [New York: Harcourt, Brace & World, 1965], 139–52.)

[2] Putnam soon began modifying his argument for internal realism in *The Many Faces of Realism* (LaSalle: Open Court, 1987). Brevity prohibits examining his subsequent developments here; his original argument is still useful as a clear illustration of a dominant tendency in recent philosophy of language and philosophy of science.

On any view, the understanding of the language must determine the reference of the terms, or, rather, must determine the reference given the context of use. If the use, even in a fixed context, does not determine reference, then use is not understanding. The language, on the perspective we talked ourselves into, has a full program of use; but it still lacks an *interpretation*.

This is the fatal step. To adopt a theory of meaning according to which a language whose whole use is specified still lacks something—*viz.*, its "interpretation"—is to accept a problem which *can* only have crazy solutions. To speak as if *this* were my problem, "I know how to use my language, but, now, how shall I single out an interpretation?", is to speak non-sense. Either use *already* fixes the "interpretation" or *nothing* does.

Nor do "causal theories of reference," *etc.* help. Basically, trying to get out of this predicament by *these* means is hoping that the *world* will pick out one definite extension for each of our terms even if we cannot. But the world does not pick out models or interpret languages. *We* interpret our languages or nothing does.[1]

Putnam was quite right about which step is fatal: to suppose that our language could have a "full program of use" and still lack an interpretation, in the sense of a specific set of relations between terms and their objects. He was also right that, on this model-theoretic view of language, the problem of establishing the interpretation of a language is one that "can only have crazy solutions." His "internal realism," the idea that truth and ontology—the way the world is—are relative to the language we use, was, it must be said, a decidedly crazy solution. Putnam held that the meaning of our terms is given by their use, and that their use is only a function of their (formalizable) syntax.[2] Accordingly, after we have come to understand our language, we have to "interpret" it, that is, we have to map our terms onto the world or parts thereof by using or constructing satisfaction relations.[3] This is the predicament that shows how fully independent thoughts or concepts are from things

---

[1] "Models and Reality," rpt. in *Realism and Reason: Philosophical Papers*, vol. 3 (Cambridge: Cambridge University Press, 1983), 1–25, p. 24.

[2] Meaning is use: "Realism and Reason," *Proceedings and Addresses of the American Philosophical Association* 50 (1976–77), rpt. in *Meaning and the Moral Sciences* (London: Routledge & Kegan Paul, 1977), 123–40, p. 127; "Models and Reality," 4; *Reason, Truth, and History* (Cambridge, Mass.: Harvard University Press, 1981), ch. 2; use is syntax: ibid., "Models and Reality," 20–22, 24.

[3] "Realism and Reason," 494, 495; "What is Realism?," *Proceedings of the Aristotelian Society* 76 (1975–76): 177–94, pp. 188–93; "Models and Reality," 19–23.

on this model-theoretic approach to natural language. However, this predicament counts as a reductio ad absurdum of that approach to analyzing natural language, rather than as a premise in an argument for "internal realism." This is because identifying linguistic usage with (formalized) syntax is spurious. Natural languages are learned and developed through concurrent referential, ascriptive, and descriptive uses of terms and sentences.[1] To link use and reference via a "non-realist semantics"[2] disregards, contravenes, and occludes the natural conditions (environmental, physiological, psychological, and neonatal) requisite for learning and understanding language.

One problem urged against the notion of truth as correspondence is to indicate to what true statements supposedly correspond. Either we repeat the statement in question, and we presume that those statements we now accept are fully adequate and so apparently immune from future revision, or else we resort to entirely unhelpful general designations such as "the world" or "reality." If realism and the correspondence analysis of truth require these sorts of reply, Richard Rorty argued, so much the worse for them.[3] Will responds to this problem in two ways. First, he points out that the philosophical problem about the ways in which or the extent to which our thoughts correspond to their objects is a broad concern about our general categories and descriptions. This concern simply is not addressed by the piecemeal repetition of particular claims about particular states of affairs. Second, he challenges the underlying assumption that conceptualization as an all-or-nothing affair; either we conceive an object, and that conception is fully adequate and unrevisable, or else we do not conceive the object at all. Will contends that a more accurate model for conception and description is found in cartography. Rejecting semantic atomism entails that concepts are interrelated; they form conceptual networks. They are thus like maps. Like maps, conceptual networks inherently leave room for filling in details and, on that basis, revising major portions of the map (network). Those revisions, of course, are found by using the map in question and, on that basis, making discoveries about the area (or

---

[1] See W. Sellars, "Pure Pragmatics and Epistemology," *Philosophy of Science* 15, no. 3 (1947): 181–202, "Concepts as Involving Laws and as Inconceivable Without Them," *Philosophy of Science* 15, no. 4 (1948): 287–315, and *Science and Metaphysics* (London: Routledge & Kegan Paul, 1968), 18–19. Similar points were also made by Wittgenstein in *Philosophical Investigations*.

[2] "Models and Reality," 22–23, 24.

[3] "The World Well Lost," rpt. in *Consequences of Pragmatism* (Minneapolis: University of Minnesota Press, 1982), 3–18.

objects) mapped. In this connection, Will emphasizes Dewey's point, that the adequacy of our linguistic and conceptual resources and abilities for discerning the characteristics of things can only be made out in the process of using those resources to discriminate the genuine characteristics of things. In the effort to discriminate the genuine characteristics of things we must of course employ whatever linguistic and conceptual resources and abilities we have; but we should not take for granted that those resources and abilities are entirely adequate. In the course of employing those resources and abilities we may find ourselves modifying them in order better to discriminate the characteristics of the things we use or investigate.[1]

In "The Concern About Truth" (ch. 3) Will shows that the "problem of truth"—the problem of what truth is—is less than a century old and stems from reaction to Kantian-Hegelian idealism and its later-day exponents. It is a specifically philosophical puzzle not afflicting practicing scientists or pre-Critical philosophers. (Historical skeptics agreed about what truth is, they just denied that anything we said could be known to be true.) The Kantian tradition discredited the Cartesian model of knowledge as revelation by developing a complex philosophy of mind and philosophy of language, the very complexity of which seemed to undermine the possibility of making, much less making truly, such statements as "the cat is on the mat." Once such statements became problematic, so did the correspondence notion of truth. Russell was inclined to affirm his ability to make such statements and on that basis to reclaim the correspondence sense of truth and to reject by reductio any philosophy of mind that entailed his inability to correctly judge the cat's location. Schlick and Ayer followed suit.[2] In claiming this ability to

---

[1] Murphy hails this as the cardinal insight of pragmatism, which, he argues, the classical American Pragmatists subverted by over-emphasizing the role or use of expressions in fulfilling our ultimate cognitive or practical aims ("Pragmatism and the Context of Rationality," esp. 164–67). Will repeatedly indicates his debts to Peirce and Dewey, and in chapters 7 to 9 he acknowledges that his account of reason belongs to and in the Pragmatic tradition. However, Will does not over-emphasize our ultimate cognitive or practical aims as the source or measure of the significance of locally useful techniques or idioms. I believe Will's debts to the pragmatists are sufficiently deep to warrant classifying him as a pragmatist. If one instead wishes to emphasize his differences from the classical American Pragmatists, then at the very least Will develops the cardinal insight Murphy finds in pragmatism.

Williams makes a similar, if not identical, objection to Rorty (*Unnatural Doubts*, 269–70).

[2] Will provides references to Russell. I augment those references here to show how pervasive was and is the assumption Will criticizes. Schlick states: "I have main-

distinguish ordinary states of affairs and make statements about them, Schlick and Ayer took no more notice than Neurath, Carnap, or Hempel of the philosophy of mind presupposed by such abilities.

In vigorous opposition to Schlick, Hempel emphasized that the comparison Schlick claimed to make was a comparison between a statement in his Baedeker's guide and the *result* rather than the act of inspecting the cathedral (namely, a comparison with the achieved recognition of a cathedral's two spires) and hence in effect compared two statements after all.[1] Since the actual comparison was between statements, and since all statements are corrigible because the psychological etiology of any observation report can always be questioned, the alleged correspondence between "facts" and propositions had to be relinquished. These ideas "obviously" implied a coherence theory of truth.[2] In this regard, Hempel formulated in semantic terms the same basic argument used by coherentists such as Brand Blanshard, who pointed out that our identification of any one particular is a matter of making a set of interdependent, corrigible judgments about it.[3]

---

tained ... [that statements can be compared with facts]. I have often compared propositions to facts; so I had no reason to say that it couldn't be done. I found, for instance, in my Baedeker the statement: 'This cathedral has two spires', I was able to compare it with 'reality' by looking at the cathedral, and this comparison convinced me that Baedeker's assertion was true ... I meant nothing but a process of this kind when I spoke of testing propositions by comparing them with facts" ("Facts and Propositions," *Analysis* 2, no. 5 [1935]: 65–70, pp. 65–66); cf. Ayer, "The Criterion of Truth," *Analysis* 3, nos. 1 and 2 (1935): 28–32, p. 30. (My discussion is drawn from *Hegel's Epistemological Realism*, 63–64, 244–46.)

[1] Carl Hempel, "Some Remarks on 'Facts' and Propositions," *Analysis* 2, no. 6 (1935): 93–96, p. 94.

[2] Carl Hempel, "On the Logical Positivists' Theory of Truth," *Analysis* 2, no. 4 (1935): 49–59 (cited as "LPTT"), pp. 50–52, 54. Hempel speaks here explicitly about revising the concept of truth.

[3] In response to the example of claiming a bird to be a cardinal and checking the statement by looking at the bird, an example exactly parallel to Schlick's use of Baedeker's guide to the cathedral, Blanshard replies: "Now, plausible as this argument is, it goes to pieces on inspection. It assumes that, corresponding to our judgment, there is some solid chunk of fact, directly presented to sense and beyond all question, to which thought must adjust itself. And this 'solid fact' is a fiction. What the theory takes as fact and actually uses as such is another judgment or set of judgments, and what provides the verification is the coherence between the initial judgment and these" (*The Nature of Thought*, vol. 2, ch. 25 §18, p. 141). Regarding correspondence as a criterion of truth, Blanshard says: "For [on this view] in order to know that experience corresponds to fact, we must be able to get at that fact, unadulterated with idea, and compare the two sides with each other. And we have seen in the last chapter [sc.

Will points out that philosophers convinced by considerations in philosophy of mind and language that facts are not knowable singly by direct acquaintance tend to argue that individual facts, things, or states of affairs must be expunged from philosophy—and conversely, philosophers who retain confidence in their abilities to know facts, things, or states of affairs singly tend to argue on that basis against such philosophies of mind and language. The pervasive, influential underlying assumption has been that, if there is no knowledge by acquaintance, then there are no individual facts (etc.) to be known. As Will notes, those influenced by Kantian philosophy tended to affirm the antecedent, their opponents to deny the consequent.[1] Both sides found this inference compelling.[2] This inference also guided Blanshard's

---

ibid., ch. 25, esp. §§18, 20, 21] that such fact is not accessible. When we try to lay hold of it, what we find in our hands is a judgment which is obviously not itself the indubitable fact we are seeking, and which must be checked by some fact beyond it. To this process there is no end" (ibid., ch. 26 §8, p. 147).

[1] Hempel's connection to the Critical tradition comes through the Marxist Neurath, who first emphasized and convinced him and the Vienna Circle generally of the corrigibility of all statements, and who avowed a coherence theory of what truth is. Neurath affirms a coherence theory of what truth is ("Sociology and Physicalism," in *Logical Positivism*, A. J. Ayer, ed., [New York: Free Press, 1959], 282–317, p. 291), as did Hempel (LPTT, 50). Carnap later protests that Neurath didn't mean what he literally said, but he does concur that Neurath rejected the correspondence notion of truth ("Replies and Systematic Expositions," in *The Philosophy of Rudolf Carnap*, P. A. Schilpp, ed., [The Library of Living Philosophers, 1963], 859–1013, p. 864). Neurath shortly repudiated the coherence notion of truth ("Erster Internationaler Kongress für Einheit der Wissenschaft in Paris 1935," *Erkenntnis* 5 [1936]: 400), but did not reaffirm the correspondence notion. Rather, he rejected the notion of truth altogether. This is still to make the crucial inference pointed out and criticized by Will.

[2] NEURATH: "In accordance with our traditional language we may say that some statements are accepted at a certain time by a certain person and not accepted by the same person at another time, but we cannot say some statements are true today but not tomorrow; 'true' and 'false' are 'absolute' terms, which we avoid. We are prepared to show that a certain theory is more 'plausible' than another theory ... and we may 'corroborate' a theory or 'weaken' it" ("Universal Jargon and Terminology," *Proceedings of the Aristotelian Society* NS 41 [1940–41]: 127–48, pp. 138–139).

REICHENBACH: "Thus we are left no propositions at all which can be absolutely verified. The predicate of truth-value of a proposition, therefore [sic], is a mere fictive quality, its place is in an ideal world of science only, whereas actual science cannot make use of it. Actual science instead employs throughout the predicate of weight" (*Experience and Prediction* [Chicago: University of Chicago Press, 1938], 188 note 20).

coherentism, C. I. Lewis's phenomenalism, and it is the crucial enthymeme undergirding Richard Rorty's dismissal of realism in *Philosophy and the Mirror of Nature*.[1] This inference is one pervasive source of the philosophical swings between "givenism" and "coherentism," one which goes unremarked by John McDowell's diagnosis of those swings in *Mind and World*.[2] The supposition that foundationalism is required to uphold realism is made expli-

---

HEMPEL: "Science [according to Neurath] is a system of statements which are of one kind. Each statement may be combined or compared with each other statement, e.g. in order to draw conclusions from the combined statements, or to see if they are compatible with each other or not. But statements are never compared with 'reality,' with 'facts.' None of those who support a cleavage between statements and reality is able to give a precise account of how a comparison between statements and facts may possibly be accomplished, and how we may possibly ascertain the structure of facts. Therefore, that cleavage is nothing but the result of a redoubling metaphysics, and all the problems connected with it, are mere pseudoproblems.

"But how is truth to be characterized from such a standpoint? Obviously, Neurath's ideas imply a coherence theory" (LPTT, 50–51).

SCHLICK: "But what then remains at all as a criterion of truth? Since the proposal is not that all scientific assertions must accord with certain definite protocol statements, but rather that all statements shall accord with one another, with the result that every single one is considered as, in principle, corrigible, truth can consist only in a *mutual agreement of statements*" ("The Foundation of Knowledge," in *Logical Positivism*, 209–27, pp. 213–14). Schlick then rejects this coherence theory of truth (ibid., 215) and relies on a version of "knowledge by acquaintance" for experiential "confirmations" which occasion the basic synthetic statements in terms of which alone we can ultimately formulate our knowledge. This is to accept the basic inference Will criticizes.

AYER: "[I]t is necessary to investigate more closely the view that in order to determine the validity of a system of empirical propositions one cannot and need not go beyond the system itself. For if the view were satisfactory we should be absolved from troubling any further about the use of the phrase 'agreement with experience'" ("Verification and Experience," *Proceedings of the Aristotelian Society* 37 [1936–37], rpt. in *Logical Positivism*, 228–43, p. 231).

WAISMANN similarly inferred from the fact that the true length of something isn't immediately given, but rather is figured on the basis of averaging a number of measurements containing slight discrepancies, to the claim that the item measured has no true, determinate length ("Logische Analyse des Wahrscheinlichkeitsbegriffs," *Erkenntnis* 1 [1930–31]: 228–48, pp. 229–30).

[1] On Blanshard, see the quotations above, p. xxviii note 3; on Lewis, see "Professor Chisholm and Empiricism," rpt. in *Perceiving, Sensing, and Knowing*, R. J. Schwartz, ed. (New York: Anchor, 1965), 355–63, pp. 356, 357; R. Rorty (Princeton: Princeton University Press, 1979), passim.

[2] Cambridge, Mass.: Harvard University Press, 1994.

citly by Simon Blackburn,[1] and it is presumed by John Haldane.[2] Similarly, Michael Williams has recapitulated precisely the debate held between realist-foundationalists and antirealist coherentists at the onset of logical positivism.[3] This debate, and the widespread assumption that realism requires a strong form of foundationalism, are based on the non sequitur exposed by Will. However, despite how pervasive and persuasive this inference has been, it is a non sequitur; the consequent does not follow from the antecedent. Its being a non sequitur does, however, cut the ground out from under the debate between the two sides, especially when a clear distinction between a criterion of truth and the nature of truth is not only noted but maintained.[4] The upshot points to a correspondence analysis of truth combined with pragmatic criteria of truth; a correspondence analysis of truth does not require using "correspondence" as a criterion, nor does it require "knowledge by acquaintance."

A major point of these two chapters is that F. P. Ramsey's "redundancy" theory of truth and P. F. Strawson's "illocutionary" theory of truth are understandable, but unwarranted, responses to the apparently embarrassing predicament mentioned above, that we can only specify the "states of affairs" which make our statements true by repeating those very statements. One clue about the non-redundancy of "statement x is true," as compared with simply stating x, is that, unlike simply saying one agrees with statement x, saying that the statement is true connotes that one has made an independent assessment of

---

[1] *Essays in Quasi-Realism* (New York: Oxford University Press, 1993), 35.   In this connection he cites Ernest Sosa, "The Raft and the Pyramid: Coherence Versus Foundations in the Theory of Knowledge," rpt. in *Knowledge in Perspective* (Cambridge: Cambridge University Press, 1991), 165–91.   However, Sosa's discussion is judiciously restricted to these two kinds of theory of justification, and avoids discussion of realism.   Sosa doesn't note the non sequitur, but doesn't need to, either.

[2] John Haldane, "Mind-World Identity Theory and the Anti-Realist Challenge," in *Reality, Representation, and Projection*, J. Haldane and C. Wright, eds. (New York: Oxford University Press, 1993), 15–37.

[3] "Realism and Skepticism," in *Reality, Representation, and Projection*, 193–214, pp. 193–205, and *Unnatural Doubts* (Oxford: Blackwell, 1992; Princeton: Princeton University Press, 1996), 231–33.

[4] Schlick distinguishes verbally between a criterion and a nature of truth, but goes on to muddle them together again ("The Foundation of Knowledge," 213–15); he at least stated the distinction. Carnap draws and insists upon this distinction ("Truth and Confirmation," in *Readings in Philosophical Analysis*, H. Feigl and W. Sellars, eds. [New York: Appleton-Century-Crofts, 1949], 119–27, pp. 119–20). Blanshard also insists that the nature and the criterion of truth are distinct (*The Nature of Thought*, vol. 2, ch. 26 §§1, 8, pp. 144, 147).

its warrant, and that one is prepared to vouch for its warrant, even if someone else originally made the statement.[1] Will's result, that Ramsey's and
Strawson's theories of truth are not warranted and do not address the real
issues involved in "the problem of truth," remains important, for Ramsey's
theory forms the point of departure, for example, for Simon Blackburn's
recent "quasi-realism,"[2] and both their theories are the progenitors of the
current antirealist "prosentential" theory of truth.[3] A major desideratum for
Will's view, of course, is to show just how a complex social account of
knowledge can be realist, since that has been widely regarded as impossible.
That is a major aim of the subsequent chapters.

4. Practices and Governance

In "The Rational Governance of Practice" (ch. 4) Will addresses what has
appeared to be a fundamental paradox facing a social account of reason. One
main point of calling procedures "rational" is to say that they are justified
or at least justifiable by rational standards, and much philosophical effort has
gone into formulating rational standards for assessing various social practices.
It is generally assumed that if rational standards provide legitimate grounds
for evaluating social practices, those standards must be independent of those
practices. Without such independence, "standards" would provide no independent assessment, and hence no legitimate assessment, of practices; critique
would collapse into circularity, question-begging, polemic, or dogmatism. This
concern can be found in both Descartes and Hume, as well as currently, for
example, in the debate about the "sociology" of knowledge. The "sociology"
of knowledge shares with its positivist opposition a narrow notion of rational
justification. Will's pragmatic account of rationality aims to replace that
narrow notion with a richer and more realistic account of rational justification.

Will argues that this paradox begins to dissolve once one recognizes the
extent to which and the ways in which rational assessment and control (or

[1] See W. H. Walsh, "A Note on Truth," *Mind* 61 (1952): 72–74. This point has
been elaborated by various authors subsequently.

[2] Blackburn's "quasi-realism" was first propounded in "Truth, Realism, and the
Regulation of Theory," *Midwest Studies in Philosophy* 5 (1980): 353–71, and reprinted
as the lead essay in his collection, *Essays in Quasi-Realism* (Oxford: Clarendon, 1993).

[3] See Robert Brandom, "Pragmatism, Phenomenalism, and Truth Talk," *Midwest
Studies in Philosophy* 7 (1988): 75–93.

"governance") is integral to our practices. Like habits, practices are, inter alia, partially determined both by our inherent physiological and psychological capacities, and by our physical and social environment. And like habits, practices are flexible; they can be adapted to and modified by a wide variety of conditions present in any circumstance of action. One reason practices are flexible is that any one practice is executed by an agent who has many dispositions to execute many different acts which accord with many different practices. As Dewey showed, in no case is a habit or a practice reducible to a simple 1:1 correlation of occasion and response. A habit or practice of an intelligent agent is conducted with at least some, usually great though often implicit, sensitivity to anything unusual in the circumstances of action which requires a modified execution of "the same" practice, or instead require a different procedure altogether. Consequently, rational governance of practices is integral to our engaging in practices at all. The governance of practices involves both the adjustment of practices to one another, and the adjustment of practices to environmental circumstances. Both adjustments occur together, and both kinds of adjustment do occur. In learning a practice, part of what we learn are circumstances in which "normal procedures" are overridden, and part of what we learn is what to do in some of those circumstances, and part of what we develop are abilities to cope with unexpected abnormal circumstances, so that we can react to them intelligently rather than blindly. That is basic to rational thought and action.

Of course, the extent to which we deliberately assess, control, or modify our practices can vary considerably. At one end of the spectrum is the routine kind of governance *in* practice represented by monitoring our normal activities for possible abnormalities (whether advantageous or disadvantageous). At the other end of the spectrum is the more reflective and radical governance *of* practice represented by critical assessment and modification, which is stimulated by unexpected developments not tractable by established procedures. Recognizing that these two aspects of governance, governance "in" and "of" practice, represent two ends of a continuum helps defuse the idea that radical or rapid changes in practices cannot be rational. This idea is most commonly known by Kuhn's phrase "paradigm shift," though the same idea is also found in Carnap's philosophy of science and its progeny.[1] This supposed problem

[1] See Rudolf Carnap, "Truth and Confirmation," in *Readings in Philosophical Analysis*, 119–27, p. 126, and "The Methodological Character of Theoretical Concepts," in *Minnesota Studies in Philosophy of Science* 1 (1956): 38–76, p. 51. The semantic background to his views on radical conceptual change is set out in "Empiri-

results from thinking of the rules governing practices as templates to guide thought and action. With this model in mind, one naturally supposes that governance *in* practice is a matter of using the "templates" appropriate to one's circumstances; that all there is to the "rational" governance of practices is to follow the dictates of the templates provided by one's paradigm, conceptual scheme, or linguistic framework. If that were the case, then major changes in the templates themselves must be nonrational.

This undesirable result assumes, however, that the rules guiding our practices are independent of those practices and determine those practices unilaterally. Will's response parallels his point about thought in "Thoughts and Things": Like thoughts or concepts, practices and the rules guiding them are to a certain extent indeterminate, they are not so specific as to provide in advance for any possible contingency; and like thoughts or concepts, practices and the rules guiding them are inherently rooted in the characteristics of the environment (both social and natural) in which they are employed and on which they act. Consequently, practices and their guiding rules are inherently mutable as new discoveries are made or new applications are developed. This mutation can be rational, provided it is conducted intelligently and effectively in view of all the relevant circumstances. Will does not argue that all large-scale or rapid changes in practices must be or are rational. His point is simply, but significantly given recent widespread skepticism about it, that large-scale and rapid change in basic principles or norms *can be* rational.

Will stresses that any and every practice is open to reconsideration or alteration. However, he shows that this fact cannot be generalized into the skeptical worry that all practices might be reconsidered or altered simultaneously. A being bereft of practices is not a social being, and consequently is not a human being. If we (*per impossibile*) rid ourselves of all our practices, we would have no procedures for so much as recognizing, formulating, or pondering our supposed predicament. In any problematic situation, there must be some practices which are accepted as stable and established, or else no situation could be recognized as problematic. (How would a problem be identified if not in the context of some procedure and by use of procedures, whether intellectual or overtly practical?) This stable body of practices always provides the framework within which problems are posed and it provides most

---

cism, Semantics, and Ontology," *Revue International de Philosophie* 4 (1950): revised form published in *Meaning and Necessity* (Chicago: University of Chicago Press, 1956), 205–21, see esp. pp. 208, 213.

of the resources for solving those problems. The resources of accepted practices may not always be adequate for resolving problems, but that should not
lead us to overlook the important fact that they very often are adequate, and
that even in those cases where they are not fully adequate, they provide
essential resources for posing, redefining, and ultimately solving problems.

In "Reason, Social Practice, and Scientific Realism" (ch. 5) Will criticizes
two widespread suppositions which block the recognition of the legitimacy
of basing the rational governance of practices in social practices. These suppositions have been widely made following the collapse of the distinction between theoretical and observation terms in the philosophy of science. Sophisticated logical positivists had long recognized that the distinction between
theoretical terms and observation terms was a pragmatic matter of degree, and
that a certain amount of "theory" went into making and reporting observations.[1] They remained sanguine empiricists until Kuhn argued that no theory-
neutral observations could be identified to select between major competing
theories, and that major theories or "paradigms" typically disagree about just
which phenomena can be explained and what kinds of explanation are important.[2] The most acute empiricist was Rudolf Carnap, whose semantics were
subject to internal refutation of the semantic atomism which would enable
observation reports to provide a check on theories. Carnap ultimately conceded
this criticism.[3] The result was a radical semantic holism which appeared to
entail two crucial consequences: First, aside from arbitrary decisions to switch

---

[1] See, for example, Rudolf Carnap, "Testability and Meaning," *Philosophy of
Science* 3 (1936): 419–71, p. 433, and *Philosophical Foundations of Physics* (New
York: Basic Books, 1966), pp. 225–26. Positivist views about the theory-observation
distinction have been subject to serious misinterpretation on this count, for example,
by Frederick Suppe, *The Structure of Scientific Theories* (Urbana: University of Illinois
Press, 2d ed. 1977), 45–49. Similarly, Paul Feyerabend mistakenly ascribes to positivism the "Constancy Thesis," the idea that only one observation language is and always
will be applicable ("An Attempt at a Realistic Interpretation of Experience," *Proceedings of the Aristotelian Society* NS 58 [1957–58]: 143–170.

[2] For discussion, see Gerald Doppelt, "Kuhn's Epistemological Relativism: An
Interpretation and Defense," *Inquiry* 21 (1978): 33–86.

[3] David Kaplan reports Carnap's concession in "Homage to Carnap," *Boston
Studies in Philosophy of Science* 8 (1971), xi–lxvi, pp. xlv–xlvii.) However, Kaplan's
remarks report on his studies in 1958 and tie his (undisclosed) objection to Carnap's
article, "The Methodological Character of Theoretical Concepts." Carnap made one
more detailed effort to avoid this kind of result in "Replies and Systematic Expositions," pp. 900–905. I develop this criticism of Carnap's empiricism independently in
Hegel's Epistemological Realism, 60–62.

"paradigms" or "conceptual schemes," one's rational thought and action are determined by one's overarching theory; Second, realism must be rescinded because observations of objects and events conform to one's overarching theory, rather than informing one of the nature of those observed objects or events.

Will calls these apparent implications the "Relativist Illusion" and the "Coherence Illusion." Radical semantic holism is implied by the demise of empiricism only if the concepts embedded in natural and scientific language are rightly modeled by formal semantics. However, words and concepts are things we work with and do things with; they are embedded in our practices, and our practices are based in nature (environmental, physiological, and psychological) as well as in our needs and interests. Critical assessment and modification of our practices would be impossible only if our practices formed a monolithic and independent whole. In opposition to this idea, that standards of rationality and justification are relative to one's "paradigm" or "conceptual scheme," Will develops two important points. First, while our practices do form sets, those sets vary widely both in how local or global they are and in how tightly or loosely integrated they are.[1] Second, even in the smallest and most tightly integrated society, every individual participates in more than one set of practices.[2] Such cross-participation in sets of practices gives us resources, and often opportunities, for resolving problems in one set by drawing resources from another. (This extends the main point of ch. 4, "The Rational Governance of Practice.")

Will identifies an important assumption which supports the relativist illusion: the idea that reason is an essentially individual, calculative phenomenon. Reason has widely been regarded as a calculative ability to infer conclusions, in accordance with clearly formulated inductive or deductive principles, from clearly formulated premises. If reason is calculative, if rational processes are limited to deductive or inductive inferences based on symbolically formulated premises, then *of course* revising the basic principles which govern the formulation of premises, or the principles governing inferences must be non-rational. And if revising the formulation of the principles or the

---

[1] In this regard, Will agrees with Clark Glymore, that adopting radical semantic holism is a serious overreaction to the demise of the so-called "theory-observation" distinction (*Theory and Evidence* [Princeton: Princeton University Press, 1980], 45), and with Michael Williams that "there is no direct move from anti-atomism to radical holism" (*Unnatural Doubts*, 287).

[2] Will first mentions this point in ch. 2, "Truth and Correspondence."

premises of reasoning must be nonrational, then revising social practices based on them must also be nonrational. However, this assumption is extreme. Is it really plausible to suppose that all of the intelligent effort required to develop, employ, assess, and revise the major premises of our theories (whether philosophical or scientific) should count as nonrational because it is not strictly deductive or calculative? One clue that rational inference is not unilateral or merely calculative is that it is often a very genuine issue whether a syllogism is *modus ponens* or *modus tollens*. Similarly, our assessment of the validity and soundness of arguments, including our detection of implicit equivocations, is not simply a calculative procedure, though it is a preeminently rational one. (This anticipates a theme of ch. 7, "Rules and Subsumption.") The assumption that reason is calculative and individual has prevented those who have recognized the social bases of language and thought from recognizing the social nature of reason itself. This is a main theme in chapters 7 through 9.

The "Coherence Illusion" is an analog to the old "Veil of Perception."[1] An analogous "Veil of Conception" appears to arise if it is true that to know objects requires identifying them, and to identify objects requires applying concepts to them. If so, then apparently we cannot know any object that was other than we conceive it to be. Most generally, the "Coherence Illusion" is this: If thought and action are based in social practices, social practices and the "knowledge" they ground cannot provide knowledge of anything other than theoretical artifacts; they cannot provide knowledge of things which exist and have characteristics that do not depend upon how we think or talk about them. Will argues that this "Coherence Illusion" stems from a basic misconception of social practices, indeed, from a misconception that the Pragmatists' original emphasis on "practices" was intended to avoid. Practices are not sui generis. Social practices are developed and employed within human communities, human communities consist of physiological (if also social) creatures who live in physical environments, and the objects and events in that physical environment are important bases of and components in social practices. Rather than interposing themselves between us and natural objects, social practices are precisely what engage us with them!

---

[1] Roughly, the idea that we perceive our sensations rather than the things which supposedly cause them. Though most familiar now from Modern Philosophy, this view and its skeptical implications were well known to Sextus Empiricus (*Outlines of Pyrrhonism*, II §§72–75).

The pragmatists emphasized our engagement in practices in order to preclude solipsism, and to preclude the idea, directly stated by Richard Rorty (though implicit in many other recent analyses), that

> the *whole* anti-solipsist burden is borne by the [social] "programming," and the "stimuli" (like the noumenal unsynthesized intuitions) drop out.[1]

In direct opposition to this, Will points out that, like our thoughts, our practices are rooted firmly and ineluctably in nature, our physical environment, our physiology, and our psychology.[2] Those are natural givens, even if they are not directly "given" to immaculate, aconceptual apprehension. Though indirect—far more indirect than empiricists ever imagined—the influence of things on our practices, and thus on our thoughts and concepts, is definite, ineluctable, and cognitively crucial.[3] Consequently, it is possible to govern our practices in view of the influence objects have on our practices, including how objects reveal themselves to us in the course of our practical interaction with them.[4] Not all social practices are intended or designed to discern

---

[1] "The World Well Lost," 17 note 1; original emphasis. This is not simply a remark in passing. Rorty thinks "justification" is strictly social and has nothing to do with relations between subjects and the supposed objects of their knowledge: "'Justification' [is] a social phenomenon rather than a transaction between 'the knowing subject' and 'reality'"; it is "not a matter of a ... relation between ideas (or words) and objects, but of conversation, of social practice ... [W]e understand knowledge when we understand the social justification of belief, and thus have no need to view it as accuracy of representation" (*Philosophy and the Mirror of Nature*, 9, 170). These reductive disjunctions are the target of Will's criticism; they show that Rorty succumbed to what Will calls the relativist illusion.

[2] Cf. Sellars, "Pure Pragmatics and Epistemology," who responded to Rorty on this count in advance by emphasizing the role of a stable and identifiable physical environment as a requirement of learning natural languages.

[3] Will recognizes that it is very difficult to determine precisely which constraints on our practices are provided by the environment, which by our physiology, and which by our psychology. For a fascinating attempt to sort these factors out, and to integrate them along lines suggested by Will's views, see Edward Hundert, *Philosophy, Psychiatry, and Neuroscience* (Oxford: Clarendon, 1989). For a précis, see my review in *Philosophy and Phenomenological Research* 51, no. 3 (1991): 722–25.

[4] "Practical interaction" is a pleonasm; but the emphasis seems necessary to counter the widespread assimilation of our practical activities to sentences about them, which are then treated in a formally structured syntax and semantics. While it is almost embarrassing to mention it, in view of the widespread antinaturalism which has resulted from recent philosophical semantics and philosophy of science, it seems

the natural characteristics of things; but if social practices in general are rooted in things and their characteristics, then there is no reason in principle that those social practices which are intended to discern the natural characteristics of things cannot do so. Will supports this general point with some brief examples from astronomy and nuclear physics.

5. Governance, Logic, and Rationality

In "Reason and Tradition" (ch. 6) Will further develops the issue first broached in chapter 5 about the nature of human reason, whether it is calculative and individual or more than calculative and social. Ever since the Enlightenment, the "Age of Reason," reason has been widely regarded as the basis of our ability to assess and revise our culturally inherited norms and institutions, in a word, our traditions. As such, reason has been regarded as independent of tradition. Accordingly, it has also been regarded as an inherent endowment of human individuals. In chapter 5, Will points out that individuals can and do make crucial contributions to social institutions, as Lise Meitner did when she figured out how to reconcile the otherwise conflicting sets of practices (in chemistry and nascent nuclear physics) which left Hahn and Strassmann puzzled over their discovery of nuclear fission. However, in making those contributions, individuals must draw heavily on their training within and their assimilation of the norms, practices, and traditions of their disciplines. Consequently, individual contributions, innovative as they are (a point Will of course recognizes), are thoroughly based in social practices. Individual innovation relies on unappreciated resources and on unappreciated possibilities of modification found within established, "traditional" practices, in response to unfulfilled aims and aspirations found in those practices, or in unexpected circumstances or turns of event; typically, in a combination of all of these.

In "Reason and Tradition," Will points out that rationality is central to the legitimacy of principles, norms, and institutions, and their legitimacy is

---

worth stressing that, although we make many artifacts and synthetic compounds, we do so only by making use of various raw materials, materials which have natural characteristics. Those natural characteristics are not themselves artifacts; they are necessary material conditions for our making artifacts. Perhaps if philosophers of science of an antirealist persuasion paid as much attention to materials science and to engineering as to the further reaches of theoretical physics, they would develop a more balanced view.

closely tied to their acceptability and their acceptance by some relevant group. How, then, does reason command interpersonal respect? The individualist answer is that, because reason is the same in each of us, if we each reason carefully, clearly, and sincerely, we will arrive at the same conclusions, because we will recognize the same first premises and follow the same principles of reasoning. The problem this view bequeaths to each of us is to determine, by ourselves, when and whether we are in fact reasoning properly or clearly, and when we are instead influenced by tradition or prejudice. Descartes propounded a set of rules by which we could attempt to differentiate our own proper and improper reasoning. Will highlights two problems with this and analogous proposals. First, if we were to abstract from a *human* mind everything it derives from its traditions, it would simply be incapable either of following or even of understanding such rules. Second, in practice, this individualist view of reason tends to fail us precisely where issues of rationality and legitimacy are most important: In circumstances of unclarity and indecision, rather than helping discern or develop mutually acceptable principles, it tends to reinforce faction.

The conflicts that arise within a tradition are not necessarily conflicts between reason and unreason; they are typically conflicts among some of the rational resources—principles of reasoning—within that tradition, which usually arise when confronting new, unprecedented developments. Such conflicts are normal, and often arise through the success of some set of practices within that tradition. The attempt to resolve those conflicts is the attempt to refashion the rational resources of the tradition in order to accommodate those developments. This, Will insists, is not only endemic but essential to reason. To appreciate the role of such conflict in the development of rational procedures, of traditions, and to assist our addressing and resolving such conflicts requires viewing reason as a social phenomenon, and recognizing that "tradition" is a part of reason, not its counterpart. (Here Will alludes to the themes of Dewey's *Reconstruction in Philosophy*.) Will develops some central aspects of a social view of reason in the remaining three chapters.

At the end of "Reason and Tradition" Will touches on the issue of the relation between individuals and their communities. This issue has been so hotly contested that a brief word about it is appropriate. Will contends that human individuals are fundamentally social practitioners. This does not, however, raise the bogey that has haunted liberal individualist critics of the totalitarian right or left, the alleged subservience of individuals to society. Will's view about social practices and individuals as social practitioners emphasizes their interdependence: there are no individuals, no social practitioners, without social practices, and vice versa, there are no social practices without social practitioners; without individuals who learn, participate in, perpetuate, *and who modify* those social practices as needed to meet their changing needs, aims, and circumstances. On this view, the issue of the ontological priority of individuals or society is a pseudoproblem. The extent to which a society concentrates influence in a dominant group or disperses it among its members is a distinct issue, quite independent of this ontological one.[1] (To be sure, Will stresses, especially in chapter 9, the wide variety of ways in which and agents by which norms are governed in modern societies.)

The subtitle of chapter 7, "Rules and Subsumption: Mutative Aspects of Logical Processes," is provocative. A deductive system is designed to conserve truth-value and to avoid mutations. Will recognizes this, just as he recognizes the importance and the power of formal logical systems. His point instead is that such systems provide a seriously misleading model of our rational processes of using rules to guide our behavior and our handling of particular objects. We can abstract our thoughts from our practices, express them symbolically, and subject those expressions to various important and powerful kinds of formal analyses. Once this symbolic abstraction is made, the axiomatic model of deductive justification is irresistible—and the "Relativist Illusion" is unavoidable because basic axioms are various, yet underivable, and so are controversial.[2] To assume that by expressing our thoughts in abstract formulae we have also extracted our thoughts from our practices and have isolated their rational core generates serious problems. These problems concern both understanding what we do when we subsume actual individuals into a practice (rather than supplying values for variables in symbolic formulae), and understanding the grounds we actually have and employ to justify maintaining or altering our practices, including our ways of thinking.

Will's main point is that our actual procedures, our rule-guided practices, involve (symbolically formulable) rules as one element of a complex situation involving our other skills, abilities, and expectations, along with the objects about which we think and on or with which we act. We subsume actual individuals (things, people, events) under "rules" when we treat them in various ways which are guided by those rules. Such subsumption has its

---

[1] For discussion of the ontological issue along pragmatist lines, see Richard De-George, "Social Reality and Social Relations," *Review of Metaphysics* 37 (1983): 3–20.

[2] Compare the discussion of Putnam's internal realism, above p. xxiv*f.*

effects on us, on other things, and on our rules. Will calls these "reactive effects." In routine cases, objects behave the way we expect, and this fulfillment of expectations, the favorable reactive effects, tend to reinforce our confidence in the rule and our use of it. These routine cases are readily modeled by logical calculi, though they abstract from the context of actual use in which these reinforcing effects occur. Will notes that Wittgenstein's paradoxes about rule-following are directed against precisely this abstraction; "rule-following" becomes paradoxical when it is abstracted from the abilities we have to identify individuals and the appropriateness of our applying a rule to them, and these abilities rely on the "reactive effects" of our subsumption.[1] In problematic cases of subsumption, objects don't behave quite as expected. (As Dewey said, one primary characteristic of objects is that they ob-ject.) In these cases, the unexpected effects can provide grounds and occasion for modifying our rules. These "reactive effects," whether stabilizing or mutative, are a crucial basis for critical assessment of rules, for justifying their maintenance or change. Reactive effects, and the possible grounds for changing our rules and practices they provide, cannot be eliminated. This is because our rules, like our concepts, have an "open texture"; they cannot be so completely specified as to preclude in advance any possible ambiguity or inaccuracy. (This recalls Will's point about thought in chapter 1.) Recognizing the grounds such reactive effects provide for assessing practices helps to resolve in practice the cleft between "is" and "ought," because it helps show how proceeding on the basis of practices can and does lead legitimately to changing those practices. Will illustrates this point with some important cases from constitutional law. These observations form the basis of Will's Lamarckian model of both maintenance and change of rules of inference.[2]

---

[1] Will reinforces the point of chapter 6 by endorsing Wittgenstein's point that our abilities to follow rules are ultimately and fundamentally social. The textual basis for such a social interpretation of Wittgenstein is canvassed by Eike V. Savigny in "Self-conscious Individual versus Social Self: The Rationale of Wittgenstein's Discussion of Rule Following," *Philosophy and Phenomenological Research* 51 (1991): 67–84.

[2] Will compares and contrasts his Lamarckian model of concept formation with Toulmin's Darwinian model in *Beyond Deduction*, ch. 1 §§7–10 and ch. 7 §§17–18. One might object that Will's subsumptive-deductive model of practical reasoning is artificially narrow because, as Aristotle or Ross recognized, practical reasoning involves determining which prima facie reasons for acting in particular ways are relevant to one's current circumstances, and determining which of those relevant prima facie reasons are important, or most important, in one's current deliberations. Such reasoning is differential, and not simply subsumptive. This is correct and important,

Will's views about the contrast between formalized logical operations and our actual practices of subsuming individuals under rules are striking and unusual enough that they bear discussion before considering how Will elaborates his basic model of rules in the final two chapters. Will himself refers to Nozick's and Dretske's views about the "closure" of knowledge under known implication. I shall consider Dretske's view on this topic, and then consider the pragmatic dimensions of establishing what Dretske calls stable "channel conditions" and the light Will's views shed on them.

Will remarks that recognizing and understanding the reactive effects of engaging in practices, including mutative effects, is essential for understanding our use of such impeccable logical principles as *modus ponens*, both in unproblematic cases of inferring Socrates's mortality from his humanity, and in problematic cases, that is, cases in which we hesitate to apply this logical principle, even when a valid inference might be made with it. The issue about the "closure" of knowledge under known implication isn't whether *modus ponens*, as a logical principle, is formally invalid; the issue is whether inference based on *modus ponens* are always appropriate whenever we have what appear to be suitable premises. The issue can be formulated with reference to the following "epistemic closure principle":[1]

---

but does not affect the main issue Will addresses, which concerns how we develop, assess, and revise the kinds of general principles which serve as prima facie reasons in practical deliberation. On some interpretations Aristotle addresses this issue with his dialectic of reasoning from particulars to generalities and back to particulars. Additionally, according to Martha Nussbaum, in Aristotle's account of practical reason the perception of particulars can provide an occasion and a basis for assessing the various general rules or prima facie reasons considered in forming a practical syllogism, including its minor premises. (See *The Fragility of Goodness* [Cambridge: Cambridge University Press, 1986], 299–303, 306, 316–17.) These points are altogether in keeping with Will's view of the pragmatic nature of human rationality.

[1] See Frederick Dretske, *Knowledge and the Flow of Information* (Cambridge, Mass.: MIT/Bradford, 1981), 81, 115, 125–34; Stewart Cohen, "Skepticism, Relevance, and Relativity," in *Dretske and his Critics*, B. McLaughlin, ed. (London: Blackwell, 1991), 17–37, pp. 19, 28–29, 33; David Sanford, "Proper Knowledge," ibid., 38–51, pp. 49–51; and Dretske, "Replies," ibid., 180–221, pp. 190–96, 220. Will refers to Nozick, *Philosophical Explanations* (Cambridge: Harvard University Press, 1981), 204–11, 869–90. Also see S. Luper-Foy, ed., *The Possibility of Knowledge: Nozick and his Critics* (Totowa, N. J.: Roman & Littlefield, 1987), especially the contributions by Nozick, Vogel, and Klein.

EPISTEMIC CLOSURE PRINCIPLE: If S knows that q, and S knows that q entails $\sim h$, then S knows $\sim h$.

On the face of it, this principle is intuitively very plausible. If accepted at face value, however, it lands us instantly in irresolvable skepticism. If I see a house, then it's being a *house* that I see entails that it isn't anything incompatible with being a house. ("$\sim h$" in the above principle could just as well be "$\sim(\sim q)$.") This includes its not being a hallucination, or an idea imparted to me by Descartes' evil deceiver, or a vision imparted to me by Putnam's cosmic super-computer while my brain is in a vat, or a dream, or a clever Hollywood mock-up, or ... The list is logically endless. The skeptical problem ensues if it is granted that we don't know that the skeptical hypotheses (Descartes' demon, or his dreams, or Putnam's brains in vats stimulated by super-computers) are false. (Some philosophers have been bold enough to insist that we do know a lot of ordinary perceptual claims, so that we do know these skeptical alternatives to be false.)

Knowing something to be the case generally involves discriminating among various possible states of affairs and identifying the one that is in fact the case. The problem is this: Which alternatives must we eliminate in order to know something? If the answer is *all* logical alternatives, then we can't do it; there is an inexhaustible supply of alternatives to its being, for example, a house I see which I can't rule out. Dretske and Nozick recommend the more modest view that we only have to eliminate *relevant* alternatives. Determining which alternatives are relevant is an important and delicate issue, to which I return below. First, it's important to see the bearing of this point on Will's issues about reactive effects and *modus ponens*. If every and any use of *modus ponens* is acceptable, then we must eliminate every logically possible alternative state of affairs in order to know any one state of affairs. If instead we only need to eliminate *relevant* alternative states of affairs, then only *some* applications of *modus ponens* are relevant. Applications of *modus ponens* are relevant when their conclusions formulate relevant alternatives to the state of affairs we (purportedly) know. Moreover, determining which applications of *modus ponens* are relevant is not simply a deductive procedure. Determining which applications are relevant is a matter of determining which "reactive effects" of making the inference and acting in accord with it are, and which are not, effective in achieving our intellectual and practical aims. In the terms Will uses in "The Rational Governance of Practice" (ch. 4) the reactive effects of acting in accordance with rules, including rules of inference, are what make governance *in* practice, as well as governance *of* practice, possible. This process is, as Will points out in "Pragmatic Rationality" (ch. 8), a pragmatically rational procedure, a procedure which involves the nondeductive assessment of a variety of broader and narrower, both competing and complementary, considerations.

Which alternative states of affairs are relevant? Which ones do we need to eliminate (or, to discriminate between) in order to know something? Dretske answers this question in terms of his information-theoretic approach to epistemology. The basic points of his theory relevant to this question are these.[1] On Dretske's view, information is a function of eliminating alternatives. If there are only two bottles of juice in the refrigerator, and you know that one is apple and the other is orange, and you see me get the orange juice, you know which kind is left in the refrigerator. Dretske's approach to determining which alternatives are relevant, and so need to be eliminated in order to know something, rests on two kinds of considerations. One consideration is natural: What alternatives are, as a matter of natural fact, possible? What alternative states of affairs do the laws of nature allow? These facts set the actual limits on the range of information any source of information can generate. The other consideration is pragmatic, and ultimately social: What are our needs and interests in the information? For a signal to carry information, the relevant alternatives must *be* eliminated; the signal must reliably indicate that only one of the de facto alternatives occurs. In ordinary circumstances, for us to gain knowledge by relying on that signal, we needn't be very stringent about ascertaining whether those alternatives are eliminated. For example, we know that there are movie sets in Hollywood which we wouldn't and couldn't distinguish from real buildings with only a casual glance from afar. But those sets in Hollywood don't pose a problem for our identifying buildings we drive past in New England. However, in critical circumstances (Dretske's example is monitoring the water level in a power-generating boiler), less likely physical possibilities become relevant *to us*, and we need to take greater precautions to ensure that those possibilities are eliminated. (Recall that the relevant alternatives are *natural* possibilities, not merely logical possibilities; skeptical hypotheses aren't automatically relevant in critical situations.) The point is that in critical circumstances, even low statistical probabilities may be relevant to our knowledge of the circum-

---

[1] For an excellent summary, see Dretske's "Précis of *Knowledge and the Flow of Information*," *The Behavioral and Brain Sciences* 6 (1983): 55–63, rpt. in *Epistemology Naturalized*, H. Kornblith, ed. (Cambridge, Mass.: MIT, 1985), 170–87.

stances in question. In this regard, Dretske's and Nozick's rejection of the "epistemic closure principle" acknowledges some of the pragmatic considerations relevant to our use in practice of logical principles, and thus illustrates one of Will's main points about rules and subsumption.[1]

It's worth considering a further feature of Dretske's views in order to bring out another feature of Will's pragmatic account of reason, and to show how his pragmatism relates to one major current in contemporary epistemology. Dretske's title, *Knowledge and the Flow of Information*, indicates his concern with the transfer of information, the transmission of information from sources of information to us as knowers. That transmission occurs through "information channels." Dretske's analysis of the conditions channels must meet in order to serve as information channels is subtle. However, the main point we need to consider is this: Information channels must be reliable or "quiescent" in the sense that they are *stable*; they do not vary or change. Hence they do not themselves generate information. Information is generated by a source, because a source *does* change. Indeed, that's what a source of information *is*. If there is a stable channel between a source and a receiver (us), then the state of the receiver co-varies with the state of the source. In that way, then, the receiver can receive information about the source by receiving information *from* the source via the information channel.

Dretske uses information theory to work out the general conditions lines of transmission must meet in order to be information channels, and he recognizes that there are some important pragmatic and even social considerations concerning whether or when alternatives count as relevant. However, he doesn't integrate these two considerations very thoroughly. Dretske treats information channels as givens; either they exist or they don't.[2] In this way,

---

[1] Michael Williams contends that "the relevant alternatives account of knowledge ... will be effective at all only if the skeptic's alternatives are generally irrelevant to ordinary knowledge claims, which is not easy to show once the skeptic's conception of philosophical inquiry is taken into account" (*Unnatural Doubts*, 188). As noted above, in "Thoughts and Things" Will shows that the skeptic's view of philosophical inquiry rests on the misleading appearance and false theoretical assumption that human beings are capable of experiencing a purely "notional" world utterly disconnected from our natural environment. Williams focuses on Dretske's earlier article, "Epistemic Operators" (*Journal of Philosophy* 67 [1970]: 1007–23), and apparently does not recognize how *Knowledge and the Flow of Information* develops the core insight of the "relevant alternatives" approach while avoiding some problems in his earlier article (*Unnatural Doubts*, 330–36).

[2] In *Explaining Behavior: Reasons in a World of Causes* (Cambridge, Mass.: MIT, 1988), Dretske acknowledges that learning creates mental structures which transmit

his analysis applies most directly to our sensory systems. Dretske doesn't address the fact that human beings, as receivers and decoders of information, have information channels that are partly physiological, partly conceptual and linguistic, and partly technological. Although there is sensation, and in some sense "perception," prior to our learning language, there is little if any perceptual *knowledge* prior to and apart from our linguistic identification of what we perceive. Explicit, linguistically based, conceptual identification is a basic part of *our* discriminating—and thus cognitively identifying—the objects and events we perceive. This is to say, many if not most or even all of *our* information channels are at least in part *artifacts*. Dretske defines knowledge in terms of beliefs caused or sustained by information. He recognizes that the information we can decode from a signal typically depends on a certain amount of background information we have about an information source and its conditions. He proposes to avoid a circularity in his definition of knowledge by appealing to a recursive procedure in acquiring knowledge, in which there is a basic level of first acquisition of knowledge where beliefs can be caused by information decoded without relying on any background knowledge.[1] It is doubtful that there is any such point in human *knowledge* (though surely in nascent experience), but even if there is, appeal to a recursive procedure masks rather than answers the question I pose here, namely: What is the role of language in our information processing? There must be a major role for it, at a very primitive stage of our cognition, if not indeed in our cognizance. Once that role is acknowledged, as it must be in view of the crucial importance of "background information" in decoding signals, then information theoretic epistemology must face the linguistically based challenges to realism addressed by Will, including conceptual schemes, their social history, and the problems these allegedly raise for realism and naturalism.[2]

---

and process information. However, he doesn't think that this introduces a fundamentally social dimension to human thought or knowledge. See below, p. xlvii note 2.

[1] *Knowledge and the Flow of Information*, 86–7.

[2] In "The Nature of Thought" (*Philosophical Studies* 70 [1993]: 185–99), Dretske argues that there can be nonsocially based thought in the case of animals and, by extension, humans. Dretske also contends that learning gives rise to representations which have informational functions (ibid., 192) and that only learning can augment a creature's representational powers from simply perceiving something to believing *that* it perceives some particular kind of thing (ibid., 193). I agree that there are cognitive representations in animals (as anyone who has seriously engaged in animal training realizes), and I agree that human thought and cognition are based in our physiology. However, human thought and human cognition also are discursive and

The same point holds, mutatis mutandis, for causal-reliability accounts of knowledge.[1]

To recall, in "Rules and Subsumption" (ch. 7) Will distinguishes between routine and problematic cases of subsumption of instances under rules, and he insists that the "reactive effects" of subsuming instances under rules are important in both kinds of cases. In cases of routine subsumption, the reactive effects of yet another successful subsumption reenforce and thus maintain that practice of subsumption. In cases of problematic subsumption, the reactive effects are usually mutative, because they give us grounds for modifying our practice of subsuming those problematic instances under rules. Will's and Dretske's views converge on this point: Whether we're concerned with ele-

---

are linguistically based. While we can learn to refine our sensory discriminations, and thus refine the kinds of discriminations common in our culture, the bulk of human cognitive discriminations rely on the linguistic categories children and students are taught, and the revisions individuals make of those categories are made by using socially developed and taught skills and resources, including linguistic resources. The different ways in which suburbanites, skiers, and the Inuit discriminate kinds of snow, the different ways in which philistines and aesthetes discriminate colors, the different ways aesthetes from the Occident and the Orient discriminate colors, and historically the different ways physical phenomena have been described and classified, are all evidence of the enormous, if typically unnoticed, influence our social circumstances have on the particular ways in which we identify objects and events, and thus the enormous influence our society plays in forming the content of specific thoughts we have. These social factors do not, however, generate the kinds of problems about explaining individual behavior which concern Dretske (ibid., 187, 197), nor do they provide grounds for rejecting realism, for reasons Will provides. (Dretske's view in this essay can work only for creatures whose learning abilities are genetically determined. However, the learning abilities of human beings are genetically conditioned but not determined. Will discusses the social and linguistic factors involved in individual beliefs in *Induction and Justification*, ch. 7, esp. §§9, 10, 13*f*. The issue is controversial and cannot be settled in a brief note. See Dretske's essay, cited above, for some good recent references.

[1] This is particularly evident in causal theories which acknowledge that discrimination among distinct states of affairs is fundamental to perceptual knowledge, e.g., Alvin Goldman, "Discrimination and Perceptual Knowledge," *The Journal of Philosophy* 73, no. 20 (1976): 771–91. Of course human beings make organic responses to the environment which differentiate between different objects or events; otherwise human infants couldn't survive and natural languages would be unlearnable. However, as noted with regard to Dretske's information theory, the vast majority of, if not all, such discriminations which count as human *knowledge*, while perceptually based, are also linguistically—and thus socially—facilitated. (This point is touched on, though admittedly only too briefly, by Alvin Plantinga, *Warrant and Proper Function* [New York: Oxford University Press, 1993], 99–102.)

mentary syllogisms, elaborate linguistic systems of classification or inference, or with sophisticated technological instruments for detecting subtle physical conditions or events, whenever routine subsumption is possible, we're dealing with a stable channel for transmitting information. Whenever routine subsumption is not possible, whenever subsumption is problematic, we're confronted with some as-yet intractable situation (whether logical, linguistic, taxonomic, technical, or scientific). Here our circumstances are variable and thus serve as sources of information, often rich ones. Viewed historically, science has succeeded in routinizing ever more exacting and subtle scales and kinds of phenomena (whether minute or vast). Once routinized, those phenomena, and our instruments and theories with which we engage and interpret them, become stable information channels with which we can then investigate new and still problematic phenomena. The new information we obtain in these ways have led in some remarkable cases to recasting our theories and to re-interpreting our experimental procedures and techniques. Those reinterpreta-tions generally have either involved preserving a sound core of prior proced-ure, or else have provided a well-motivated replacement for prior procedures and theories. Dretske's point is that information can be conveyed so long as channel conditions are in fact stable. If investigators succeed in establishing a reliable procedure or technique, then that procedure or technique *is* an information channel, even if the initial understanding of that procedure or technique requires subsequent revision. Will's account of the "reactive effects" of our subsuming particulars under our rule-governed practices, and our reliance on those effects to assess our rules critically, whether to validate or to revise them, highlights the pragmatically rational character of these kinds of episode in the history of technology and science. Will augments his ac-count considerably in the final two chapters.

In "Pragmatic Rationality" (ch. 8) Will draws together the considerations raised in the previous chapters in order to argue three main points. First, the pragmatic processes by which we revise our procedures and their rules are not distinct in kind or occurrence from the calculative or deductive proced-ures by which we apply procedures and rules to particular objects or events. They are instead two complementary aspects of rational thought and action. Second, focusing exclusively on the calculative procedures of deducing conclu-sions from major premises leads to seriously misidentifying and misunder-standing the rationality of the ways in which we modify our practices and their principles. This misunderstanding has occurred in many areas of philoso-phy, where the deductive calculation of conclusions has taken various forms: making predictions within a formalized scientific theory or linguistic framework, puzzle solving within a paradigm, applying (rather than determining) the law in judicial judgments, or arguing for normative conclusions on the basis of one's moral intuitions. In each of these cases, the direct and inevitable result of regarding only our deductive procedures as rational is that any significant change in our most basic procedures and principles must be non- if not irrational. In Hume, only custom can guide life, while reason can only be a handmaid of sentiment (emotion). In Carnap, choices of linguistic frame- works cannot be justified, because justifying reasons can only be given within a linguistic framework. In Quine, choices of basic ontology are equally free and unarguable. In Kuhn, changes from one paradigm to another are irrational. In the law, judicial determination of the law can only be a matter of the arbitrary preferences of the judge (legal realism). In moral philosophy, the fundamental divergence and irreconcilability of basic moral intuitions must grudgingly be acknowledged, perhaps by ceding the case of emotivism.

In partial opposition to these kinds of conclusions, some legal theorists have recognized that cases of judicial determination certainly do include careful assessment of various relevant considerations, both narrow and broad. Similarly, some historians of science have recognized that scientific discovery rests on carefully considering various observational, experimental, and theor- etical factors. Will contends, third, that these kinds of cases in which proce- dures and their principles are modified and expanded can be rational, if they are performed intelligently, and that a proper account of reason must include these ampliative aspects of reasoning along with the calculative, deductive aspects of reason as their necessary complement. Recognizing these two complementary aspects of reason helps to resolve numbers of otherwise recalcitrant problems in philosophy and in the philosophical assessment of other domains and problems.

Some of the significance of Will's views about the philosophic gover- nance of norms can be highlighted by showing the extent to which Barbara Herman's insightful reconstruction of Kant's ethical theory, *The Practice of Moral Judgment*, at several crucial points verges on Will's pragmatism.[1] Herman contends that Kant's views must be augmented in at least four ways. First, she argues that Kant's test of the Categorical Imperative cannot func- tion without a rich set of "Rules of Moral Salience," which help us identify the morally salient features of our circumstances. These provide the basic

---

[1] Cambridge, Mass.: Harvard University Press, 1993; cited as "*Practice.*"

data on which moral judgment and moral deliberation are based.[1] Second, she distinguishes moral judgment from moral deliberation. Moral judgment is routine and is generally guided by the Rules of Moral Salience together with familiar principles and procedures. Moral deliberation occurs relatively rarely, when an agent identifies morally relevant features of his or her circumstances which may require or allow an exception to standard procedures.[2] Herman's distinction between moral judgment and moral deliberation parallels Will's distinctions between governance "in" and "of" practice and between routine and problematic subsumption (chs. 4, 7), and like Will, Herman recognizes that there is no distinctive procedure (or algorithm, deductive procedure) for the problematic subsumption involved in moral deliberation.[3]

Third, in order to account for the consequences of actions within Kant's framework of assessing actions by assessing their maxims, Herman introduces "maxims of response," which concern how agents react to the results of their actions.[4] She introduces maxims of response on the basis of a simple but important observation:

> We know that to act effectively for any but the simplest ends requires preparation, then efforts, and a somewhat open-textured set of responses to the way well-intentioned efforts may go awry.[5]

Herman's use of "open texture" in this connection recalls Will's points about the open texture of concepts and rules (chs. 1, 7). Her observation reflects the pragmatic character of human rationality, the way in which we take what Will calls the "reactive effects" of our actions into account in assessing and modifying our procedures (ch. 7). This point provides the basis for recognizing the role of reactive effects in assessing and revising our principles of action, the existence and importance of which is suggested in Herman's fourth supplement to Kant's moral theory.

Finally, Herman notes that Kant recognizes the need to complete his system of ethics by specifying a series of corollaries concerning how to apply the a priori principles of ethics to particular agents in their specific circum-

---

[1] *Practice*, 93.
[2] *Practice*, 145–46, 201.
[3] *Practice*, 157.
[4] *Practice*, 98.
[5] *Practice*, 102.

stances.[1] To understand how such empirical facts relate to Kant's principles of practical reason requires what Herman calls "Middle Theory."[2] Middle Theory "is the theory of the practice of moral judgment," linking theory of value and theory of applications. It articulates "the contingent structure of rational agency" and it investigates the empirical circumstances of deliberation which expose rational agency to misuse. Some of these circumstances are inherent in our species, others are contingent on social, institutional, or other historical conditions. Middle Theory thus expands our list of moral categories and it charged with assessing and revising the Rules of Moral Salience. Because Middle Theory both shapes and is shaped by our practices,[3] it requires a pragmatic account of rationality like Will's. Herman recognizes that the revision of our principles and practices must be "internal."[4] For criticism to be both legitimate and internal requires addressing both of the illusions Will dissolves, the "Coherence Illusion" and the "Relativist Illusion" (ch. 5). Once Herman acknowledges that not only the Rules of Moral Salience, but also moral theory itself is subject to critical revision,[5] she verges on recognizing Will's point that even our highest practical principles are justified and are subject to amplification and revision based on the reactive effects of their employment.

Now Herman tries to retain the rationalist elements of Kant's ethics by appealing to Kant's alleged a priori fact of reason that we are obligated to act on the basis of the Categorical Imperative[6] and by retaining Kant's account of human dignity as the fundamental value guiding all our moral thought and action. On Herman's account, Kant's Formula of the "Realm of Ends" expresses the idea of a social plurality of self-legislating autonomous agents. This idea implies that, to the extent we are social beings, institutions and practices necessary for social life can only be justified—they are only legitimate—if they are consistent with recognizing each agent as an equal and autonomous member.[7] As a source of ultimate and intrinsic reasons for

---

[1] Kant, *The Doctrine of Virtue*, in *The Metaphysics of Morals*, M. J. Gregor, tran. (Cambridge: Cambridge University Press, 1991), Part II, §45; Herman, *Practice*, 233.

[2] *Practice*, 233.

[3] *Practice*, 236.

[4] *Practice*, ix.

[5] *Practice*, 185.

[6] *Practice*, 85–87, 93.

[7] *Practice*, 237.

accepting or rejecting maxims, rational agency has a special kind of value, called "dignity."[1] However, Herman does not offer any particular grounds to support her use of Kant's a priori claims, and by the end of her analysis it appears that the alleged intrinsic value of "dignity" does not play the role she ascribes to it. Instead, the operative principle of justification in her account appears to be that legitimate principles must (inter alia) be mutually acceptable.[2] The core idea of respecting persons as rational agents is to act on principles which they, as rational agents, can in principle accept.[3] If this is correct, then the further development of the research program she sets out in *The Practice of Moral Judgment* requires adopting the pragmatic account of rationality developed by Frederick Will.[4]

6. Philosophic Governance of Norms

As is fitting, Will's final chapter, "Philosophic Governance of Norms," brings together and extends the analyses developed in the preceding eight chapters. Will's main negative point is that viewing norms as explicit, over-arching principles or rules from which we deduce guidance to particular actions, inevitably faces us with insuperable philosophical and historical problems. First, if we follow the justification of our acts regressively up the deductive chain of reasons, we inevitably confront irresolvable problems about divergent principles, intuitions, conventions, or just plain skepticism. (Wittgen-stein's paradoxes about rule-following count as objections to precisely this view of norms.) Second, if we view rational justification solely in this deduc-tive way, we will inevitably find major periods of social and scientific transi-tion rationally intractable; they will invariably look to us like mere changes of fashion. The only way to solve these problems about the nature of justifi-cation is to change our understanding of norms by adopting the pragmatic

---

[1] *Practice*, 237–38.

[2] This is a complex point which cannot be explored further here. For discussion see my "How 'Full' is Kant's Categorical Imperative?," *Jahrbuch für Recht und Ethik/Annual Review of Law and Ethics* 3 (1995): 465–509, esp. §5.9.

[3] *Cf.* Onora O'Neill, *Constructions of Reason* (Cambridge: Cambridge University Press, 1989), ch. 7, esp. pp. 138–39. I develop this point in "Do Kant's Principles Justify Property or Usufruct?" *Jahrbuch für Recht und Ethik/Annual Review of Law and Ethics* 5 (1997), esp. §§3, 4.

[4] Herman repeatedly indicates the exploratory character of her account, and its need for further development, e.g., *Practice*, viii, 72, 112.

liv   Pragmatism and Realism

view according to which rational norms are inherently embedded in our practices, and are subject to rational assessment and modification only because they are thus embedded.

Some writers in ethics have proposed to avoid this regress to first principles—and to avoid Will's kind of pragmatism—by appeal to the following non-deductive schema: (1) If conflicts and confusions in commonsense moral judgments can be clarified and resolved by some principle P, and if these judgments can be systematized and explained by P, then P is an ultimate moral principle; (2) Conflicts and confusions in commonsense moral judgments can be clarified and resolved by some particular principle Q, and this principle can explain and systematize these judgments; (3) Therefore principle Q is a fundamental moral principle.[1] Setting aside questions about "fundamentality," several points could be made about this schema. The most immediately relevant are these. This schema avoids conflict about first principles (premise 1) only by relocating it in controversy about any candidate particular principles Q (premise 2). More important, any particular principle Q must clarify, resolve, explain, and systematize commonsense moral judgments in a *normative* way, a way which shows why those moral judgments are right, valid, or (in sum) justified. If principle Q justifies commonsense moral judgments by deductively entailing them, then this schema does not provide a genuine alternative to the deductivist model of justification, and it shares the problems inherent in that model. If principle Q justifies commonsense moral judgments in some nondeductive way, this alternative mode of justification must be explicated and the question remains whether it differs from Will's pragmatic account. There are good reasons to suppose that ultimately this kind of justification coincides with Will's pragmatic account of justification of norms. To show how some principle Q clarifies, resolves, explains, and systematizes commonsense moral judgments, we must already be able to ascertain at least many commonsense moral judgments which are right, valid, or justified. (If principle Q showed that a commonsense moral judgment was

---

[1] This strategy can be found, for example, in Hardy Jones, "Are Fundamental Moral Principles Incapable of Proof?," *Metaphilsophy* 10 (1979): 153–60, pp. 155–56, and Marcus G. Singer, "The Ideal of a Rational Morality," *Proceedings and Addresses of the American Philosophical Association* 60 (1986): 15–38 (cited as "Ideal"), pp. 27–28. Jones argues persuasively that this strategy is employed by Henry Sidgwick, *The Methods of Ethics* (London: Macmillan, 7th ed. 1907). This strategy is also close, if not identical, to the Rawlsian method of "reflective equilibrium" and it is used by those who seek to elucidate the wisdom and insight of commonsense morality.

justified when it isn't, that would be counterevidence against that principle.) The pragmatic character of the clarification, resolution, explanation, and systematization of commonsense moral judgments becomes more evident once it is recognized that many commonsense moral judgments change historically with changes in the conditions of life and changes in our insight into or understanding of the nature, activities, and purpose(s) of human life. These changes can be subtle, but if "fundamental" moral principles are to be justified by their power to explain and systematize them, this raises the very real possibility that those principles are also variable and corrigible. This points away from an ideal of a noninstitutional One True Rational Morality which alone is supposed to provide a basis for criticizing commonsense (positive or institutional) morality, and toward recognizing the pragmatic point Will makes, that normative principles and particular judgments are interdependent and mutually corrigible.

The point about historical variability of commonsense moral judgments is controversial and easily misunderstood, but cannot be explored in detail here. Significant historical variability is compatible with the universal "principle of justice" that what is right for one (kind of) person is right for any relevantly similar person in relevantly similar circumstances.[1] However, such "universal principles" are abstractions from and very incomplete representations of norms as concrete modes of practice.[2] Furthermore, the challenging issues concern the basis on which the relevant similarities and differences among persons and circumstances are ascertained and justified. More importantly, even when exaggerated to counterfactual extremes, the point of historical variability has much less to do with variability and much more to do with highlighting the basic character of the justification of norms represented in the above schema. As in Will's pragmatic account, so too in this schema: General normative principles are justified through their integration with the particular judgments they inform, and they are normative only insofar and as long as

---

[1] This is Marcus Singer's strategy. He distinguishes moral principles—which are exceptionless, always relevant, and cannot conflict—from moral rules (and in particular from "neutral norms" and "local rules") which admit of exceptions, are not always relevant, and some of which are subject to change. See *Generalization in Ethics* (New York: Atheneum, 1961), chs. 2, 5.

[2] Cf. below, ch. 7. Whether abstract principles are self-sufficient or are abstractions from concrete practices is a complex and controversial point which cannot be justified by brief introductory remarks. The merits of Will's view of norms on this count must be ascertained by how well it illuminates and resolves problems about the character of theoretical and practical reasoning, both in theory and in practice.

they inform those particular judgments within the context and activities in which and about which they are made.

Some significant recognition of this point can be found even in a staunch opponent of pragmatism such as Marcus Singer. Singer extols the Kantian ideal of an a priori, noninstitutional one true rational morality.[1] However, elsewhere he comes much closer to Will's pragmatism. Singer cites E. F. Carritt's doctrine of the "Primacy of the Particular":

> When we criticize a particular moral judgment as being inconsistent with a principle, it is ultimately with other particular judgments that our comparison must be made. For the principle may be an inaccurate generalization.[2]

Singer admits that this sounds almost self-evident, but then inverts Carritt's doctrine:

> When we criticize a (general moral) principle as being inconsistent with a particular moral judgment, it is ultimately with other (general) principles that our comparison must be made. For the (particular) judgment may be an inaccurate particularization.

Singer then comments:

> The truth seems to be rather that neither pole, neither the particular nor the general, is necessarily prior. Sometimes we have certainty at one end of the spectrum and not at the other, and other times the situation is reversed. ...

---

[1] Cf. "Ideal." One of Singer's reasons for holding this view is his assumption that it alone can provide a basis for criticizing positive morality (ibid., 17). This, however, remains an assumption on his part, one which Will's analysis shows to be unwarranted. Genuine criticism and self-criticism do not require Platonism or Kantian *a priori*sm. (See below, chs. 4–9.) Singer appears to believe that because the principle of justice is a priori, it is neither subject to pragmatic critique nor in need of pragmatic justification. The pragmatic account of the a priori cannot be discussed here, but it may be mentioned that Kant's account of the a priori was deeply flawed and that pragmatism offers a very sophisticated account of the a priori. See Philip Kitcher, "How Kant Almost Wrote 'Two Dogmas of Empiricism' (and Why He Didn't)," in *Essays on Kant's Critique of Pure Reason*, J. N. Mohanty and R. W. Shahan, eds. (Norman, Okla.: University of Oklahoma Press, 1982), 217–49; and Ralph Sleeper, *The Necessity of Pragmatism: John Dewey's Conception of Philosophy* (New Haven: Yale University Press, 1986).

[2] Carritt, *The Theory of Morals* (London: Oxford, 1928), 70.

The general is already implicit in the particular, and the particular is actually
already implicit in the general.[1]

This observation confirms that general normative principles are justified
through their integration with particular moral judgments. Because the proper
integration of normative principles and particular judgments is sought with
the ends-in-view of guiding effective and appropriate action, this kind of
holism is tantamount to pragmatism. This shows that the nondeductive schema
sketched above provides no alternative to Will's pragmatic account of norms
and their justification, because it in fact conforms to Will's view. This is not
surprising in view of the fact that the argument schema Singer and Jones
endorse is abductive, a mode of argument first explicitly identified and analyzed by the founding father of pragmatism, C. S. Peirce.[2]

Will's primary aim is to understand the nature of norms. He does this in
pragmatic terms, treating norms frankly as sociopsychological entities. The
norms a group accepts are, qua accepted, norms. It is then a further question,
which norms are better or more justifiable than others? This question Will
has not attempted to answer, though his views on the nature of norms suggest
many important points relevant to it. This is not to deny the importance of
this further issue. Rather, it is to stress that attention has been distracted by
preoccupation with this question from the more basic question regarding the
nature of norms, their generation, assessment, and revision. This distraction
has resulted in recalcitrant misunderstanding and question-begging among
practitioners and normative theorists. Only with an answer to the basic questions about the nature of norms—including their generation, assessment, and
revision—firmly in view can we properly approach the more common question, which norms are the best, or are better than others? Will's answers to
the more basic questions do not make answering this latter question easy, but
they do make clear the wide and rich array of resources pertinent to answering it.

Will emphasizes again that norms cohere more and less tightly into
groups, and that only as grouped together can norms in fact guide our thought

---

[1] "Universalizability and the Generalization Principle," in *Morality and Universality*, N. T. Potter and M. Timmons, eds. (Dordrecht & Boston: Reidel, 1985), 47–73,
p. 60. Cf. Singer, "Ethics and Common Sense," *Revue Internationale de Philosophie*
40, no. 158 (1986): 221–58, pp. 245–46.

[2] See Peirce, *Collected Papers*, C. Hartshorne, P. Weiss, and A. Burks, eds.
(Cambridge, Mass.: Harvard University Press, 1931–58), vol. 5, 145, 172, 189.

or action. In chapter 9 he augments these points in two ways. These extensions develop Will's view of the governance of norms beyond Dewey's, and they help redress the occasionalist character of Dewey's instrumentalism. First, the extent to which we govern our norms in practice unreflectively or reflectively can vary considerably. More important, Will emphasizes that the more obvious or "manifest" aspects of norms are only part of each norm. Every norm also has a rich implicit or "latent" aspect which connects it with many other norms, both local and remote. He illustrates some of the breadth of these latent aspects of norms by referring to the broad concerns bearing historically on the shift from geocentric to heliocentric astronomy, or currently on the abortion controversy.

Some of the significance of Will's view of the "latent" aspects of norms can be brought out by considering the contrast between defining and explicating concepts and by comparison with Gerd Buchdahl's views on scientific theories. Ideally, definitions fully specify the necessary and sufficient conditions for the use or application of a concept. Explications provide partial definitions which clarify and may revise what is implicit in a concept in use. Both Kant and Carnap recognize the difference between explicating and defining concepts, they both recognize that only arbitrarily invented concepts can, strictly speaking, be defined, and so they both recognize the importance of explicating central, basic concepts found in our everyday and scientific discourses.[1] This notion of explication is a genuine insight on their part, and is far more informative and realistic than modern notions of clear and distinct ideas or recent notions of conceptual analysis. However, neither Kant nor Carnap recognize the pragmatic point Will makes, that to explicate a concept is to articulate conceptually the manifest aspects of a norm or norms; it is to clarify the linguistically formulable aspects of social practices which have complex nonlinguistic roots in our activities and in the structure of the social and physical environment in which we conduct our activities and pursue our needs (both theoretical and practical).

One problem confronted in the heyday of linguistic analysis is the paradox of analysis. Roughly, the problem is that a conceptual analysis (the *analysands*) must have exactly the same meaning as the concept(s) analyzed (the *analysandum*), and yet the analysis must be informative in ways that appear

---

[1] Kant, *Critique of Pure Reason*, A727–8/B755–6; Carnap, *Logical Foundations of Probability* (Chicago: University of Chicago Press, 1950), 3–7.

inconsistent with this identity in meaning.[1] This paradox arises on the mistaken assumption that our conceptual resources must be transparent to us because they are strictly linguistic. Once we recognize that our conceptual resources are part and parcel of complex forms of practice, then the kind of transparency which gives rise to the paradox of analysis is exposed as a myth, a linguistic analog to Cartesian transparency of consciousness. This reinforces the importance of conceptual explication over analysis or (strict) definition.

Gerd Buchdahl greatly expanded the notion of explication in scientific contexts by showing that scientific theories take shape and have explanatory power only within a rich setting comprising three kinds of components: a probative component, an explicative component, and a systemic component.[2] The probative component determines the evidential support or probability of a theory. It concerns the detection, selection, and colligation of observational and experimental data, as guided by hypotheses, and their processing through various methods, such as induction, confirmation, corroboration, or Bayesian principles of probability. The systemic component determines the rational coherence or unity of a theory. It concerns the systematic articulation of the theory in view of consilience of inductions, the sociohistorically conditioned development of research programs, and other intertheoretical relations and background information. The explicative component determines the intelligibility or "possibility" of the theory. This conceptual explication or metaphysical foundation of the theory produces the "hard core" conceptual scheme of the theory in question and determines the ontological status of the explanatory concepts and principles of the theory. This explicative component interacts with broader issues concerning the plausibility of the theory, and these issues

---

[1] On the paradox of analysis see C. H. Langford, "The Notion of Analysis in Moore's Philosophy," G. E. Moore, "Reply to My Critics: III. Philosophic Method," both in *The Philosophy of G. E. Moore*, P. A. Schilpp, ed. (New York: Tudor, 1942), 319–42, 660–77 (respectively); Richard Hare, "Philosophical Discoveries," and Paul Henle, "Do We Discover Our Uses of Words?," both rpt. in *The Linguistic Turn*, R. Rorty, ed. (Chicago: University of Chicago Press, 1967), 206–17, 218–23.

[2] Buchdahl summarizes his view in "Neo-transcendental Approaches Towards Scientific Theory Appraisal," in *Science, Belief and Behaviour*, D. H. Mellor, ed. (Cambridge: Cambridge University Press, 1980), 1–20, and in *Kant and the Dynamics of Reason* (London: Blackwell, 1992), chs. 1, 3 (see Figures 1.3 and 3.4). His earlier book, *Metaphysics and the Philosophy of Science* (London: Blackwell, 1969) demonstrates brilliantly that this kind of setting is an important and legitimate concern in modern philosophy which survives logical positivism's critique and rejection of traditional metaphysics.

about plausibility also affect the systemic articulation of the theory. The plausibility of a theory is determined by heuristic maxims and regulative principles such as simplicity, economy, continuity or discontinuity, conservation of data or theoretical scope, or preferred types of explanation.

Buchdahl's considerations reveal that traditional notions about confirmation of single principles or hypotheses by enumerative induction or statistical probability alone are woefully oversimplified because of the enormous number and kinds of factors which bear on the development and assessment of scientific theories. His considerations also reveal that the "underdetermination" of theory by data does not, of itself, have the drastic skeptical or relativist implications often associated with it. This clearly is very much in accord with Will's pragmatic realism. However, there is a further point of particular interest in connection with the latent aspects of norms. Buchdahl argues persuasively that these three kinds of considerations bear on the development and assessment of scientific theories. Will's point about the latent aspects of norms highlights the converse of Buchdahl's insight: The considerations Buchdahl highlights bear on scientific theories because those theories have rich latent aspects which bear on those broader kinds of considerations.

Finally, it is significant to note that Kant, Carnap, and Buchdahl each reject realism, but in each case, their rejections fail for the same kind of reason, indeed for the reason highlighted by Will in "Thoughts and Things" (ch. 1). Did we not live in a naturally structured world of relatively stable and identifiable macrolevel objects and events, we could not be self-conscious (Kant), there would be no relative frequencies of events which could be better (or worse) organized or predicted by linguistic frameworks (Carnap), and we would have no commonsense or scientific "life world" whose ontology we could (re)construct (Buchdahl).[1] Commonsense realism may perhaps be revisable, but it is not dispensable. The crucial point is that the revisions of commonsense or scientific notions occur, not by the kinds of confrontations of data and theory or probability functions which have entranced empiricists, but by the kinds of pragmatic processes highlighted by Will.

Will stresses that the controversy and indecision which accompanies such assessment and revision of deep-seated norms is neither avoidable nor, ultimately, regrettable. (This is not to say that particular acts made in the heat

---

[1] I defend these criticisms, independently of Will and on grounds internal to their views, in "Affinity, Idealism, and Naturalism," *Hegel's Epistemological Realism*, ch. 4, and "Buchdahl's 'Phenomenological' View of Kant: A Critique," *Kant-Studien* (1997).

of controversy may not be regrettable.) Only through such controversy do we have opportunities to achieve new insights and principles. The various considerations adduced by parties to such disputes each represent some facet of a society's norms and practices. The challenge during such controversy is to find a new way of recomposing those facets into a feasible set of integrated practices. In this regard, Will emphasizes, the grounds for changing norms are the same in kind as the grounds for maintaining them, namely, their reactive effects within and on our practices. The legitimacy of a norm, whether it is already accepted or is newly proposed, is a function of how well it can serve to compose the whole complex of associated norms and practices and thereby to guide our activities, both collectively and individually.

One of Will's main points is that we *do* engage in such critical and revisionary activities. Much as we may want an algorithm to resolve social or scientific controversy, that Leibnizian hope is doomed by the fact that were there such an algorithm, it and its legitimacy would be equally controversial. We will do a much better job, and will much better appreciate the job we do, if we recognize the pragmatic rationality we in fact exercise, individually or collectively, during such rationally pragmatic reconstruction of our norms and practices.

Will's book, it should be plain, presents a sustained, provocative, and insightful pragmatic analysis of some very fundamental philosophical issues regarding the assessment and justification of cognitive and practical norms. After studying the analyses developed here, the interested reader can find these themes developed further in Will's second book, *Beyond Deduction*.

Kenneth R. Westphal

Sources and Acknowledgments

"Thoughts and Things" is the presidential address delivered before the Sixty-seventh Annual Meeting of the Western (now Central) Division of the American Philosophical Association in Cleveland, Ohio, May 2, 1969. It originally appeared in *Proceedings and Addresses of the American Philosophical Association* 42 (1968–69): 51–69.

"Truth and Correspondence" originally appeared in *The Philosophical Forum* 9, no. 1 (1977): 60–77.

"The Concern About Truth" originally appeared in George W. Roberts, ed., *The Bertrand Russell Memorial Volume* (London: George Allen & Unwin, New York: Humanities Press, 1979), 264–84.

"The Rational Governance of Practice" originally appeared in *American Philosophical Quarterly* 18, no. 3 (1981): 191–201.

"Reason, Social Practice, and Scientific Realism" originally appeared in *Philosophy of Science* 48, no. 1 (1981): 1–18.

"Reason and Tradition" originally appeared in *Modern Age* 27, no. 2 (1983): 171–79.

"Rules and Subsumption: Mutative Aspects of Logical Processes" originally appeared in *The American Philosophical Quarterly* 22, no. 2 (1985): 143–51.

"Pragmatic Rationality" originally appeared in *Philosophical Investigations* 8, no. 2 (1985): 120–42.

"Philosophic Governance of Norms" originally appeared in *Jahrbuch für Recht und Ethik/Annual Review of Law and Ethics* 1, no. 1 (1993): 329–61.

We wish to thank each of the editors, journals, and publishers who gave their permission to reprint these essays here. I also thank the Center for the Humanities at the University of New Hampshire for defraying some of the initial costs of producing this volume.   –K.R.W.

1

Thoughts and Things

There is no reason why "thought" ... [considered as an activity, a "species of conduct"] ... should be taken in that narrow sense in which silence and darkness are favorable to thought. It should rather be understood as covering all rational life, so that an experiment shall be an operation of thought.

–Peirce, 1905

One must not take a nominalistic view of Thought as if it were something that a man had in his consciousness. Consciousness may mean anyone of the three categories. But if it is to mean Thought it is more without us than within. It is we that are in it, rather than it in any of us.

–Peirce to James, 1902

1   Among the more widely received views in the Western philosophical tradition there is one, common to a variety of positions and hence finding expression in a variety of ways, concerning the nature of thought, its relation to things, and consequently its role in the development of our knowledge of things. The view in question does not commonly appear, at least in recent philosophy, as an explicit thesis or theory about thought. It functions much more implicitly as an assumption underlying the treatment of such closely related topics as ideas, concepts, criteria, definition, verification, and so on. The central feature of the view is that thought, considered just as thought, has a certain autonomy in relation to things, a certain fundamental independence of them. Of course when thoughts are employed to convey information about

1

things they are dependent in an obvious way upon things for their truth or falsity. But apart from this true or false relation, and various subsidiary relations connected with it, thoughts, considered simply in themselves, are not, according to this view, dependent upon things. In order for me to entertain thoughts concerning the kind of stone in the Washington Monument, it is not necessary for me to think of the stone as marble, which it is. I may think of it as granite, which it is not; but apart from the more or less serious discrepancy now obtaining between my thought and the stone, the thought that the stone is granite is no less a thought than the less discrepant one that it is marble, or the even more discrepant one that it is sandstone or chalk. What establishes that there are no more passenger pigeons is not that it is hard to think of them, but that they are hard to see.

As John Dewey would have said, the view in question is surely in part a legacy of the mind-body dualism that underlies a considerable portion of modern philosophical thought. The durability of the view is displayed in the way it lingers, exerting an appeal and affecting decisions in the reflections of a variety of philosophers who in their more explicit metaphysical pronouncements show little attachment to the older, fuller versions of this dualistic scheme. It is not a question of whether our thoughts, as psychological phenomena, are in some way determined to be what they are by things. The denial that there is such determination is not a part of the view in question. It is commonly and compatibly associated with the further view that things of various sorts play an important part in the generation and conditioning of thought. Beginning with our brains, central nervous systems, and sense organs, and continuing far beyond these in our physical environment, there are all kinds of states and events in the world of things, that are commonly conceded to affect the character of thought, just as, for example, my own thought is affected by the pressure of the blood in the arteries of my head, and by the intensity of the light on my desk, as I write these words.

But in the view under examination the kind of determination just exemplified is taken to be altogether a matter of the generation and conditioning of thought, and to be not a matter of the character or identity of the thought itself. The relations between our thoughts and their generating and conditioning antecedents and concomitants in things are what, in certain philosophical discussions earlier in this century, were called "external" rather than "internal" relations. They are relations that are external to the terms they relate in the sense that the terms related are contingent in respect to each other; so that while it may be a matter of contingent fact that objects of kind B are always associated with objects of kind A, this association is not a necessary or logical one. It is not essential to B, not a matter of its character or identity as B, that it be associated with A. An A failing to accompany B may amaze and disturb us, but it cannot, as it were, disturb B. B is what it is, independently of A, independently of whether A accompanies it always, sometimes, or even none of the time.

What is essential to a thought, on this view, is the character it has as an event or state realized in the private theater of the mind; consciousness, head, or brain of some thinking being. However the metaphysical constitution of this theater may be conceived—whether as a Cartesian mind or a Hobbesian brain—it is the event or state, the scene occurring in this theater, that is the thought as distinguished from the contingent accompaniments of it. In the most common versions of the view the theater has been identified with consciousness, so that it is sufficient in order for the character of a thought to be known directly and infallibly by some thinking being, that it occurs in the theater or thought-forum of that being. But this feature is not essential. What is essential, rather, is the conception of thought as located in and restricted to the medium of the mind or body of the thinker, and yet capable, by virtue of its peculiar character, of laying hold of, representing, referring to objects beyond. The character and power of representation of thought are conceived as residing altogether in the event or state in this medium, and hence as independent of the things represented, or any other objects beyond the medium, in the world of things.

2   A striking example of this independence of thought from things is presented by Descartes as in reflection he confronted his supposed demon. The capacity of the human mind to fall into error that is represented in the person of this demon, though it extends far, is nevertheless limited, as the dramatic pronouncement "*Cogito, ergo sum,*" is intended to signal. In order for me to be deceived, I must exist. Not even a demon can deceive a non-existent person. Similarly not even a demon can make it that a being that thinks badly, or in error, does not think at all. Here in the realm of thought is a preserve from the contingencies of error upon which even the most powerful demon cannot encroach.

If we construe the term "thought" as widely as Descartes did, to include acts of will, of affirmation and denial, as well as the passions, and sensations, there are a variety of errors of which our thought may be capable that are not cognitive ones, but rather, for example, moral ones, prudential ones, and so on. Recognizing this in the *Meditations*, Descartes chose the narrower term "idea" to refer to that species of thought to which the conception of cognitive error may properly be applied. "Some of my thoughts," he wrote,

> are, as it were, images of things; and to them alone strictly belongs the title "idea," *e.g.*, when I represent to myself a man, or a chimera, or the sky, or an angel, or even God.[1]

But although it is in these representational thoughts, these ideas, that "truth and error, in the strict sense, are to be found," according to Descartes, nevertheless truth or error does not reside in any idea in itself. So long as ideas are "considered only in themselves," as he proceeded to observe at once,

> and not as referred to some other thing, they cannot, strictly speaking, be false. Whether I imagine a she-goat or a chimera, that I imagine the latter is no less true than that I imagine the former.[2]

It is in the *judgments* we make with ideas that falsity and error are possible. Considered in themselves, ideas are ways of thinking, mere modes of consciousness. So considered, without reference to anything beyond, they "hardly afford," Descartes said, "any material for error."[3]

One way of putting the point of Descartes here is that the capacity for error in thought lies, not in our thoughts of things, but in our thoughts about things. My thought about the stone in the Washington Monument—that it is marble—is capable of being true or false. But the thought of the stone itself, the idea of this, is simply the thought or idea. Where in that is there material for error, any opening for the demon to effect deception? When I set out to characterize the stone truly as marble, I may fail because of the character of the stone. It may, if it is granite or something else, thwart my intention. But how can the thought of the stone itself go wrong? It cannot be other than the

---

[1] *Descartes' Philosophical Writings*, N. K. Smith, ed. and tran. (New York: Modern Library, 1958), Med. III, 195–96.

[2] Meditation III. The above translation diverges from that of Kemp Smith chiefly in the repeated use of the verb "imagine" in place of "image." Cf. *Descartes' Philosophical Writings*, 196.

[3] Meditation III, 196. Kemp Smith remarks: "To Burman's objection that they would then yield *no material whatsoever* for error, and that the reservation 'hardly' does not hold, Descartes makes a not very satisfactory reply." *New Studies in the Philosophy of Descartes* (London: Macmillan, 1952), 233 note 7; emphasis added. [Cf. below, ch. 6.—*Ed.*]

thought it is, namely the thought of the stone; it cannot, as it were, miss the stone. I cannot, it appears, try to think of the stone and fail. For to try to think of it, I must already think of it in order to make that endeavor. So that if I am trying to think of it, if I think that I am thinking of it, if I take myself to be thinking of it, then I am thinking of it. In the case of thought, intention is the act, apparently, so that it is impossible in such cases to intend and fail.

Ideas thus have a certain integrity, a certain impregnability against the wiles of the demon, precisely, as Descartes views it, because "in themselves" they advance no claims that could be judged true or false. It is when ideas are employed in the making of judgments, that the possibility of error becomes epidemic. When I employ the idea I have of a body to judge that I have a body, or that bodies are utterly distinct from minds, the powers of the demon must be reckoned with. He represents the possibility that while I have the ideas of these things, there may be "no Earth, no heavens, no extended thing, no shape, no magnitude, no location"; furthermore that "every time I add 2 and 3, or count the sides of a square; or judge of things simpler, if anything simpler can be suggested," I am deceived and my judgments untrue. To be sure, as I proceed with the development and clarification of my ideas, achieving in them not only clarity but distinctness of conception, there are some judgments, like that there are bodies, and these utterly distinct from minds, that become so obvious that a pure and attentive mind accepts them without reservations. They can be brought within the realm of the dubitable only by raising that general doubt of the capacity of the human mind to distinguish truth from error which the demon represents. But this doubt can be raised. And in raising it one recognizes that the development of thought, the attainment of dear and distinct ideas, and the articulation in judgments of complex relations among these ideas, could proceed in its own realm independently of the world of things. I might have all the ideas I now have, and form judgments of their connections, without there being a world of things that these ideas seem to represent. My confidence that there is such a world is not guaranteed by the ideas, and the judgments that, when I attend them, these ideas lead me to make. These ideas could be exactly what they are if there were no such world, only the demon constantly leading me to make false judgments about it. It is only when the demon is exorcised and a good God revealed in his place, that the reliability of dear and distinct ideas as a guide to truth about things is finally ensured.

Some of the immediately ensuing developments of this metaphysic of thought among Descartes's rationalist followers are now a familiar story. The elaborate alternative views advanced by the Occasionalists, by Spinoza and Leibniz, though fanciful from the point of view of common sense, are understandable, as generations of students have discovered, when they are viewed in the philosophical context in which they arose. Then the strangeness of the views yields to an appreciation of their appropriateness as responses to the severe conditions under which these men were led, by their metaphysical inheritance, to account for the apparent complex interrelations between our thoughts and the world of things.

3   The general view of thought that, meanwhile, was being developed by the empiricist philosophers, though in many respects different from that of Descartes and his rationalist followers, was, on the point under investigation here, remarkably in agreement. The development of ideas under the stimulation of sensation was conceived by the empiricists in a radically different way, a way which led to the imposition of severe limitations on what could be achieved in the way of ideas and in the way of judgments or affirmations employing them. But these ideas were regarded similarly independent from the world of things, except, of course, for the true-false relation our judgments or affirmations could have with these things. Here, rather than the Cartesian grand project of ensuring the veracity of those judgments we find ourselves inclined to make, through the existence of God, the empiricists favored a more piecemeal means of verification, namely through sensation. But the modesty of this means, though attractive in its own way, and a relief from the intellectual bravura of the rationalists, led to its own difficulties. Very little in the web of thought that required verification, if this was to be an acceptable theory of knowledge, could be accounted for in this way. The vast and irremediable imbalance between drafts and resources that was thus installed at the heart of this intellectual economy—celebrated for centuries as the Problem of Induction—was sufficient to ensure the eventual bankruptcy of the system.

On the point under investigation here the empiricist followers of Descartes were even more faithful to their leader, more firm in maintaining the independence of thought from things, than their rationalist cousins. It is of course not adequate to the complexity and subtlety to be found in the empiricist philosophers to say that they thought of ideas as images. Such persistent adherence to a blatantly false view would tax the capacity of a Hobbes. Certainly this is the way they sometimes thought, even in the face of great difficulty, as did Berkeley in his discussion of abstract ideas. And certainly the root metaphor in the empiricist theory of ideas is the image. Items of some sort are given to us in experience, in sensation, and something rubs off, something is deposited in us by the experience. And this deposit, capable of representing that which deposited it, is the idea. An idea, commonly an image, is, if not an image, like one in that it may with some plausibility be regarded as a self-interpreting representation of its object.

To an American student of British philosophy is attributed the comment that it is a wise idea that knows its own impression.[1] Though directed at empiricism the significance of this remark is not restricted to that philosophy. It is a wise thought that knows its object. The view that ideas are copies of impressions, to which Hume gave much currency, seemed to provide a simple and plausible explanation of what it was to have an idea of something, what it was to think of something, as contrasted with apprehending its immediate, sensuous feeling. The difference between the sensuous feel of X and the thought of X, said Hume, is merely a difference between the force and vivacity of the feeling in each case. To apprehend the smell of the rose is to have a certain immediate feeling; to think of the smell, to have the idea of the smell before the mind, is simply to relive that certain smell, except in a greatly diminished degree. This can be done, of course, apart from the rose and its real emanating odor. Granted that without the odor apprehended by sense in the first place it would not be possible for me to relive it in imagination. But once I have this capacity—once, as Hobbes would have put it, there are certain motions in my brain—I have the idea of the smell. For me to have the idea of X it suffices that I have, or am able to awaken reverberations of, the sensation of X. Nothing more is required; not the existence and cooperation of X, or of any other thing. What limitations there are on my

---

[1] This wry comment recalls the following more general pronouncement of Hegel: "Vorstellungen überhaupt können als Metaphern der Gedanken und Begriffe angesehen werden. Damit aber, daß man Vorstellungen hat, kennt man noch nicht deren Bedeutung für das Denken, d.h. noch nicht deren Gedanken und Begriffe. Umgekehrt ist es auch zweierlei, Gedanken und Begriffe zu haben, und zu wissen, welches die ihnen entsprechenden Vorstellungen, Anschauungen, Gefühle sind." [In general, representations can be viewed as metaphors of thoughts and concepts. But just because one has representations doesn't mean that one knows their significance for thought, that is, that one yet knows their thoughts and concepts. Conversely, it is one thing to have thoughts and concepts, and quite another to know what are their corresponding representations, intuitions, or feelings.—Ed.] *Enzyklopädie der philosophischen Wissenschaften*, Einleitung, §3 Anmerkung; *Werke in 20 Bände* vol. 8, 44. Cf. also Wittgenstein, *Philosophical Investigations*, G. E. M. Anscombe, tran. (London: Macmillan, 1953), Part II, §iii:
"What makes my image of him into an image of him?"
"Not its looking like him."

capacity to have ideas of things, given the initial sensations and the reverberations of these in imagination, are not imposed by things, but by my capacity to recall the reverberations and to manage varieties of combinations of them. It is by this capacity that I conceive things, both actual and possible, whole domains and systems of things, this world, and other possible worlds.

Thus, regardless of their differences on various points about thought, its relation to sensation, and its limits, the empiricists and the rationalists were in basic agreement concerning the independence of thoughts in relation to things. Whatever thoughts are, whether modes of mental substance, neural phenomena, or motions in the brain; whatever their derivation, whether from innate capacity or from characters inscribed by experience; in their essential capacity as thoughts or ideas, representing or referring to things, they are not in any necessary way dependent upon things. In the minds of some, such a presumption must have seemed no more than a summation of the state of affairs exhibited case by case in the relation between individual thoughts or ideas and the objects they represent. Unlike ordinary physical acts that we engage in, our acts of thought do not require real objects in the world to complete themselves. Or, as it is sometimes said, they have a capacity to provide themselves with their own objects. There is no flask from which you can fill a wine cup that does not exist; but you can think of such a cup, even spend a lifetime searching for it. And the same kind of independence of represented objects in the world of things is exhibited by our thoughts of kinds of things. In their capacity as representations, our ideas of such things depend no more than any other representations of them do, upon the real existence of the objects represented by them. The colors of the passenger pigeon in the Audubon folio were not dimmed nor the lines altered, when the last of its archetypes, victims of a heedlessly expanding human species in North America, passed into oblivion.

4   Our thought about thought, our way of conceiving conceptions, owes much to the metaphor—model, if you prefer—of pictures and portraiture. This mode of developing an understanding of one thing by assimilating it to the model of another is one of the most fundamental techniques by which we expand thought and achieve a broader and more penetrating understanding of things. But just as our understanding can be increased by the apt employment of such analogies, so it can be confused and misled by their inapt employment. And the danger is increased if it is weakened in the first place by a misunderstanding of the basic model itself.

Fundamental as is the conception of representation in our understanding of the relation of ideas to the world of things, we are misled by this conception if we regard it as underwriting a view of the matter in which the development of such representations is regarded as the production in the medium of thought of facsimiles, gossamer replicas, of the things represented. We are misled if we are led to think of these productions—which of course need not be reproductions—as being, when considered just as thoughts, independent of the world of things, and dependent only in their capacity of conveyers of information concerning that other world, in their capacity to be not simply ideas, but, in their employment in propositions, to be also true or false.

While in some ways the model does encourage such presumptions about the nature of thoughts, as representations, and things as objects of representation, there are also in it some signals of warning. The painter Philip Ernst, father of Max Ernst, once painted a picture of his garden, and omitted a tree which spoiled the composition. Then, "overcome with remorse at this offense against realism," we are told, he cut the tree down.[1] But it is not in such isolated extravagant episodes that the inadequacy of such presumptions about representational thought is revealed. The inadequacy is revealed rather in many more subtle and pervasive ways in which the capacity of one thing to serve as a representation of another depends on a multitude of things beyond the vehicle of the representation and the represented object. The history of the visual arts seems to testify amply that the mechanisms and conditions of representation are not fixed by any eternal laws. The attempt to found such, for example, on scientific laws of perspective seems to have been mistaken. The possibilities of representation with line and color are not now in the Western world what they were in the years before Matisse and Picasso, just as they were not then what they were for artists in Africa or the Far East. And these differences are not due solely to variations in the media in these cases, to variations in the pigments, the vehicles, the means of application, and the surfaces to which they are applied. The state of affairs is similar in the various kinds of representation that we embrace in the wide concept of human thought. It is not the case that our capacity to represent to ourselves, to think of items in the world of things, requires no cooperation from this world. No more in the medium of thought than in other media is it the case that representing something is entirely within the power of the individual setting out to effect that representation. As the above general reflections hint,

---

[1] Tuchman, Barbara, *The Proud Tower* (New York: Macmillan, 1966), 302.

so particular examination of our thoughts themselves not only fails to confirm, but positively challenges the received view of the independence of
thought in these matters: the view that in this particular area of human
activity the intention literally is the act; that consequently there is a special
infallibility to our efforts in this realm, since thoughts are in their own way,
like the Forms in Plato's metaphysic, independent of the vicissitudes of
change and error in the world of things.

5   There are a variety of places in the philosophy of thought at which the
inadequacy of this view lies close to the surface and needs little digging to
uncover. Two of these, the subject of referring expressions and the related
one of presupposition, have been the object of considerable attention in recent
publications. Another one, equally interesting but not so intensively discussed,
is that to which, following the nomenclature used by Waismann, it has
become customary to refer to as the "open texture" of concepts. Let us look
at this briefly. The phenomenon to which this expression is applied is not
altogether a newly discovered one, having been noted briefly by philosophers
as far back as Locke and Leibniz. Besides Waismann, other recent philosophers, among them Wittgenstein and Austin, have paid some attention to the
phenomenon and made suggestions concerning its philosophical significance.
The phenomenon in question is a certain looseness or porosity in our concepts that leaves open, in the application of terms conveying these concepts,
the possibility of borderline cases of an interesting kind. It is easy to imagine
situations in which one would be at a loss to say that some common terms,
like "cat" or "man," either did or did not definitely apply. Suppose we encounter one of Waismann's hypothetical creatures, for example, one that in
all other respects appears to be a cat but later grows to a gigantic size, or
shows some other queer characteristics such as the capacity to be revived
after death. Should one say of it that it is a new species of being, not a cat,
or that it is a cat with extraordinary properties? Or what about a being that
looks like a man, speaks like a man, behaves like a man, but is only nine
inches tall? Or what about that creature in Austin's garden? After we have
made sure it's a goldfinch, a real goldfinch, it does, in Austin's words
"something outrageous (explodes, quotes Mrs. Woolf, or what not)." "We

don't say we were wrong to say it was a goldfinch," Austin writes, *"We don't know what to say. Words literally fail us."*[1]

As Austin's last comment suggests, and Waismann and Wittgenstein agree, something about our language is revealed here. Waismann, presumably following Wittgenstein in this matter, traces this to a certain incompleteness of definition of the terms in question. If we think of definition of what are called "empirical terms" as a matter of providing rules of application for these terms, the incompleteness of definition here is the incompleteness of these rules, their insufficiency to provide in all conceivable situations an answer to the question whether the term applies. We are not equipped in the definition of these terms with "rules ready for all imaginable possibilities."[2]

Why is this so; and to what extent is it so? On the latter question Waismann's account is somewhat indefinite. Open texture is said to be "a very fundamental characteristic of most, though not all empirical concepts," the suggestion being that it is not only not a fundamental characteristic of some empirical concepts, but not a characteristic of them at all. This suggestion does not reconcile easily with the positive statement, made later, that "No definition of an empirical term will cover all possibilities."[3] Included among those concepts of which open texture was thought by Waismann to be a fundamental characteristic are clearly all concepts of the kind of things that philosophers call "material objects."

A better clue to the extent of this phenomenon among concepts lies in the answer to the question why it is indeed a characteristic of some. Waismann's explanation is that the incompleteness of definition in these cases is due to the *"essential incompleteness* of an empirical description."[4] Open texture is a necessary feature of a concept like that of a cat, because the definition of "cat" is necessarily incomplete; and this is in turn because it is logically impossible to complete the description of such an object. Waismann's illustration of this is the impossibility of his ever completing a description of his own right hand. "I may say different things of it," he writes,

---

[1] John Austin, "Other Minds," in *Logic and Language: First and Second Series*, A. Flew, ed. (New York: Anchor, 1965), 342–80, p. 354 (§I), original emphasis.

[2] Frederick Waismann, "Verifiability," in *Logic and Language*, 122–51, p. 125 (¶4). Cf. Wittgenstein, *Philosophical Investigations*, Pt. I, §80.

[3] "Verifiability," 129 (¶11); emphasis added.

[4] "Verifiability," 127–28 (¶10); original emphasis.

I may state its size, its shape, its colour, its tissue, the chemical compound
of its bones, its cells, and perhaps add some particulars; but however far I
go, I shall never reach a point where my description will be completed:
logically speaking, it is always possible to extend the description by adding
some detail or other.

In contrast with describing a triangle by giving its three sides, or specifying
a melody in the musical notation,

There is no such thing as completeness in the case in which I describe my
right hand, or the character of a person; I can never exhaust all the details
nor foresee all possible circumstances which would make me modify or
retract my statement.[1]

But the reason adduced here is not sufficient to account for the effect. The
fact that I cannot pack into a description of a particular object or being like
a hand or man every characteristic it has does not explain the capacity of
some unspecified characters to render indeterminate the application of the
term "hand" or "man," while there are many others that would not. In
defining a musical instrument, say a guitar, we do not specify its color,
where the maker should affix his name or the material of the finger board
and frets. I never saw a purple guitar, and, following the verse of Gelett
Burgess, may never hope to see one. But it is possible for me to hope not to
see one, precisely because there is no real conceptual difficulty in the thought
of a "purple guitar" that prevents my conceiving what it is I hope not to see.
In its entry under the name of "guitar" the Second Edition of *Webster's
International Dictionary*, published in 1953, did specify something about the
character of the strings: that three be of silk wound with wire and three of
catgut. At this time countless guitars were in use with steel strings, the now
popular nylon strings were entering the market, and it would have been
merely eccentric for anyone then to contend that putting such strings upon an
instrument raised any serious question about whether it could rightly be called
a "guitar."

6   Although Waismann's account of the matter is thus not adequate, his
intuitive philosophical sense was leading him in the right direction in the

---

[1] "Verifiability," 128 (¶10).

search for an explanation of the phenomenon. Somehow it is due to a discrepancy between that aspect of a thing that can be caught in a defining description, or, as some would have it, a "criterion" of it, and the thing itself. It will be recalled that in describing the imagined quandary with the putative goldfinch, Austin says that in such a case "words literally fail us." And a few sentences later, speaking in another idiom, he says, that the future can always "make us revise our ideas about goldfinches or real goldfinches or anything else." The occurrence of prodigies of this kind would lead certain words to fail us, not in the simple way of clearly signifying conditions or occurrences in the world that are not realized there, but by becoming somehow unhinged in their application to the world, so that it is no longer clear what they signify, how they do apply. But if this is so, then the fact that these words do not fail us now in this particular way indicates something about the character of that world, at least up to now. Our success in employing linguistic practice involving words of this kind must be due in part to the fact that the world in which this practice goes on is not populated to any great extent, with entities of the kind supposed, that they remain far the most part in the category that Leibniz referred to as "bizarre fictions."[1] Though having the idea of a purple guitar does not require there being an archetype of that idea in the world of things, successful employment of the language of musical instruments—of lutes, violins, horns, organs, and the rest—depends in fundamental and far-reaching ways upon the character of the world in which this successful employment takes place. And if it is granted that having a concept of a thing is derivative and hence dependent upon such a practice, then it appears that having a concept of a thing is thus indirectly dependent upon things. For when do we say that someone has developed a concept, has got the idea, understands what is meant by the words "man," "goldfinch" or "guitar," or at another level, of "filibuster" or "judicial restraint"? Not, of course, just when he has developed certain imagery, nor when he reports that he does have the idea, understands the words, not even when a certain look of understanding appears in his eyes when he enunciates the words. To develop a concept of a thing like a bird, whether it be a goldfinch, phoenix, or great roc, is to be initiated—not always well—into a

---

[1] "Fortunately we are spared these perplexities by the nature of things; but still these bizarre fictions have their uses in abstract studies, as aids to a better grasp of the nature of our ideas." *New Essays Concerning Human Understanding*, P. Remnant and J. Bennett, trans. (Cambridge: Cambridge University Press, 1981), Bk. III, Ch. VI, §22.

complex practice which involves both men and things, though not necessarily phoenixes and rocs.

Thinking is an activity which we engage in not only in the world of things, but by means of things in this world, supported and sustained by them. And when these things fail us in certain ways, as they sometimes do, then, to extend Austin's pronouncement, words do literally fail us, because our thoughts fail us. How different this is from the misguided metaphor, engendered by what, with some simplification, I have called the "traditional view" of the relation between thoughts and things! I refer to the metaphor of the human mind as a kind of private factory, weaving, perhaps out of materials provided by sense, thought-textiles representing with equal ease and independence of this world a vast array of possible worlds which this world only intervenes upon by continuously flashing signals about which of the array is to be taken as real. This "traditional" view has been sometimes opposed in Western philosophy by another, which in its extreme forms, suggests that it is with some falsification, if not also presumption, that we view ourselves as the agents in our thought processes. Rather our finite minds are centers in which something far greater than we, something that it would be misleading to identify as thought, realizes itself in thought. The metaphor suggests itself here of a clock, as it marks the hours, not creating these divisions of the day, but, if it works well, reflecting divisions determined by the motion of the earth in relation to the sun and other heavenly bodies; or of a barnyard cock who in crowing not so much announces the rising sun as serves as a vehicle through which the rising sun announces itself. This confrontation of metaphor is useful in dramatizing and emphasizing, for those of us who have had lapses of dogmatic slumber in these matters, the variety of views which it is possible for philosophical reflection on them to take. But, having struggled free from one extreme position, I do not wish my momentum to thrust me into another. I want to maintain that the cock, and not the sun, does crow; that, like Descartes, you and I do think; but that, conceding the simplification that is necessary in a brief statement, we think with the help of things.

7   When one looks at matters from the perspective of this point of view, the aspect of certain fundamental topics in the theory of knowledge is significantly altered. In concluding, I shall touch briefly on several of these alterations.

7.1 *Verification.* One of the persistent difficulties encountered in the traditional view has already been referred to in the portrayal of two historical versions of the view. It is the difficulty of understanding how, when thoughts or ideas are regarded as so separate from and independent of things, it is possible for those who have these thoughts to ascertain whether the judgments they make with them are true. On this matter Descartes and his empiricist followers presented a classic philosophical cleavage, a more recent form of which was the controversy over the coherence and correspondence theories of truth. For Descartes the criteria of truth lay in thought itself, in the clearness and distinctness of the ideas and the immediate certainty in judgment to which these features of our ideas give rise. But on the question of the justification of taking an internal feature of thought as a sign of its correspondence with things, Descartes was, as centuries of commentators have emphasized, vulnerable. His appeal to the veracity of God for that justification seemed to require him to use beforehand, in the thought used to prove God's existence, the same justification that only God's existence was supposed to provide.

The empiricist philosophers rejecting the supposition that internal features of thought can be used as signs of its fidelity to things, appealed instead to a separate source of information on this matter, namely the deliverances of sensuous intuition, of direct aesthetic feeling. But this move, within the framework of this general metaphysic of thought in which they were operating, did not so much enable them to avoid the Cartesian circle as fragment it into a vast number of small ones. Or rather, in order to avoid a multiplicity of circles at each point at which sense is appealed to, to verify thought, it was necessary to conceive of these deliverances as quite independent of thought. For if thought is implicated in the messages we receive from sensation, if it is required to discern or decode these messages, then what we employ in the verification of thoughts, namely the messages as decoded, are not witnesses altogether independent of thought, so that once again thought is being called upon to justify itself. On the other hand, if thought is not in any way implicated in these messages, if what is delivered to us by sense is utterly independent of thought, if, as it were, they do not speak to us in the language of thought, how can we know what they say? How can they verify or falsify any thoughts? Supposing that there is a realizable state in the procedure of acquiring knowledge of things in which something or other is accessible to consciousness entirely apart from thought, how can what is revealed in such consciousness be anything more than, to use the language of Francis Bradley, some completely unspecified "that," uncharacterized by any "what"? And if that should be the case, how can this stage of the procedure perform the verifying and falsifying function that is necessary on this view if knowledge acquired in it is to function as what is commonly referred to as "the foundations of empirical knowledge"?

As much of the specific difficulty encountered here lies in the metaphysical separation of thoughts and things, so the difficulty takes on a different and less baffling aspect when the severity of the separation is itself reduced. Reflecting upon these matters one begins to see that certain of the ages-old and comfortable categories in which we naturally begin to think are going to have to be revised, or at least reviewed, since it appears that we can be unthinkingly led into error by the easy commonsense way we draw distinctions between thought, sensation, and perception, and speak of the *thought* or *idea of this*, the *concept of that*. But continuing to speak in the language in which the problem arose, and in terms of which the whole view of thought and its difficulties have been presented here, one may say that, as in our thought we are dependent upon things, so these things exert some guidance on the development of our thought, on our language. In order to understand the way in which thought gets confirmed or corrected by things, one does not need to stake all on the supposition that there is a special unthinking way in which we acquire a knowledge of things. In our thoughts themselves, things are implicated and in a variety of subtle ways make their characters known to us. For this reason the grand philosophical project of devising possible ways in which, by the grace of God or pure sense, some coordination may be effected between altogether independent thoughts and things—that project is a gratuitous one. What remains in its place is the difficult task of achieving understanding in detail of the way things are implicated in our thoughts. It is not the end, but the mere beginning of the story, to say that our thoughts are what they are by virtue of our relations with things, that their very roots lie in things. We shall need to comprehend in detail how in our very thinking we employ and depend upon a vast nexus of relations with things; how it is by virtue of these relations we manage to refer to things, to represent and think of them; and finally how, in view of all this, we should conceive of that particular, distinctive relation we expect things to have with individual expressions of thought when we speak of truth and error. Progress in achieving this comprehension will be impeded, the comprehension suffer obscurity and distortion, so long as, victims of this old metaphysic of thought, we continue to mistake the more obvious ingredients of thought which may plausibly be conceived as independent of things, with thought itself. It is not essential to this metaphysic that we identify thoughts with acts of the soul or with states of mind. We do not depart from it, but rather change the idiom, when our identification is with muted sounds of inner speech, incipient contractions in the larynx, patterns of neuron discharge in the brain, or the behavior patterns of computers. We need to learn afresh the moral of the children's story: It is not the whistle that makes the steamboat go.

7.2 *Deduction.* Another, closely related topic which takes on an altered look is that of the fruitfulness, in yielding knowledge of things, of deductive method, the method which proceeds by elaborating, refining, explicating ideas, and determining relations between them. This, like the preceding topic, has been an enduring source of difficulty in the traditional view of thought, particularly in its empiricist versions. If thought is as it is represented in the view, what the mind can learn as it busies itself with its ideas is restricted to the relations of these ideas, and, necessarily, stops short of things. The propositions discovered in this way are, as Hume said, "without dependence upon what is anywhere existent in the universe," and hence tell us nothing about the universe.[1] But if this is so, if the method is barren in this respect, how can we account for what at first view seem to be substantial fruits of it, great achievements, for example, in the seventeenth century that seemed both to scientific practitioners like Galileo and Descartes, and to sympathetic observers like Hobbes, to have been made largely, not by the observation of bodies in motion or at rest, but by endeavoring to think clearly about them?

One of the consequences of the view of thought I have been advancing bears directly upon this topic. The dependence of thought upon things, its vulnerability, simply in its capacity as thought, to changes in the world of things, and the capacity of thought somehow to illuminate some features of things, are different faces of the same coin. I may not be able to determine simply by reflection, to borrow an example from Langford, that Jones has a cube in his hand. But, knowing that he has a cube in his hand I can determine by reflection that it has twelve edges. The task is not to explain away the power of thought in determining that cubes have twelve edges, but to understand it. Part of Kant's answer to this question, the more metaphysical part, is that those characteristics which objects can be determined to have by the understanding alone are characteristics contributed by the understanding itself, characteristics somehow determined by the very character of an understanding, and hence not within our power to change. The eternal fixity of this element in knowledge was one of the points at or which Kant's theory of the a priori was subject to attack. The more recently revealed

---

[1] [*An Enquiry Concerning Human Understanding* §4 Pt. I ¶1.—*Ed.*]

vulnerability of such supposed a priori features as Euclidean geometry and Newtonian causality suggests that, whether there is or is not such an element, determined by thought simply as thought, there is also a revelation in thought of the character of things because of the role of things in supporting, guiding, making our thoughts possible. One way in which it is possible for the elaboration of thought to contribute to knowledge is by disclosing, in thought, the signatures of the helping hands of things.

7.3 *Induction.* One of the best known of the difficulties attending the traditional view in its empiricist versions concerns, not the beginnings of knowledge at some point where thought and things meet, but its expansion from this point. If we suppose the beginning items of knowledge to rest upon some foundation independent of thought, how is it possible for thought to expand knowledge beyond these admittedly restricted first steps? The most general and familiar form in which this question arises in this philosophy is in the Problem of Induction, the problem of how, beginning with the immediate deliverance of sense, and the records of these in memory, one could expand upon these by what Hume called "reasoning from experience." Here again the metaphysical separation of thought from things installed by the view has a deleterious effect. By the separation thought is rendered impotent, as Hume easily showed, to perform the role it must play if knowledge of things is to be expanded in the desired way. The independence of thought from things has been purchased at a disastrous, but what Hume nevertheless regarded as a necessary price. For it is a feature of that independence that what can be established by thought, and hence contributed by it to our general stock of knowledge, is not knowledge of things, but, at most, a codification, recasting, reformulation of information concerning things derived from other sources.

Relinquishing the view of thought at work here effects a most remarkable change in the aspect of this putative problem. If, altering one's views on this matter, one supposes that our thoughts are dependent upon things in the ways described, then in the conduct of thought, in the development of ideas and tracing relations between them, we are dependent upon features of the world extending far beyond the domain of what we are alleged to have direct knowledge of in the sensation or feeling of the specious present, or in the records of this in memory. There are many genuine and some very difficult questions that arise in particular cases and particular areas concerning the justification of conclusions we draw in expanding upon what we can establish in a more or less direct way by perception or memory. But the so-called general Problem of Induction is not one of these. We cannot consistently argue our necessary ignorance of all unseen things on the grounds of the incapacity of thought to establish conclusions about them, if in formulating these conclusions, we depend upon the character of just the kind of unseen things we profess not to know. This characteristic of certain skeptical philosophical problems, that the very development of the problem requires one to treat as assured what in the problem one professes to doubt, has been remarked by a variety of philosophers and employed by some as a basis of transcendental arguments designed to dispel the doubts. The one great paradox, dominating all others, in the philosophy surrounding the Problem of Induction is this: that upon the view of things embodied in this celebrated Problem, anyone who *has* this Problem must already have solved it.

2

Truth and Correspondence

Truth, as any dictionary will tell you, is a property of certain of our ideas. It means their "agreement," as falsity means their disagreement, with "reality." Pragmatists and intellectualists both accept this definition as a matter of course. They begin to quarrel only after the question is raised as to what precisely may be meant by the term "agreement," and what by the term "reality," when reality is taken as something for our ideas to agree with.

–William James

For the Truth ... [consists in] this: not that external things correspond with my representations [*Vorstellungen*]—these are only correct representations held by me, the individual person—but that the Objectivity [i.e., the essence, apprehended in thought, of the existing thing] corresponds with the Concept [*Begriff*] [the developed conception of it as fully rational, actual, real]... Truth in the deeper sense consists in the identity between the Objectivity and the Concept.

–Hegel

Truth is that concordance of an abstract statement with the ideal limit towards which endless investigation would tend to bring scientific belief... There is nothing to prevent our knowing outward things as they really are, and it is most likely that we do thus know them in numberless cases, although we can never be absolutely certain of doing so in any special case.

–Peirce

1   The object of this paper is to explore the notion of correspondence which is a central notion in the theory of truth, and, in the process of the explora-

21

tion, to criticize and discredit a particular view of this notion which has unfortunately become so identified with the topic that it has preempted discussion of it.

2   This view is commonly referred to as *the* correspondence theory of truth. Its limitations have retarded understanding of the notions of truth and correspondence, and the formidable objections to it have widely been regarded as insuperable obstacles to the association of these notions in a reasonable correspondence theory.

3   The problems of this one particular theory have been rendered prominent in recent philosophy, as they were at the beginning of this century, by the declining fortunes of empiricism and, more important, by an increasingly adverse judgment concerning one of the central tenets of this philosophy, namely the thesis that somewhere in the processes by which we develop knowledge of the world a strict distinction can be drawn between fact and theory, datum and inference, the immediately and mediately known. In recent philosophy of science a debate over this issue concentrated upon the validity of the distinction between observational and theoretical terms.

4   The fortunes of a theory of truth elaborating the notion of correspondence seemed to be so closely linked with the fortunes of this seriously challenged thesis that, having given up the thesis, one seemed committed to the conclusion that the endeavor to understand truth in terms of some kind of correspondence between our thought and its objects was an infeasible, if not thoroughly unintelligible project.

5   But the apparent difficulties thus generated for the correspondence view of truth lay, not in the conception of the correspondence relation itself, but in certain ancillary theories employed in the elaboration of one particular version of the conception.

6   One of the theories employed is a semantic one, another a theory in the philosophy of knowledge and of mind. The first expresses a doctrine of semantic atomism; the second a doctrine of what might be termed "conceptual independence."

7   The independence in question here extends much further than the presently popular term "conceptual" suggests, applying not only to what we would naturally refer to as *concepts*, but more generally to the whole repertory of our intellectual resources which are broadly linguistic, though not strictly conceptual, and, further, to portions of these resources that are not even strictly linguistic. Though the terminology of "concepts" is thus in serious ways inappropriate, it is widely current and for present purposes may be followed here, with the understanding that as it is employed the word

"conceptual" is a code word, signifying a very broad range of both linguistic and nonlinguistic phenomena and cognitive practice.

8   It is in the language of conceptual systems that debate is now carried on concerning what in an earlier day would have been referred to as systems and relations of ideas. Conceptual independence is a more modern expression of the independence of ideas, and of the mental generally, a doctrine so persuasively promulgated in the philosophy of Descartes and elaborated in modern empiricism, beginning notably with Locke's "new way of ideas." The problem of conceptual relativism, of possibly irreducible alternative conceptual systems, is the familiar present form of the older problem posed for earlier philosophers by the installation in their philosophies of this independence. Descartes' problem about the trustworthiness of clear and distinct ideas, and Locke's about the reality of ideas, are early examples. And given the independence, the challenge of the problem is rendered sharper today by the decreased attractiveness to present-day philosophers of the kind of solution, illustrated in both Descartes and Locke, in which, in place of an account of the correspondence of thoughts with things, one is given general assurances of correspondence deriving from the alleged existence of a benevolent God.

9   Within the confines of an empiricist and theologically neutral theory of knowledge the indicated remedy for the difficulty thus posed for the correspondence notion of truth was the semantic atomism set forth in a variety of ways in the empiricist theory of meaning; for example, in Hume's thesis that ideas are the weak replicas of sensory impressions. Given the independence of concepts or ideas, this general doctrine relating the significance of ideas to sensations appeared to be the only plausible way of reestablishing philosophically, albeit in a restricted way, a connection between two domains which the doctrine of independence had logically put asunder.

10   Although traditionally these domains have been most often spoken of in Cartesian terms of mind and matter, for the present purposes employment of this particular metaphysical idiom is not necessary. For exploring the consequences of the notion of correspondence one may, for example, speak of language in place of mind or thought, and ideal language in place of ideal thought. The domain of the ideal, hypothesized language shared remarkably a primary character of the domain of clear and distinct ideas in Descartes, namely, that of a mode of being, a segment of life, a domain of entities which may be conceived of as capable of being developed and cultivated in independence of them. When language is taken as a modern replacement of thought or ideas in the traditional rationalist or empiricist schemata, the putative independence is reinforced by what has seemed to some as the

possibility of viewing a language, at least in its idealized, purified forms, as an uninterpreted system of symbols organized internally in a geometrical or axiomatized order.

11 For the purpose of understanding knowledge and the central concern in knowledge for an articulation between two supposed independent domains, it was necessary for this philosophy to provide some aperture in the logical curtain which had been erected between them. Some sort of epistemic pineal gland was needed, one preferably, for obvious reasons, of restricted dimensions. The most likely candidate for this purpose, viewing the matter linguistically, was ostensive definition, or, more widely considered, ostensive demonstration or explanation.

12 So long as the exceptions to the insularity of thought were restricted to the supposed matching of impressions with ideas—proceeding in one direction in definition and in the reverse in verification—it seemed possible for one to retain the basic conception of correspondence within the confines of independence theory, granted that the price paid for this retention was this restricted area of anomaly in the theory, which like the original pineal gland, constituted a logical discrepancy which could be considered tolerable only because it was minor.

13 This feature of the situation was radically altered by the multiple considerations which in the last twenty-five years have increasingly supported criticism and the call for rejection of the fundamental thesis of semantic atomism, the doctrine that the connection between percept and concept, fact and theory, is established by the piecemeal correlation of elements of one supposed independent domain with elements of another. Implausible as it may have been, apart from the independence doctrine, to suppose that the fate of the correspondence notion hung upon the slender thread of atomism, within the independence doctrine the atomism was essential, and the effects of its rejection upon the correspondence notion destructive.

14 The principal reason for the supposed connection between the correspondence view of truth and the doctrine of semantic atomism thus lay in an actual connection that does hold between this view of truth and the semantic doctrine, when the view is developed and speciated in a philosophical background embodying the further important doctrine of conceptual independence. From the influence of this doctrine upon the view flow many consequences closely connected with the semantic doctrine, among them the distinction between observational and theoretical terms. This is why, when the fortunes of empiricism are in ebb, when the distinction between observational and theoretical, and with it semantic atomism in general, is in increasing disfavor,

the very notion of correspondence, which is mistakenly taken to be the source of these doctrines, seems to be increasingly questionable and hence increasingly unavailable for the elucidation of a broad, theoretical account of truth. 15 In one respect, what was being effected in the denial of the observational-theoretical distinction was a confirmation of the Kantian doctrine of the essential role of categories in the development and structure of knowledge. And with that confirmation likewise effected was a reinstatement of an apparently insurmountable difficulty in the project of explicating truth in terms of a relation between our thoughts, judgments, hypotheses and something not our thoughts, etc., which we think, judge, or hypothesize about. It was as if the only alternative to the conceptual narrowness of Kant was the excessive permissiveness of Protagoras.

16 The omnipresence of categories, concepts throughout knowledge—which in Kant led to the doctrine of the inaccessibility for knowledge of things-in-themselves—seemed again to lie athwart the enterprise of comparing thoughts with and adapting them to things other than thoughts. It seemed to reduce any such enterprise necessarily to an internal exercise in thought, one of comparing thoughts with thoughts, exploring the relations among thoughts, conceived as items of an internal realm fundamentally independent of items of other realms which may, on occasion, be their objects. This kind of view was commonly presented and easily refuted by critics as "the coherence theory of truth." But the refutations were flawed by a serious ignoratio; for the theory of truth which was the ostensible object of the refutation was itself a feature of a broad theory of knowledge in which there was no place for thought conceived in the internal, independent Cartesian fashion which the presentation and criticism presupposed.

17 The difficulties of correspondence so conceived were amply confirmed by the results of various philosophers who, not accepting the Kantian doctrine, attempted to explicate correspondence in terms of a matching or conforming relation between judgments or propositions, on the one hand, and states of affairs, on the other.

18 It was not difficult for critics of these projects to expose the illusory character of any claims of success. What is disclosed in the exhibited correspondence between the statement that the cat is on the mat and the state of affairs of the-cat-being-on-the-mat, is not an isomorphism between some, say, linguistic product and some nonlinguistic entity, but a correspondence between two linguistic products, a correspondence which, grammar being what it is, could not be otherwise. In short, a grammatical correspondence between two similar utterances was mistaken to be a correspondence between one of

the utterances, or the proposition advanced in it, and some entity, i.e., the fact or state of affairs, thus easily leading those making the mistake into the practice of populating the world with those dubious, linguistic *Doppelgänger* against which many sober philosophers like J. L. Austin have warned.

19 There seemed to be a quandary here similar to that exploited by the tortoise in Lewis Carroll's fable, "What the Tortoise Said to Achilles."[1] Like the tortoise the critics of correspondence had simply to ask the protagonists of the view, as elaborated in this way, for some specification of the putative state of affairs, for some way of picking it out and understanding it. No response to the request was an implicit admission of the failure of the view, while on the other hand, any response, being, to use a Peircean phrase, inevitably some kind of thought-sign, some kind of sign of the state, rather than the state itself, left one with a correspondence between two signs rather than a correspondence between a sign and some nonsignal entity.

20 The apparent quandary seemed to some to confirm a suspicion that there was something fundamentally illusory in the correspondence notion and in the theory embodying this notion. A natural response to this was the "no rela-tion," performative, or (somewhat better) illocutionary analysis of F. P. Ramsey and Peter Strawson. The Ramsey-Strawson theory accounted well for the repetitive aspect that seemed to force its way into those accounts of truth attempting to explicate correspondence as a relation of congruity between judgments or statements, on the one hand, and states of affairs, on the other. What was emerging, according to this theory, in spite of the intentions of those performing the analysis, was the real re-affirming, endorsive function of "true" and similar terms, a function which, in concrete analysis, easily estab-lished its reality in contrast with the insubstantial, illusory function which philosophical preconceptions unsuccessfully were trying to foster upon these terms.

21 One might be tempted to view efforts to explicate in this way the corre-spondence notion of truth as simply a largely harmless, if ineffective, scholas-tic word game, were it not for the fact that the illusion that correspondence could be conceived and achieved in this relatively simple way acted as a most effective curtain obscuring the more complex, more difficult, but more realistic ways in which correspondence needs to be understood in theory and achieved in practice. The illusion in question not only contributed to the neglect of the genuine philosophical concerns represented in the questions

---

[1] [*Mind* N.S. 4 (1895): 278-80.—*Ed.*]

about truth and correspondence, by diverting attention from them. It also had the effect of rendering these concerns more difficult to understand and minister to.

22 Philosophers, with the statement firmly in hand that the cat is on the mat, and with attention concentrated upon the search for the supposed metaphysical double of this statement, are naturally less alert to those aspects of the concern about truth which attach to the statement itself. The reiteration of the statement and the concentration upon detecting from some quarter the sound of its metaphysical echo, tend to preclude the consideration of much more fundamental questions concerning the form of thought and action represented in the statement, concerning the vast intellectual apparatus of referring, predicating, and inferring which this statement represents, of the general suitability of the logical structure which this particular apparatus embodies, in comparison with other feasible, contending alternatives. The displacement of attention from the statement to the supposed state encourages the prolongation of dogmatic slumbering with respect to the statement itself and the vast complex of presupposition which philosophical acceptance of the statement, and the particular logic it embodies, represents. The acceptance of the statement as representing a proper linguistic or cognitive performance is at the same time, though of course we rarely think of this, acceptance of a certain complex practice of which this statement is an instance, a set of related practices, not only of meaning, discriminating, characterizing, but also of opposing, of verifying, denying, inferring, and so on.

23 The question about correspondence is essentially a question about the suitability of the forms of thought, of statement, inference and the rest, to the general subject-matter to which they are applied. Or, viewed in the reverse direction it is a question about the tractability of the subject-matter to these forms. How well, for example, and how ill, do we think of electrical current in a wire according to the analogy of the passage of liquid through a pipe?

24 To the extent that, in the philosophical investigation of truth, we simply take for granted that our practices of referring, predicating, inferring, etc., are in order, we pass over and neglect what is the heart of the matter, namely, the general question of the suitability of these practices for communication and investigation in the domains in which they are applied. And the effect, of course, is that of reserving these practices from fundamental philosophical criticism.[1] Nor was this effect altogether inadvert, since the intention of

---

[1] [Cf. ch. 7 below.—*Ed.*]

some writers—e.g., Russell—was to restore the practices, and the logical superstructures which could be erected upon them, from the kind of metaphysical discredit which they had suffered at the hands of the idealists. (Cf. Bradley's criticism of substantive, adjective, and relation in *Appearance and Reality*; Royce's treatment of finite minds and objects in his argument for the Absolute.)

25 But to the extent that these intellectual practices were reserved from, rather than preserved by, criticism, they became the basis of a kind of dogmatism or absolutism with respect to the most fundamental questions of correspondence and truth. In such a view the main lines of the accepted conceptual systems of common sense and commonsense science were taken as settled—though not as explicitly as in the categories in Kant—and the task of developing knowledge was conceived as that of filling in with context (the descriptively predicates, and their relations) what the predetermined forms left open to contingency.

26 It is this kind of a priori and absolute way with the questions at hand to which John Dewey objected when he attacked "antecedent reality" as the object of scientific and other inquiry.[1] When he was criticized on this matter, Dewey emphasized that he, like most of us, accepted, what his infelicitous exposition seemed to have put in question. Coming to have knowledge of the position of the cat, placing the cat on the mat in thought, is of course vastly different from setting the cat physically on the mat. The achievement of knowledge here, unlike the photon striking the electron, does not alter the position or velocity of the cat. What Dewey wanted to emphasize in saying that antecedent reality is not the object of language is that the features we come to ascribe to reality in the development of knowledge through inquiry are ones the reality of which must be made out, or ascertained, in the inquiry. If the language of subject and predicate, or of the relatively independent objects of molar physics, applies in the domain of microphysics, this is something to be discovered in inquiry and not to be predetermined by us in advance. Likewise the extent to which the electron is an object which moves according to Newtonian principles is something which has to be discovered by us. We do not ordain it.[2]

27 Comparing ancient Greek science with modern physical science Dewey said that the Greek science "operated with *objects* in the sense of the stars,

---

[1] *The Quest for Certainty* (New York: Minton Bach, 1929), chs. V and VIII.
[2] [See ch. 3, p. 45 note, for references.—*Ed.*]

rocks, trees, rain, warm and cold days of ordinary experience" while modern physical science "*substitutes data for objects*."[1] "*Objects*," he went on to say, "are finalities; they are complete, finished; they call for thought only in the way of definition, classification, logical arrangement, subsumption in syllogisms, etc." When the comfortable "qualitative objects of ordinary experience" are taken as "finalities," when the investigation of nature is limited to what can be assimilated into a conceptual scheme modeled upon and restricted to such objects, the limits so imposed become obstacles to inquiry. What Dewey was thus objecting to in the provocative and misleading language about antecedent reality not being the object of inquiry is this kind of scientific and metaphysical ossification. And it is ossification of this kind which was encouraged by those who considered the main problem in understanding the correspondence notion of truth to be that of discovering somewhere the replicas of a fixed, predetermined conceptual scheme.

28 On Dewey's behalf it needs to be recognized that it is difficult to explain what needs explaining in these matters in familiar, accepted philosophical terminology. To take the familiar term "correspondence" as an example, a central and sound thesis of those who urge the correspondence theory of truth was one that did not fit altogether this familiar notion. The aspects of lack of fit, when the term was not adapted to these particular surroundings, were a source of difficulty, mistake, and misunderstanding.

29 If we say that a central concern in the topic of truth is the large-scale correspondence, agreement, fitting or aptness of our conceptual systems, a natural question is, "Correspondence with what?," "Aptness for what?," and so on. If we say *what*, if in elaborating our theory we give a comprehensive account of what the congruent entities are (or is, if there is but one), we presume, to the extent that we take our account to be accurate and comprehensive, to know now what future inquiry will reveal and so fall into the trap of which the talk about antecedent reality was intended to provide a warning.

30 Characterizing the second term in a two-place relation as "things," "substances" or "substance," or "objects"—any such characterizing is presumptive if it implies completeness, or at least incorrigibility, in the conceptual scheme, or aggregate of such schemes, by which these congruent items have been revealed. And if, retreating, we say "reality," or "the world," it is proper for us to be challenged to show that what we are doing in resorting to these

---

[1] *The Quest for Certainty*, ch. V; original emphasis.

terms is more than concealing presumptions of absoluteness in the details of these conceptions behind a protective veil of generality and obscurity.

31 For when we submit for redemption such a term as "world," what possibly can we receive in return, as Richard Rorty argued a few years ago in the *Journal of Philosophy* (October 12, 1972), but the familiar coin of our accepted beliefs and assumptions, namely stars, people, tables, and grass, and other conceived designata of our well-entrenched present conceptions. This seems to put in serious question the acceptability of the very idea of a world which determines the truth of views embodying these conceptions. For the idea now turns out to be the trivial and truistic one that what makes our beliefs true or false is that things are or are not the way we believe them to be. "Things" now having been construed as the objects of our well-entrenched present conceptions, as whatever the "vast majority of beliefs not currently in question are currently thought to be about," and the question whether things correspond to these conceptions correspondingly translated into the question whether what these beliefs are currently thought to be about are what they are currently thought to be about, no other than a affirmative answer to the question about the correspondence between conceptions and things is possible. An effect of this way of dealing with the question about the second term in a two-place relation is thus, by conferring automatic correctness upon the current conceptions of "things," "objects," etc., in terms of which the question is raised, to render these conceptions immune from the very kind of philosophical criticism which in the correspondence theory were intended to be raised.

32 On the other hand, if repelled by this self-serving absoluteness, one refrains from cashing into specific terms the conception of the "world" or "reality," one is left with a purely vacuous notion, the ineffable something I-know-not-what or thing-in-itself of much historical notoriety. And in either case a natural conclusion about the "world" of philosophical realism and correspondence theory seems to be that this notion is an inutile, if not positively harmful one, is, in the language of the title of Rorty's paper, "A World Well Lost."

33 The most prominent weakness in this dilemma aimed at discrediting the conception of a world capable of determining by agreement or disagreement the truth of our ideas is the poverty of resource which it conceives to be available to us in filling out, giving context to this conception. It is the very same poverty which repeatedly has been exposed in Berkeley's notion of a world composed of ideas. Without question a great and essential part of our conception of the world is our conception of whatever objects, events, states,

and so on we are now able, by the development of our conceptions, to discriminate and determine as really existing. But conception is by no means an all-or-nothing procedure. One of the most pervasive truths about our conceptions, whether of homely objects, scientific ones, or broad philosophical ones, is that they are capable of an indefinite amount of change and development.[1] Thus a feature of my conception of Aristotle, or Hegel, or Wittgenstein is the recognition in it that any one of these conceptions is capable of great expansion, correction, and revision, without thereby losing its identity.

34 It is similar with a conception of a world, a world view. Such a conception does include in a basic way whatever the vast majority of accepted beliefs is currently thought to be about; but it is not restricted to this. Just as there is provision in my conception of Aristotle for much more than what in any specific way I do or can think of when I think of Aristotle, so there is provision in my conception or Aristotle's conception of the world for more than the supposed objects of his or my accepted beliefs. As Milton Fisk wrote in an accompanying comment upon Rorty's article, "Surely ... the realist who rejects a world of ineffable things-in-themselves need not accept the view that current concepts adequately represent the world."

35 It is by no means clear, but it appears that one deep source of the contrary view, to the effect that the choice is between a completely ineffable and completely conceived world, *tertium non datur*, lies in a philosophical view of the way knowledge develops, namely, exclusively by accretion rather than also by transformation, and in a corollary view about the development of concepts, notions, ideas. It fits such a general view to think of the objects of our thought as intended by us in a specific, atomic way, so that an object must be either an object of explicit conception or reference or no object of conception at all. Until it is added as an explicit object of conception it must count as unconceived. But the clarity and neatness of this view seems to be purchased at a great price in realism.

36 A more realistic model for understanding increase in conception, and for thinking of a conception of a world that is more than the object conceived in it, is the map of a partially known planet, or part of a planet like Earth. What is explicitly represented, drawn on the map, is a basis, a skeleton of information defining, but not fully defining, the feature of the quadrant, continent, or whatever is its object. It is not inconsistent with its character as

---

[1] [Cf. chs. 1, 5, 7–9.—*Ed.*]

a map, but rather essential to it, that it leave room for refinement, detail, and even in some cases revision of basic outlines. No one supposes that the features represented in a map of North America are definitive of, say, the geography of that continent. The discovery of hitherto unrepresented details, the drawing of a new map including these, do not mean that the older map was not a map of North America. The historical fact is that many incomplete, inadequate, and radically erroneous maps of the early explorers still count properly as maps of this same continent. Recognition of this feature of the development of our conceptions would doubtless have been easier in recent British and American philosophy if it had not been so closely associated with a figure widely viewed as the philosophical counterpart of the Prince of Darkness, namely, Hegel.

37 A notion of a world is dispensable, and, the historical record discloses, can be positively harmful, if the notion is that our present categories or conceptual schemes are exhaustive and inviolate, that the world as known and the world as it is are so completely identified that little or nothing is provided for in the notion beyond what is present and accounted for in our present system of conception. A world incompletely and imperfectly conceived may still be a world and the object of our conception, just as a number inadequately conceived may still be a number conceived, for example, as numbers were conceived before the discovery and admission of nonrational numbers. And the same holds for the familiar objects of everyday experience which we comprehend, conceive in ways somewhat different from those of Egyptians in the time of Ramses II or Romans in the time of Julius Caesar. Though we may have no doubt that our understanding of these objects—rocks, sand, and earth; cats, dogs, and horses—is capable of improvement, has not, to use Peirce's conception, reached that state upon which opinion will converge if life and investigation indefinitely continues, we may also have no doubt that in such an ideal opinion some place will be found for these, cats will be discriminable from dogs, rocks from clay, and both from the clouds, the river and the sea.

38 The concern for truth is a concern for correspondence. We act to meet this concern at a variety of levels, as when by observation we seek to determine whether the cat is on the mat, or, by the collection of evidence of a somewhat different sort, whether Oswald fired the shot that killed the President. At this level we are concerned not so much with the adequacy of spatial-object talk or agent talk in general, as with the use of a particular sample of this talk to say something about the cat's relation to the mat or Oswald's role in the assassination of the President. The decision here may be

the fairly simple one of choosing which of two alternative examples of this talk, "is on" or "is not on," or "did fire" or "did not fire," best fits the situation. At a very different level we inquire concerning the adequacy for the occasion with which we are engaged of the kind of thought or language of which these alternatives are instances: If the surface of the pencil facing the earth is adjacent to the book, and the book is in a similar position with respect to the satellite vehicle in orbit about the earth, is the pencil on the book? If the Secret Service agent's finger moves the trigger, leading to a fatal shot being fired, in consequence of the agent's elbow being jogged by someone in a stampeding crowd, is it still quite clear that the locution, "The agent fired the shot" fits the occasion?

39 At a much wider, though related level, we consider the question of the aptness in general of ways of speaking and thinking in various domains of life and inquiry, and, with that, the general appropriateness of the complex of practices with which these ways are integrally related and which these forms of speech and thought, in their own particular modes, represent. In the examples cited these forms represent, in the first case, such practices as those of identifying creatures like cats and objects like mats, making elementary spatial and temporal determinations, and whatever further determinations, including perhaps that of a support relation, are required in order for us to be able to speak of creatures like this as being, in respect to an object like this, in whatever state the word "on" conveys in a situation like this. In the second case the practices include those of identifying individual men, instances of the operation of fire-arms, the discrimination of death as a terminal state of a living person, the discernment of causal agency, and the attribution of responsibility.

40 In spite of the perplexities to which the analysis of correspondence has led, in spite of the many culs de sac encountered in the road of analysis, there is something fundamentally sound and of absolutely first importance to philosophy in the intuitive idea of truth as a congruity to be sought, tested, achieved or of speaking and thinking and what it is what we speak and think about. Questions about correspondence of the wide generality which such questions assume in philosophical inquiry substantially coincide with the questions which in much recent philosophical writing have been dealt with in terms of alternative conceptual systems.

41 The identification of questions about correspondence at the philosophical level with questions of this kind seems to lead to the substitution, in the elucidation of correspondence, of one extreme philosophical predicament for another. Instead of the sequestration of thought in general, and the conse-

quent problem of somehow providing that contact of thought with its possible objects in which truth might be thought to consist and be ascertained, our apprehension of these objects is viewed as depending in a universal and necessary way upon thought or speech forms. Apprehension of objects by thought and speech is bought at a price of raising a question of how our apprehensions could be given the kind of independent assessment which the conception and appraisal of correspondence requires. Might not our assessment, because of the interconnection of thought and speech with objects, always bear the marks of, be influenced by, the very modes of thought and speech which are under investigation? Thought and speech, instead of being isolated from their objects, have now become so implicated in the apprehension of objects, that the possibility of an independent judgment of the suitability, of instances of thought and speech, as modes of apprehension of objects, seems to be rendered problematic.

42 It is not essential to the major purpose of a paper designed to expose the general character of correspondence, as that is a desideratum in our quest for knowledge, that it contain solutions to the problems which we encounter from time to time in the assessment of specific instances of correspondence. But a word about the much advertised bogey of conceptual entrapment may be desirable. It is one consequence of the way correspondence has been conceived and pursued in recent philosophy, that it is possible to think of ourselves as the intellectual inmates of one, grand, totalitarian conceptual system: its beneficiaries to the extent that it is good; its victims, if bad. But this way of conceiving our relation to our conceptual systems is surely hyperbolic, if only for the reason that as a matter of fact we are not the prisoners of any one conceptual system. Just as we are the members of no single social community, we are the tenants of no single linguistic or thought structure, no single set of categories, no single intellectual paradigm. As plurality of communities has been one of the sources of freedom in modern democratic societies, as checks and balances, notwithstanding their logical untidiness, have proved to be elements of a workable system, so part of the story of the possibility of intellectual freedom in conceptual matters is that in these matters, in any moderately civilized society, men are not, except by their own failures to exploit their opportunities otherwise, like subjects of any single intellectual conceptual, cognitive sovereign. It is not that in their aspirations toward molding our intellects these different authorities do not aspire to expand and even achieve hegemony. The tendency of practices to expand is a natural consequence of success, and, in its most ambitious forms leads to such universal methodological and metaphysical programs; those of mechan-

ism, materialism, positivism, organicism, and idealism being familiar cases in point. In the arena of the intellect the impulses of competing systems and programs to expand yield competing ways of thinking, competing hypotheses to deal with problems, and different ways of conceiving problems which yield competing sets of categories and conceptual systems. Except in societies in which those in power—political, economic, ecclesiastic, etc.—have both an interest in and the capacity to achieve and maintain intellectual conformity, competition, both orderly and unruly, rather than monopoly is the normal state of affairs.[1]

43 In such a state the major task is not to attain competition through the overturning of a monopolistic power but rather that of encouraging and maintaining healthy competition, it being possible here only to mention that not all competition is healthy, not all means of competition proper and fair. One part of this task which is closely related to a topic already dealt with in this paper is that preventing ourselves, as individuals or collectively as intellectual communities, from becoming, through the material attachments we develop, the self-immured prisoners of forms of thought and speech which we have engaged with long and with success. To a vast extent, custom may be the great guide of life, as Hume proclaimed. But as an English poet (in his own time laureate of his nation, yet now so separated from us in outlook that he can scarcely speak to us) had a dying King Arthur observe, one good custom may corrupt the world.

44 However successful in the quest for correspondence a given conceptual scheme may be in some area of life and inquiry, we must, if we are not to become victims, as well as beneficiaries, of that success, not permit it to blind us to whatever signs there may be of aspects of misfit, of failure in respect to correspondence. Still less may we permit successful performance of a conceptual scheme in one area to be unthinkingly taken as a guarantee, rather than, at best, a promise, great or little, of performance in any area in which the aspirations and problems of both life and inquiry are prima facie widely different. In particular, a way of thinking and speaking may have demonstrated great competence in the exploration of patterns of inference concerning objects like those dealt with in everyday life, and yet be much less competent, even generally incompetent, with respect to the exploration of situations and problems confronted in mechanics. So obvious a point had to be learned through arduous efforts, and failures to proceed otherwise, in the

---

[1] [Cf. ch. 4 below.—*Ed.*]

development of modern physical science.[1] Similarly, a pattern of thought and symbolic formulation may be appropriate for conceiving the relations of connections and sets and yet may be inappropriate, as much debate in the past few decades seems to show, for the formulation of general causal statements and of the refined, and hence somewhat altered, descendants of these in scientific laws. And a way of thinking appropriate for these may fail in a significant way when the attempt is made to import and apply it to such widely different areas as those of the development and evaluation of norms of conduct in ethics and politics, and in law. Recalling Dewey's animadversions on antecedent reality, one may say that antecedent conceptual schemes are not, need not be identical with consequent ones. Presuppositions about the matters at hand, which form a necessary basis for all inquiry, for the very occurrence of the problems and questions to which inquiry is directed, if taken to constitute paradigms to which the results of investigation must unfailing conform, easily degenerate into prejudice, obscuring what a less cramped inquiry might reveal if ways of thought and speech were permitted, by alteration in response to clues uncovered in inquiry, to perform this revelatory service.

45 Our languages and conceptual systems, with their broad categories, modes of reference, modes of predication, and so on, cannot be well understood for philosophical purposes (though for other purposes more limited ways may suffice) so long as we persist in conceiving languages primarily on the model of isolated systems of symbols, and concepts then as nodal features of such systems. Languages and concepts need to be conceived more concretely on the model of a human and hence social institution, or, perhaps preferably, as discriminable features of a complex array of such institutions. And when we so conceive them, the perplexity about correspondence generated by the isolated, dualistic view of them is relieved, yielding to a variety of more specific questions and problems about how the kind of correspondence that is necessary for truth can be conceived in theory and pursued in practice.

46 In the life of our cognitive institutions, scientific and otherwise, men and their environment, concepts and the conceived, speech and the bespoken, are integrally related. Concepts and speech do not need extreme measures to introduce them to the world. They have the world as their home. We do not begin with language or thought apart from things or objects and then face the problem of how we manage to speak or think of these; they were there,

---

[1] [Cf. chs. 5, 6 below.—*Ed.*]

engaged in and literally constitutive of the institutional practices from the start. Without them the practices would not exist.[1] Things or objects have played an important, indeed indispensable role, in shaping the practices, just as money and trade have played determinative roles in shaping the institution of banking, and as sun, moon, and stars, have played their own roles in shaping the institution of astronomy (and also astrology). The articulation of our linguistic and conceptual practices with the world, the fitness of our linguistic and conceptual practices with the world, the fitness or correspondence of our language and conceptual systems to their objects, is constantly being exploited and missed, grasped and mistaken, gained and, of course, lost.

47 Thus the world, of which we are a part, and various of its features, states, or objects continue to have the capacity to affect our language and conceptual systems in a variety of ways. Things—to speak thus loosely and collectively—can guide us in our epistemic endeavors, if we have the good fortune and wit to discern their guiding signs. They can nudge us, frustrate us and so prompt us to bring our conceptual and linguistic practices into conformity with aspects of the world which we at the time may only dimly recognize. They can signal us through the retrograde motion of Jupiter that revisions are needed in our astronomy and our conception of the relations of earth, sun, and moon. They can prompt us by means of the peculiar properties of newly isolated deuterium that alteration is due in the way we think of a physical element.

48 In one of his aphoristic remarks Wittgenstein observed that in its study of language, "Philosophy may in no way interfere with the actual use of language; it can in the end only describe it .... It leaves everything as it is."[2] The above remarks on truth and correspondence reflect a somewhat different point of view. Whether we will it or not, our language and conceptual systems, and with them the articulation with the world achieved in them, are not ordained, once for all, and in all respects, by a benevolent Creator, by genetic or other biological determinants, by the inexorable march in the world of the powers of production, or by common sense. Language changes, concepts change, ways of speaking and thinking generally change as life and knowledge change. Indeed what we think of as conceptual change is one broad feature of change in life and thought. It is more a kind of change, sometimes

---

[1] [Cf. ch. 1 above.—*Ed.*]

[2] *Philosophical Investigations*, I §124.

of a most profound sort, in *how* we think than one in *what* we think, more
an alteration in our resources of speaking and thinking than one in the
effectiveness with which in speech and thought we simply put to use resources already in being. The kind of increase in knowledge afforded by
conceptual change comes more from the discovery of a kind of thought or
speech that will fit, grasp, match, and thus reveal something in the objects of
investigation, than from the discovery and proper categorization of objects
which there are available resources of thought and speech already competent
to fit, match, grasp, and record. Speaking loosely we discover "things" by
discovering ideas which match them, by doing something of the sort Descartes would have called developing clear and distinct ideas, rather, than by
discovering things with which the ready resources of thought and speech, the
well-formed formulae of accepted symbolisms, are already competent to deal.
49 There is no little irony in the fact that the possibilities of conceptual
variation, viewed synchronically, should be regarded by some philosophers to
be a most serious obstacle for determining in any fair, unbiased, undistorted
way, the character of objects and features of the world, when, these same
possibilities, viewed diachronically in the history of science, have been one
of the most productive methodological resources of modern physical theory.
What has not been so well recognized, though the matter was emphasized by
some philosophers of an earlier generation, notably Peirce and James, is how
the successful exploitation of this resource illustrates ways in which the
concern for correspondence, which has been the object of much unrewarding
puzzlement and controversy in conception, is pursued and achieved in practice. Here again, as frequently elsewhere, conception has suffered in isolation
from act, theory in isolation from practice. Philosophical investigation may,
or may not, in its exploration of the articulation of thought and language with
aspects of the world with which they are engaged, be able to do more than
"describe ... [leaving] everything as it is." Whatever further it may do,
whatever further steps there may be, surely a first step *is* "describing" this
articulation, realistically grasping its character, understanding it as it is.

3

The Concern About Truth

> In the *Tractatus*, I was unclear about "logical analysis" and ostensive demonstration [*Erklärung*]. I used to think that there was a direct link [*Verbindung*] between Language and Reality.[1]

1   The aim of this chapter is not to solve the "Problem of Truth" but rather to locate, elucidate, and render more accessible to philosophical treatment a major philosophical concern to which the phrase "Problem of Truth" not very aptly refers. One of the consequences of increased understanding of this concern is a realization that its object is not a problem in any common sense of this term. As with our concerns with poverty or disease, peace or prosperity, the object of this concern is not some definite intellectual or practical puzzle for which a key may be found and a definitive solution effected. This characteristic by no means diminishes the importance of such concerns, while an appreciation of it is valuable in promoting realistic, sustained devotion to them. There is no scarcity of problems to be encountered in dealing intelligently with the philosophical concern about truth, and happily we are by no means without resources for dealing with them. But the first need, and that

---

[1] Wittgenstein, comment to Waismann, 1 July, 1932, S. Toulmin, tran., in A. Janik and S. Toulmin, *Wittgenstein's Vienna* (New York: Simon and Schuster, 1973), 222.

to which this chapter is directed, is to penetrate some of the obscuring dress
in which the concern often appears and discern some of its main features.
2   The career of the "Problem"—I will hereafter omit the qualifying quotation marks—has some odd and intriguing features. In their anthology in the
theory of knowledge, Nagel and Brandt open the discussion of the topic of
truth with the following observation:

> Although the pursuit of knowledge is often said to be a "search for truth,"
> those engaged in it are rarely concerned with the nature of the alleged object
> of their search. Certainly few investigators in the natural or social sciences
> have devoted much thought to defining what truth is; and there is no
> evidence to show that failure to do so has been a handicap in the conduct of
> scientific inquiry.[1]

Similarly, Pitcher begins the Introduction to his collection of contemporary
articles on truth with the observation that although the concept of truth, the
meaning of the term "truth" is a concern of philosophers, "the great philosophers of history [i.e., the great historical figures] said surprisingly little about
this concept: they were far more interested in truths than in truth."[2]

The divergence remarked by these writers between a concern with truths
and a concern with truth itself is interesting and bears investigating. It may
be suggested at once that the divergence, though real, by no means signifies
that the two concerns are not deeply and importantly related. That it no doubt
widely seems otherwise is chiefly due to the fact that in much work on the
topic of truth the concern represented in it has been misconceived. In consequence, often the means employed in ministering to the concern have ended
up by obscuring and distorting it. This helps to explain the frustration one
often experiences in pursuing many recent discussions of the topic, the
feeling that somehow, though much energy has been expended, the main
issues remain untouched, the main difficulties unscathed, and that after all
this diligent effort, one is left singularly empty-handed.

Intense cultivation of this topic dates less than a century ago, as Pitcher
notes, and was surely in good part a reaction to the then large-scale hegemony in Western philosophy of the Kantian-Hegelian Idealism. It is not too
much to say that the concern about truth which was expressed in the lively

---

[1] *Meaning and Knowledge*, Ernest Nagel and Richard B. Brandt, eds. (New York:
Harcourt, Brace and World, 1963), 121.

[2] *Truth*, G. Pitcher, ed. (Englewood Cliffs, N.J.: Prentice-Hall, 1964), 1.

controversies over the Coherence, Correspondence, and Pragmatic Theories of Truth, was aroused by the accusations of critics of Idealism—among whom Russell was a leader—that the theory of knowledge of this philosophy, however illuminating concerning some aspects of our thought and judgment, was extremely negligent and inadequate concerning the primary question of the truth of that thought and judgment. However limited we are in this thought and judgment, these critics thought it important to emphasize, we do pursue truth, do want, among other things, and not least, this characteristic for our allegations or judgments about how things are. We are not content to realize this aspiration only vicariously in the absolute, and not ready to accept for ourselves, in place of it, an ersatz commodity composed of such ingredients as personal satisfaction, public utility, and evolutionary success.

The "Copernican" revolution in the theory of knowledge effected in the critical philosophy of Kant and his idealistic successors was strikingly effective in discrediting one of the central features of the Cartesian philosophy, which was the notion that knowledge should be conceived in terms of what might be called the paradigm of revelation. Whether the means by which the objects of knowledge revealed themselves was the natural light of reason or experience, the dominant view before Kant in modern philosophy was that there is a source or sources of knowledge by which knowledge of things, including ourselves, is given in some direct, revelatory way. At some fundamental stage in knowledge, if not throughout, we know what we were told by this source, and sometimes this source informs us of the nature of things by "presenting" to us the things themselves, actually ushering them into the forum of consciousness, conceived to be a milieu so pellucid that in it something needed only to be, in order to be known. Philosophical wisdom with respect to this source naturally consisted in listening, letting the source speak, not permitting our own impulses to anticipate nature, to drown out, or to garble the information accessible to us in this way.

The effect of the Kantian philosophy, when its implications were eventually worked out and accepted, was to install in place of this theory one in which the necessary condition of knowledge is not the suppression but the employment of what we as knowers, individually and collectively, bring to the knowledge process. Knowledge is something we produce, as an artist or craftsman produces artifacts. These are not delivered to him ready-made, if he but assumes an artistic or productive posture; nor does he create or spin them entirely out of himself, like a spider. Recognizing that what the artist-craftsman of knowledge brings to the process of forming cognitive products is always a mixture of skill and ignorance, deftness and clumsiness, inspiration and delusion, good and bad materials, one sees also that the new theory of the knowledge process requires a new way of thinking of items of knowledge and of what we do when we evaluate candidates for this position. Gone from the new theory was any place for archetypes, disclosed to a passive knower through the natural light of reason or the deliverances of sense. This seemed to have a revolutionary, subversive bearing upon the question of how we should conceive the character of truth as attributed to our alleged cognitions, as indicated in the following line of reasoning. If there are no archetypes which may be conceived as both independent of our cognitive processes and yet somehow accessible to us for the purpose of conceiving and judging the fidelity of our cognitive products—our propositions, judgments, hypotheses, allegations—then the notion of truth itself as applied to these products must be revised to dispense with such archetypes, either in their old metaphysical dress of "objects" or "things," or in the new habiliments of "facts" or "states of affairs."[1] Adherents of the critical philosophy in the main were disposed to affirm the antecedent of this hypothetical pronouncement, dissenters to deny the consequent. And when the dissenters emphasized that we obviously do judge the truth or falsity of our cognitive products in relation to some "objects" or "items" accessible to us, the adherents agreed, but urged that in order to make the theory of truth fit our actual practice in pursuit of it, we must conceive the judgmental, relating procedure differently. We must conceive of truth as consisting not in a relation between cognitive products and things altogether different from them, but in a relation between these products themselves. (And, of course, in a very different metaphysic, they likewise conceived of the "products" differently.)

There are various things to be objected to in reasoning like this. Some hint of its fragility upon critical impact may be gleaned from considering that although we cannot now see Abraham Lincoln's face and must derive what information we have about his facial appearance from such sources as photographs, portraits, and descriptions, it by no means follows that all the information we now have is information about photographs, portraits, and descriptions, and not about Lincoln himself. Nevertheless many philosophers

---

[1] "Wondering at how something in experience could be asserted to correspond to something by definition outside experience, which it is, on the basis of epistemological doctrine, the sole means of 'knowing,' is what originally made me suspicious of the whole epistemological industry" (John Dewey, "Propositions, Warranted Assertibility, and Truth," *Journal of Philosophy* 38 [1941], excerpted in Nagel and Brandt, 152–60, p. 157).

who found the general philosophical conclusion unacceptable sought like Russell to escape from it chiefly by rejecting the epistemological premises from which it seemed to follow, rather than the reasoning which made it seem to follow. In this respect Russell's theory of knowledge was literally reactionary in relation to the Kantian revolution, and Russell did not mince words in characterizing much of nineteenth-century philosophy carrying out this revolution as an unfortunate aberration.[1]

The controversy over the Correspondence and Coherence Theories of Truth (and incidentally over the Pragmatic Theory as well) was thus in good part a very abstract expression of issues raised in reaction to a certain kind of theory of knowledge. The strong insistence by many writers that truth must be conceived in terms of correspondence between our judgments (beliefs, statements, etc.) and some features of a world independent of these judgments expressed a conviction that in making such judgments we are engaged in the project of discerning and portraying the existence and character of things, broadly conceived, in this world, and that our concern for truth in these judgments is a concern for accuracy in this discernment, fidelity in the portrayal. The general theory of knowledge to which objection was being made was one which seemed to many to be on principle negligent of this concern. Within the confines of this theory it did not seem possible for one adequately to understand and construe the concern, so that the effect of the theory was, at one level, a lack of understanding of it, and, at another, to the extent that philosophical theory in the matter is translated into action, a lessening of devotion to it in practice.

The basic reason for the inadequacy charged to the kind of theory of knowledge in question, both the idealist and pragmatic varieties, was the emphasis in the theory that universally our knowledge of things, our judgments, hypotheses, and so on, even our very consciousness of matters of which we are most intimately aware, is always a product of a complex of determining conditions other than, and extending far beyond, the states of

---

[1] "I respect Descartes, Leibniz, Locke, Berkeley and Hume, all of whom employed the analytic method. I do not believe that Kant or Hegel or Nietzsche or the more modern anti-rationalist have contributed anything that deserves to be remembered." Also: "I regard the whole romantic movement, beginning with Rousseau and Kant, and culminating in pragmatism and futurism, as a regrettable aberration. I should take 'back to the 18th century' as a battle-cry, if I could entertain any hope that others would rally to it." See "Dr. Schiller's Analysis of *The Analysis of Mind*," *Journal of Philosophy* 19 (1923): 645–51, pp. 647, 645 respectively.

affairs, objects and events we take ourselves to know. The judgment that a certain state is realized is never produced by that state alone. Always it represents a result of the confluence of various determinants, which may or may not include that state, and which, even if they do include it, must be recognized themselves also to affect our reaction in judgment to and consciousness of that state. All this is illustrated constantly and abundantly in the knowledge of material objects we derive by means of sight and the other modes of sense perception. And the resultant question posed was this: if our cognitive apprehension or consciousness of objects, and our representation of those objects to ourselves and others, is conceived to be effected in a variform type of activity on our part, often spoken of as "judgment," which is generated and formed by such a complex of influences, how can we determine, and, even more fundamentally, how can we even consistently consider, whether there are objects corresponding to our apprehensions or representations of them? It was this sort of question to which Berkeley long ago was responding, in his own idiom of thought, when he maintained (*Principles*, §8) that "an idea can be like nothing but an idea," and that "it is impossible for us to conceive a likeness except only between our ideas." A century later the same basic point was urged by those who argued that a fuller understanding of the main doctrine of the *Critique of Pure Reason* led to the conclusion not only that the alleged question of the relation between phenomena and things-in-themselves could not be answered, but also that the question itself could not survive careful critical examination.

A further important consideration in the evaluation of this doctrine was the increasing realization that the determinants of judgment were not only more complex than was recognized in the *Critique of Pure Reason*, but also more subject to variation from time to time and from place to place, in different intellectual, social and scientific contexts. The fact that these determinative conditions of our judgments display so much variation and are so liable to change, seemed to render intolerable the conclusion that judgments, so conceived, are the sole vehicles of knowledge. For surely truth, conceived as conformity between judgment and objects, is a primary desideratum in knowledge. How could a theory of knowledge be maintained from which this concern is on principle extruded?

3   One can be sensitive to the force exerted by reasoning of this kind without succumbing to it. Some appreciation of this force, of the way in which a culminating effect of the reasoning was to render problematic the relation between our judgments, thoughts, or beliefs and some system of

objects and relations, some "prior and independent reality" (John Dewey's sometimes deprecatory phrase) with which they might be thought to correspond, is essential for understanding what the objectors to the critical philosophy of knowledge were attempting to elucidate and ensure in their theories and analyses of "propositions," "states of affairs," and the "correspondence relations" between these.[1] Furthermore—and this is essential for understanding the matter—one can understand how this kind of elucidation and analysis was bound to be ineffective, bound to fail to minister to the deep philosophical concern from which it arose.

One point of difficulty only in the vicissitudes of the analysis of correspondence may be attended here. If the judgment or proposition that, say, the cat is on the mat, is true, then there must be some corresponding feature of the world, the present situation in the room, or whatever, some state of affairs, which has this relation with the judgment. Pressed by their critics to specify what this feature is, the correspondence analysts typically and necessarily were driven to appeal to the very form of judgment or statement which was under examination, to employ the form, not necessarily to make a judgment, but to formulate and refer to one in some mode of indirect discourse. What corresponds to the proposition "The cat is on the mat" and makes it true, if it is true, is the state of affairs that the cat is on the mat, and the same holds correspondingly of the state of affairs to be specified in believing or stating that Desdemona loves Cassio or that Mary is baking pies now. Of course, this is all too easy. In speaking in this way we are saying what we were instructed to say when we learned the formula to the effect that p is true if, and only if, p. What the formula expresses is incontestable, and not negligible. But on the matter at hand it is not helpful, valuable as it may be for some purposes, to have a firm grasp of the relation between the various linguistic expressions or propositions which is codified in this equivalence formula. What makes the proposition true that the number 5 is prime

[1] "Scientific conceptions are not a revelation of prior and independent reality," *The Quest for Certainty*, 165; cf. 185, 195–96. Dewey's exchange on this matter with Arthur E. Murphy in the Schilpp Dewey volume is helpful in revealing that, at least when directly confronting the issue, Dewey wished to have the emphasis in such a pronouncement put on the "revelation" part rather than the "prior and independent reality," i.e. to be interpreted as rejecting the view that scientific knowledge is derived by revelation rather than the view that in science we do attain knowledge of such realities. See Dewey, "Replies," in *The Philosophy of John Dewey*, P. A. Schilpp, ed. (Evanston and Chicago: Northwestern University Press, 1939), 515–608; pp. 556–59, 563, 565.

is the state of affairs of the number 5 being prime; and what makes the proposition true that God is three persons in one, if it is true, is presumably just that state of affairs, whatever it is. As a way of proceeding to elucidate the corresponding state of affairs in the case of true propositions, this easy way was thoroughly unsatisfactory. It was very questionable whether the change of linguistic mode was sufficient to specify so rich a set of entities, having just the characteristics desired; and the entities, if specified, seemed to cry for the application of Ockham's Razor. So F. P. Ramsey early, and P. F. Strawson later and in more detail, noting certain parasitic and idle features of philosophical truth theory, proposed a view of our locutions about truth in which the principal function of saying of a certain statement that it is true was not to speak about the relation between the statement and some putative corresponding state, but rather to assume and express toward the statement, on the part of the speaker or any others for whom he presumed to speak, a confirming, endorsing, conceding attitude.[1] And John Austin, though himself convinced of the fundamental rightness of the notion of correspondence for the purpose of elucidating truth language, warned against the tendency of philosophers, to which the Ramsey-Strawson view seemed an extreme and mistaken reaction, to indulge, when speaking of truth, in the linguistic production of dubious entities. Here the twin dangers are, he said, that "we suppose that there is nothing there but the true statement itself, nothing to which it corresponds, or else we populate the world [and indeed "grossly overpopulate it"] with linguistic *Doppelgänger*."[2]

Confronted by the challenge to specify what is the state of affairs which makes it true that the cat is on the mat or that Charles I died on the scaffold, what indeed could one do? The dilemma was very much as Austin estimated it: a hard choice between the linguistic conjuration of dubious entities, or a secure theory that afforded relief from the metaphysical extravagance, but at perhaps too high a price. Was there as Austin put it, "nothing there but the true statement itself, nothing to which it corresponds"? If the project of specifying states of affairs is the consequence of a judgment that there is "something there"; if success in this project is necessary before one can consistently maintain that ascription of truth to our judgments

---

[1] Ramsey's views date from 1927; see Pitcher, ed., *Truth*, 16–17. Strawson's "Truth" appeared in *Analysis* 9 (1949), excerpted in Nagel and Brandt, 160–66.

[2] Austin, "Truth," *Proceedings of the Aristotelian Society*, sup. vol. 24 (1950), rpt. in *Truth*, Pitcher, ed., 18–31; and in Nagel and Brandt, 166–76.

conveys not just that these are judgments we are led by various considerations and for various purposes to make, but that they do capture and convey how things are; then perhaps our commonsense inclination to think that there is something there is just some form of transcendental illusion. But is that project so closely connected with the theory? Austin himself thought not, and tried to elucidate the matter of statement, fact, and the correspondence relation between them in terms of historical acts of stating, historical situations, and demonstrative and descriptive conventions binding specific acts with specific situations.

Much of the criticism which Strawson made of Austin's efforts in this project is persuasive.[1] Strawson argued also that some of the major defects in Austin's account were due to the fact that, setting out to deal with one topic, Austin ended up treating another. The criticism advanced here of attempts generally to elucidate the concern about truth expressed in the Correspondence Theory is similar. In the exercise of identifying judgments or statements, facts or states of affairs, and a correspondence relation between these types of entities, carried on early and late by Russell, Austin, and others, the project of dealing with the basic concern from which the theory derived had somehow miscarried. The attempts which regularly led to the introduction of various kinds of dubious entities were well intentioned; behind them lay a legitimate concern. We shall be poorer in our understanding of human knowledge if we permit our proper skepticism of these entities to obscure and cause us to neglect the concern from which they arose.

4   One may properly react to Russell's early discussion of truth in *The Problems of Philosophy* with doubt that much more is known after the truth or falsehood of Othello's judgment that Desdemona loves Cassio has been explained in terms of the correspondence between the complex composed of Othello, Desdemona, loving, and Cassio—namely the judgment itself—and another complex composed of Desdemona, loving, and Cassio "in the same order." Surely a good bit, perhaps all, of what Russell is saying is that if Othello judges that Desdemona loves Cassio, he judges truly if, and only if, Desdemona loves Cassio. What is said is a philosophical truism. But behind and expressing itself inadequately in this truism appears to be a deep philosophical concern with entities like Othello's belief or judgment, which are by no means figments of philosophical imagination, and things, circumstances,

---

[1] Strawson, "Truth."

states or whatever to which they have to be closely related if they are to be beliefs or judgments at all, and further, if they are to be true.

There seems to be more here than an impulse, to which Russell was inclined less than many philosophical writers, to make two linguistic phrases grow where only one grew before. Behind our natural impulse to say with Russell that what makes the judgment about Desdemona true, if it is true, is the complex composed in a certain way of Desdemona, loving, and Cassio, i.e., the state of affairs of Desdemona loving Cassio, is an intention to emphasize, as Russell himself indicates, that necessary to the truth of the judgment is the existence in some frame of reference (here Shakespeare's play) of a woman named "Desdemona" and also an affection, relation, attachment on her part for a man—not a dog, a horse, or a variety of sweet wine—named "Cassio."

Obviously what is being identified here as the concern about truth is a very old concern, one that has been primary in philosophy throughout its history in the Western world. The view attributed to Thales, the bold specu-lation that water was the principle or substance of all things, implies at once that when we say that the traveler perished in the desert for lack of water, our way of speaking in some respect does not reflect the actual situation as well as we conceivably might, since surrounded by the sand the traveler, though dying for water to drink, was as surrounded by water in some form as completely as the Ancient Mariner. Similarly Democritus, as reported by Sextus Empiricus, said that "by convention" there is sweet, there is bitter, and hot, and cold, and similarly color, "but in truth there exist atoms in the void." Among many of the early writers discussing primary and secondary qualities in modern philosophy the concern is even plainer. Descartes, as is well known, held that in judging the piece of wax to be sweet or fragrant, we depart widely from the truth if we conceive the wax to be an independent substance having the very characters of sweetness and fragrance which it arouses as adventitious ideas in us. So Locke recommended that we think of the secondary qualities of matter as powers between which and the sensed qualities of colors, sounds, tastes and so on, there is "no resemblance ... at all," the qualities in the bodies being nothing but certain modes of bulk, figure, and motion which under certain circumstances produce these sensations in us. And so Hume, in his more pronounced skeptical and phenomenalist moods, urged that in careful thought we would conceive causes or powers themselves as nothing resident in the objects to which in common thought and speech we attribute them, but rather as a propensity or habit in us. And so, in less metaphysical contexts, we find ourselves obliged to say that of course accurately speaking what we call the rise of the sun is not a rise at all, but an apparent rise, due to the rotation of the point from which our observation of the sun is made.

The historical facts just cited are but a minute selection from a long familiar story. What is neither so familiar nor merely factual is the construction put upon the facts here, the assimilation of them with the primary philosophical concern which is represented in the Problem of Truth. If this assimilation is correct, the concern is by no means a new one. And the Problem itself is new or especially prominent in recent philosophy, because it arose as a response to a relatively new, sweeping and powerful challenge to the satisfaction of the concern which seemed to many to derive from a persuasive and dominant theory of knowledge. But in speaking thus of an *old* "concern" and a *new* "problem," there is no intention to exploit here the vagueness of principles of individuation applied to philosophical problems, nor to advance a case which derives its plausibility from a special and idiosyncratic distinction between terms. Possibly this way of speaking tends to obscure some important things about the philosophy of truth, for the challenge to the satisfaction of the concern could also fairly be said to have generated a new concern. There has been a strong historical tradition of looking at matters in a way that conforms to this latter way of speaking. This is the tradition which sees in philosophy of knowledge from the time of Kant the development of a view which was in a new way "critical," raising in a newly searching way the capacity of human reason to know reality. Following this way of speaking, the concern about truth merges with the Problem of Truth, and the Problem, that of understanding the nature of truth in the face of a philosophy which in a mystifying way threatened to draw a veil between us and the real world, is one which during most of Western philosophy did not attract the attention of the great figures because the veil had not yet been manufactured.

While adoption of a way of speaking about these matters is not a major concern here, there is a point of doctrine emphasized in one way of speaking which, however one speaks, needs to be insisted upon. This is that the major philosophical question agitated in the controversies over the theory of truth represented a new way of thinking—perhaps it should be thought of as a mutation—about an aspect of knowledge which had previously been the concern of philosophers, though not so perplexing and frustrating a one, because of the prevailing confidence of philosophers outside the skeptical tradition that there were ways of dealing with it. This is not to deny that there were differences of philosophical doctrine concerning the character of these ways. But on the main point the precritical tradition in philosophy seems to have been right. There are indeed and have always been ways of dealing with the concern which was dealt with in such an abstract and exacerbated form in the more recently agitated Problem of Truth. The ways are of special but by no means exclusive interest to philosophers. They constitute an armoire, a repertory of intellectual skills and methods, of common sense and theory, which changes as knowledge and methods of investigation change, which did not spring fully equipped from the noble brow of technical philosophy, but which is both an intellectual resource in being for that philosophy and a subject of in critical understanding, appraisal, and possible emendation.

5   If the Problem of Truth is understood as an expression of the kind of philosophical concern which has been portrayed here, the fact that few investigators in the natural and social sciences devote much thought to this specific Problem is not odd, just as it is not odd that the great historical figures in philosophy have had little to say about the particular questions which the Problem embraces. The relation of scientists, historians, philosophers, theologians, poets, and others to what has been referred to here as the concern about truth, and to the issue met from time to time in attempting to minister to that concern, is an altogether different matter. A scientist busy in the project of discerning and elucidating the conductivity of metals, the features of unsaturated and saturated solutions, or unsaturated or saturated markets, has little occasion in the normal conduct of inquiry (this being one of the things which make it normal) to pause for reflection upon and investigation of the large-scale validity of the composite logical, mathematical, linguistic, experimental-observational, social, and historical institution in which he has been indoctrinated and trained and in the disciplined practices of which he is now engaged. But what is normal is not universal. And as some of the historical examples cited testify, there are many occasions in the development of the institutions of knowledge, scientific and otherwise, when the guidance of inquiry, the development of theory and the design of observation and experiment wait upon, demand, just this kind of philosophical investigation. This may be carried out, as in the past, sometimes by persons whom we should naturally call "scientists," such as Galileo, Gilbert, and Newton, and at other times by those whom we more naturally think of as philosophers, such as Descartes, Hobbes, and Locke, their work illustrating that, as Émile Meyerson put it, ontology is an integral part of (*fait corps*

avec) science itself and cannot be separated from it.[1] All these scientist-philosophers, or philosopher-scientists, were alert to some aspects of the question, not whether truth should be "defined" as coherence or correspondence or what not, but whether and how the system of thought and judgment in which they and others were operating could be made to respond more sensitively and reflect more accurately the nature of the objects, events, states, or whatever it was that seemed to be expressing itself in the phenomena which were at the focus of attention. This same concern was not neglected, but robustly cultivated by the great ancient and modern philosophers: think, for but one example, of the Cave, the Line, and the Forms in Plato. What most of these philosophers, Plato again, or Aristotle, or Descartes, or Locke, did not have was the problem of squaring their concern with a complex theory of knowledge and mind, such as was developed in the nineteenth century and seemed radically to subvert it. Thus, Descartes judged that once clearness and distinctness had been achieved in our ideas, the only substantial reason for doubting the capacity of these ideas to serve as vehicles of knowledge lay in the possibility of the ideas being implanted in us by a malevolent jinni. Even Locke, who disagreed with Descartes concerning the possibility of our developing a science of necessary truths concerning bodies, did not question our capacity to develop "real" ideas of bodies, that is, ideas which so far as they went, did "agree with the real existence of things." He attributed our incapacity to have a science of bodies to our lack of "adequate" ideas, this term for him conveying the special requirement that the ideas so characterized represent their archetypes "completely" and "perfectly." Thus, in order to have adequate ideas of bodies, he thought, we should need to be able "to penetrate into the internal fabric and real essence" of them, from which essences, he supposed, their properties would be deducible, just as properties of a triangle are deducible from "the complex idea of three lines, including a space."[2]

6   The comment on Locke makes this perhaps an opportune place to try further to specify what is central in the philosophical concern about truth and distinguish it clearly from what is not. The question about the cat and the

[1] *Identity and Reality* (1930), K. Loewenberg, tran. (New York: Dover, 1962), 384.

[2] *Essay Concerning Human Understanding*, A. C. Fraser, ed. (New York: Dover, 1959), Bk. II, chs. 30–31, Bk. IV, chs. 3, 12.

mat, or about Desdemona, or about Charles I is no simple question about what makes it true that the cat is on the mat, and so on. At one level the answer to the cat question is perfectly obvious; it is the cat's being on the mat that makes the judgment true, if it is true. But if, when we talk in this way, we have a nagging feeling that we are somehow begging the question, are somehow winning a point and papering over a difficulty with an easy verbalism, we should take heed. For at a deeper level the question is about the adequacy of the thought and language (let us, for brevity talk principally of language: not the words, of course, but the practices with the words) which are exemplified in one or another of these judgments or statements. It is a question about the adequacy of this kind of language to capture and represent real features of whatever it is with which it is engaged, the something (or somethings) which apart from our efforts to capture and represent it obviously cannot be captured and represented, must otherwise remain for us a something we know not what.

When we inquire about the truth or falsity, the correspondence with fact, of specific individual judgments, propositions or beliefs, we are already involved in, employing and presuming the adequacy of a complex system of linguistic practices.[1] To ask about truth, about correspondence, in such a context, is to suppose that the language is already so well articulated with whatever it is we are dealing with that judgments can be made, propositions formulated, beliefs entertained; it is to suppose that the articulation between language and subject matter is sufficiently well achieved that such specific questions about truth and falsity can be asked. When we form the phrases which we employ to pick out or specify individual judgments we normally without further thought suppose that the linguistic machine by means of which, employing these phrases, we refer, describe, represent, and so on, is already in place, in operation and in order. We suppose that with the phrases and the other appurtenances of language we can, for example, mark off some subject, however minute or vast this may be, which can be discriminated by ourselves and others, and with respect to which it is our interest to express ourselves.

We similarly suppose that we can individually signify a great variety of features which we use in discriminating various subjects, be those subjects as

---

[1] As Josiah Royce urged many years ago, a bushman, in contrast with a mathematician, lacks even the capacity to make mistakes about the properties of equations. *The Religious Aspect of Philosophy* (Boston: Houghton, Mifflin, 1885), ch. 11, "The Possibility of Error."

concrete as the homely material objects which form the furniture of our lives or as abstract as political constitutions or logistic systems. And with these means we suppose ourselves able to signify to ourselves and others the presence of selected features in discriminated subjects, so that the cherry does not need to be present to us in order for us to appreciate that it is red, nor for us to be able to consider and say that it is white, or even say that white is the color of cherries.

When we consider the truth or falsity of Othello's judgment about Desdemona, our judgment that the cat is on the mat, we are already operating the machine, could not consider these matters unless we were. And when we ask if one or other judgment was, or is, true, we suppose that the machine is operating well. And because we suppose this, when we ask what makes the judgment that the cat is on the mat true, we naturally say "That it is on the mat," "Its being on the mat," or something similar. Of course, if the machine is operating well, it is the cat's being on the mat which makes that judgment true, if it is true. But what if the machine is not operating well? What if the question about judgment and fact is not a question to be answered by operating the machine, but rather a question about the machine, about its operation, or more particularly, about the operation of this particular part of it. Then the echo-redundancy which made us somewhat uncomfortable with our answer is of more than stylistic significance. It signifies that in setting out to provide an answer to a question about the well-ordering of some part of the machine we have insensitively used that very part, in effect begged the essential question. So familiar are we with the operation of the machine at this point, so at ease with its employment, that like much language it has become transparent. As with our eyes, we are more apt to become aware of the complex practices of judgment we constantly employ and rely upon when they display malfunction: when we experience the logical analogues of improper focus, blindness with respect to certain features of objects, or the pathological generation of apparent features of objects or apparent objects themselves. There is no fault, of course, in using the judgmental machine unthinkingly to make judgments, just as there is none in using the internal combustion engine for locomotion without constantly dwelling upon the physical and chemical processes developing the energy which make the vehicle move. It is a fault, however, when, in response to a question about some part of the machine, a challenge of its capacity to perform in a certain manner, we use the challenged part of the machine to produce our answer, thus presuming the very capacity on the part of the machine which was challenged in the first place. And when, having done so, we apply our results

to the development of a philosophical view of truth, a natural view to take is
that the word "true" and similar words enable us to do what otherwise would
be tiresomely repetitive, namely, confirm (agree, concede, etc.) a judgment
made, a story told, without making the judgment, telling the story again.

In setting out to answer the kind of questions about our judgmental and
linguistic practices which arise out of our concern for truth, while we may
not presume the adequacy of just those features of our practice which are in
question, we may, and indeed must, presume the adequacy of others. Otherwise there could be no challenge to meet, no question to answer. The avoidance of circularity does not require one to doubt, or try to doubt, all ways of
calculating in order to consider fairly the validity of some; and the same goes
for proving, measuring, seeing, and so on.

An outstanding feature of that particular historically occasioned expression
of philosophical concern which was the Problem of Truth was the extreme,
global character which the concern assumed in this form of expression. This
alone is sufficient to account for the intractability of the concern when the
attempt is made to treat it in this form. Furthermore, when we are released
from a preoccupation with this form, we are freer to recognize, what has
been before our eyes all along, some of the less hyperbolic, less intellectually
paralysing ways in which the concern continues to express itself, as life,
knowledge, language, and judgment change, and some of the resources with
which on occasion we have been able to deal with the concern in successful
ways.

7   References to the practices of ordinary speech are now less imposing than
they were a decade or so ago, and for some good reasons. But recognition
of the deficiencies, ambiguities, and downright contradictions of these practices should not blind us to the excellence of them when regarded, not as a
composite of items of philosophic wisdom, secure and irrefragable in detail,
but as examples of an epistemic tool, constantly adjusted to its tasks through
myriad, diverse applications, and, though glaringly imperfect in many respects, in many others wellordered, efficient and sensitive beyond comparison with any putative rivals. When we say that the cat is on the mat, we
must recognize that what we signify when we use the word "cat" and, in
particular, speak of "the" cat, when we speak similarly of "the" mat, and
when we signify that there is now this situation of the former being "on" the
latter—we must recognize that what we signify is liable to so much elaboration, revision and rectification, were there occasion for such, that at times we
must wonder how we succeeded in doing what we did in saving this, know-

ing so imperfectly what we were about. Nevertheless the language is apt, is a model of aptness. For if we are not able securely to discriminate creatures and objects of this kind, and such elemental spatio-physical relations as one body resting upon another, it is hard to imagine in what system of linguistic practice we can take the nouns and relational phrases to fit their objects and hence to be a reliable guide to the kinds of entities, features and composite states incorporating these that partly make up our world.

Various philosophers, speaking sometimes in the material mode about things, and sometimes in the formal mode about our language, have urged, in effect, that whatever metaphysical wisdom we can attain must be a development of the metaphysic already contained in our commonsense language of the portions of the world with which we are intimately concerned: the material objects we deal with, other living things, other creatures, and other persons. Some have gone so far as to suggest that the manner of development must be circumscribed so severely that in it nothing can be added to the original story, the endproduct being a way of speaking perhaps more precisely and, for certain purposes, more efficiently, of objects, events, features, already included in the original story. While such a view may be appealing to us in moments of philosophical perplexity and frustration, it is surely wrong, and for a variety of reasons, one of which lies close at hand. That is that our commonsense language and metaphysic are not so fixed as this view suggests, and the causes and motives for change do not all come from the kind of specialized examination that philosophers make of them. They change themselves. Within them are forces which prevent them from remaining static, even if we willed and tried to ensure this.

Once a change has been effected and ratified in extended use, it is sometimes hard to recapture the extent of the theoretical, practical, and emotional difficulties from which and with which it emerged. Galileo before the Inquisition, and Descartes taking residence in Holland, are but two of the more spectacular reverberations of the emergence of a way of speaking about a familiar feature of our daily lives which has become a fairly secure part of common sense if not, for pretty plain reasons, a part of common speech. Though we still speak of "the sky" or "the heavens," we no longer suppose, as we do with the cat or the mat, that our phrases refer to a definite physical entity, in this case a dome as physically real as, though vastly more extended than, those of St. Paul's Cathedral in London or St. Peter's in Rome. Similar in some respects, but vastly dissimilar in others, is the gingerly way in which, when we are not doing arithmetic, but thinking philosophically about it, we treat the noun phrase "the number five" or even the simple noun "five." We can readily understand how arithmetical inquiries, emerging from and always conducted against a background of our commonsense language of objects, easily followed a way of speaking which seemed to imply a Platonic view of numerical objects. On the other hand, reflection upon the manifest differences between the number five, the cat, and the mat, must give us pause, which further reflection may or may not transform into full stop.[1] Similarly, when we began to think of the fine structure of matter, we thought of it as composed of "solid, massy, hard, impenetrable, movable particles" in respect to these properties similar to bodies we are acquainted with, though vastly smaller and "even so very hard as never to wear and break in pieces."[2] When thinking thus we naturally supposed each such particle to have at each moment a definite position and motion. And yet there are now strong grounds for regarding our conviction that this must be so as a metaphysical prejudice, to which we were disposed by the linguistic judgmental machine we naturally and necessarily imported into a new area of inquiry. Whatever may hold for molar objects, and however strong may be our derived inclination to attribute both definite position and motion to the electron, there may be no good reason to suppose that there must be relational features of the electron corresponding to this attribution.[3]

The time is now past when the term "animal magnetism," applied to a person capable of producing a hypnotic state in another, could be more than an interesting metaphor. This is not because some piercing metaphysical eye enables us to penetrate the real essence of the hypnotist and determine that there is nothing there corresponding to the term. Rather it is because increased information about human mental processes, including phenomena of attention, suggestion and motivation, enables us to understand better what

[1] An exploration of some metaphysical aspects of our language of numbers and properties (cf. below, this section), utilizing the resource of recent Anglo-American analytic philosophy, makes up the major portion of David S. Shwayder's *Modes of Referring and the Problem of Universals* (University of California Publications in Philosophy 35 [1961]).

[2] Newton, *Opticks*, Query 31; see also *Principia*, Bk. III, "Rules of Reasoning in Philosophy."

[3] The existential implications of some aspects of the language and methods of physics, and an illuminating contrast between the "Logic of Idealization" and the "Logic of Existence Assertions" in physics, is contained in Dudley Shapere's "Notes toward a Post-Positivistic Interpretation of Science," in *The Legacy of Logical Positivism*, P. Achinstein and S. F. Barker, eds. (Baltimore: Johns Hopkins University Press, 1969), 115–60.

characters we should ascribe to human beings and how increasingly inapt is the ascription deriving from this apparent importation from physics. Much less settled in the same field of inquiry is how to judge the complex attributions of features to human beings which are part of that tradition of modern psychology stemming from Freud. Does the doctrine that the ego represses the id at the bidding of the superego express some sober fact? Is it pure mythology? If not, and if the rich personal characters which Freud's use of these terms often connotes are discounted, what are the features and processes in us which these dramatic stories signify, in at least a semimythical way, and in what kind of language can they be represented more soberly and accurately?

Some feature of our language and thought which have been of special philosophical interest illustrate well what a broad problem we confront sometimes, what extensive considerations are relevant to the consideration of the aptness of the language and thought to its subject, to the question to what extent substance does correspond to subject, characters to predicates, and so on. In modern and recent philosophy much effort has been expended on the language of "good" and "bad" employed in both ethical and aesthetic contexts. One vein in the tradition of ethical philosophy, following a mode of treatment exemplified by Hume, urges that our straightforward use of such predicates in the formulation of ethical judgments easily misleads us into thinking that villainy and dishonor represent qualities in the man guilty of treason in the same way as predicate reporting his height, blood pressure, or basic rate of metabolism. Logically prior to the question whether "good" represents a simple property discerned by ethical intuition is the question whether it is a property at all, and if so, what kind: a question, it may be noted, remarkably similar to that posed by the dictum of Democritus concerning "sweet" and "bitter" and "hot" and "cold." This, in turn, is a question which one cannot deal with thoroughly without considering in the end what it is to be a property of an object, what are the kinds of difference which distinguish predicates which do represent features, do in this sense correspond to their objects, from those which do not. This is no inquiry to be carried out in abstraction from the uses of our language and the complex institutions, scientific, ethical, and otherwise of which these uses are parts. What can be divined from a close consideration of the syntactic forms, or of the obvious, rudimentary features of their semantic application, must be supplemented by and assimilated into a broad philosophical inquiry directed to achieving a comprehensive and coherent view of these institutions, the practices which they embrace, the ends for which these practices are engaged in, and the results which in them are achieved.[1]

The verb "think" in the indicative mood requires a subject. This was surely a very minor consideration in Descartes' endorsement of the view that mind should be conceived as a thinking thing, though some of his arguments seem to take advantage of this syntactic fact. When we say that the speaker thought for a moment before giving his answer, there is an obvious level of examination at which no philosophical theory is necessary in considering whether what we said is true or false. But there is also a deeper level, some appreciation of which is necessary before one can understand what has been identified here as the philosophical concern for truth in its application to this and various other locutions. At this level we are concerned not with this particular instance of judgmental activity, but with the kind of activity of which it is an instance. We are concerned with the linguistic practice, with the distinctions made in such a practice, and with how apt these aspects of practice are to the subjects with which they are employed, how well articulated they are to features of this subject, what they represent, and how they represent them.[2] Again, whether we may construe the language of "I think" and "He thinks" as referring to mental substances is not something that can be divined from the grammar, but must be divined concerning the grammar in an extensive examination of, to put it oddly, of course, how adequate this *theory* of "I think" is, construed as an instance of the philosophy of mind. This requires, as the evaluation of theory typically requires, an examination of the considerations that can be advanced for and against. The wide range of these considerations embraces many familiar and diverse items in the

---

[1] Compare, for example, Charles L. Stevenson, *Ethics and Language* (New Haven: Yale University Press, 1943); P. H. Nowell-Smith, *Ethics* (Harmondsworth: Penguin, 1954); Brand Blandshard, *Reason and Goodness* (London: George Allen and Unwin, 1961); Arthur E. Murphy, *The Theory of Practical Reason* (La Salle, Ill.: Open Court, 1964).

[2] Similarly one of the key questions posed by Wittgenstein's discussion of sensations in the *Philosophical Investigations* is not whether the writhing, groaning man who says he is in pain is deceiving us, but rather whether we deceive ourselves philosophically when we "construe the grammar of the expression of sensation on the model of 'object and name'" (I §293). Conversely, the principal question facing the Environmental Protection Agency in the case of the industrial plant charged with polluting the air is not the philosophical one of whether colors or odors are to be viewed as properties of material things (though in analogous circumstances, e.g., in a dispute over conformity to aesthetic standards, the corresponding philosophical question may become pertinent).

history of the philosophy of mind, derived from such diverse sources as Plato's *Phaedo*, Descartes' *Meditations*, Hume's *Treatise*, and, more recently, the Carus Lectures of C. J. Ducasse,[1] Russell's *Analysis of Mind*, Ryle's *The Concept of Mind*, Wittgenstein's *Philosophical Investigations*, and Sartre's *The Transcendence of the Ego*.

8   The activities with which we respond to what has been identified here as the concern for truth are many, various, and complex. And, it appears, so long as intellectual and practical life continues, they are interminable. They abound in everyday life, in science, history, and belles lettres, in the technical arts and practical disciplines, and so on. Furthermore, what we actively do, in contrast with what gets done in and through us, without conscious activity on our part directed to this end, represents but a portion, and by no means the only important portion, of the total process of response.[2]

As philosophers, scientists, and professors of other intellectual disciplines we are especially concerned with what we actively do. In investigating the adequacy of a domain of our language and thought to capture and represent real features of whatever it is with which we are engaged, we are, of course, at the same time investigating, exploring, and discriminating these features themselves. And there is no simple decision procedure—indeed, in the common sense of this phrase, there is no decision procedure, simple or complex—for this activity; there is no universal algorithm for metaphysics.[3] When Lavoisier began investigating combustion, part of his resource was a language-in-being involving the term "phlogiston." This term was taken to signify a substance intimately involved in combustion, taken so because at the time it appeared that combustion could best be understood as involving a release of this substance from combustibles. We can now see that those who thought in this way were misled by, as it were, a metaphysical shadow; they mistook the shadow of oxygen, a genuine substance, for a substance itself. For this realization we are indebted to Lavoisier and others, scientists and natural philosophers, who have thus helped us to understand at one and the same time both what kinds of things there are in the world and what is a more adequate language for speaking of them. At the present time we have a language-in-being in which we take ourselves confidently to refer to persons

---

[1] [*Nature, Mind, and Death* (La Salle, Ill.: Open Court, 1951).—*Ed.*]

[2] [This theme is developed throughout the subsequent chapters.—*Ed.*]

[3] [Cf. ch. 7 below.—*Ed.*]

as agents, as distinguished from their bodies or specific organs of these
bodies, such as their brains; and we confidently use predicates to ascribe
characters to these agents. But how about these subjects and predicates? Are
individual persons independent, real entities in exactly the way that our
ordinary ways of speaking presume them to be? How will they appear in any
scrupulously careful accounting of the contents of the world?

The concern about truth, identifiable in such examples as these, is a
concern about the broad constitutive outlines of our knowledge of the world
in the various domains in which we presume that we have such knowledge.
So, Russell's concern about the circumstances of the death of Charles I, and
the disposition of Desdemona's affections, was a concern about the thorough
adequacy of the common features of our language and thought in which we
pick out objects or persons and attribute to them properties and relations.
Confronted by a philosophy which cast suspicion on just these features, for
example, individual substances and persons, it was natural for Russell to
express his confidence in them by proclaiming in effect that what makes the
judgment that Desdemona loves Cassio true, if it is true, is the presence (in
the world of *Othello*) of a real being, Desdemona, with a real amorous
passion for another real being, Cassio. Though natural, this was preaching
calculated to appeal only to the converted, to those already equally confident
of the metaphysic Russell was espousing. Others, more cognizant of the
significance of his performance, were more apt to be impressed by the
facility with which the language, interrogated about its own adequacy, could,
like an agreeable Epimenides, be made to endorse its own presumptions.

Two different, though not unrelated, questions were being conflated here.
One is a broad philosophical question of the general adequacy of the linguistic and thought forms of which this specific judgment is an example, a
question about the adequacy of the categories of substance, accident, property,
and the rest, in comparison with alternatives. The other is a specific, concrete
question about correctness of this one individual judgment, exemplifying these
categories, in comparison with other similar ones, such as the judgment that
Desdemona does not love Cassio, is indifferent to him, positively dislikes
him, and so on. To construe an answer to the specific concrete question as
an answer to the broad philosophical one is a mistake of the first magnitude.
But it is just this which is being done by those who set out to answer the
philosophical question of truth in respect to a given judgment by appealing
to those suspicious replicas of the judgment itself, namely, corresponding
complexes or states of affairs. At the level of use, a question about the
correctness of categories used can hardly be responded to except by reaffirm-

ing, re-exemplifying the use. What makes my allegation true that a certain named person is related by the directed relation of loving to another named person is that there are two such persons so related. Except for the aspect of reaffirmation or confirmation, which Strawson emphasized, such an affirmation of truth is redundant, and as empty of philosophical substance as he maintained.

9   In contrast with the variform activity and response in which over the years the concern about truth has been ministered, the Problem of Truth, to which much attention has been given during certain periods of this century, stands, not as a particularly clear response ministering to the concern, but rather as a philosophical response to what appeared to be a strong and sweeping challenge to the concern itself. This challenge arose not from difficulties encountered in activities ministering to the concern, but in a philosophical view which in a fundamental way cast doubt on the efficacy of those activities and thus brought the concern itself into disrepute.

During the periods of controversy over the Problem, the clash of arms over it tended to obscure the actual responses we make to the concern, including the activities we consciously engage in in response to it, and the results achieved in them. Immersion in the literature still has the power to produce the same effect. Against this, the aim of this chapter has been primarily to pierce the obscuring cloud of controversy and expose more clearly the nature of the concern, and, secondarily, to freshen recognition of some of the activities in response to the concern and some of their results. Far from being fundamentally misconceived, the general human enterprise directed to this concern is a healthy, ongoing affair, in the constitution of which there is no guarantee either of invariable success or unremitting failure. What we can expect of it, as of other human enterprises, is a mixture of such outcomes. On the proportions of these we may hope that philosophical understanding will have some favorable effect.

For the questions which arise in the conduct of this enterprise are on many occasions, and not untypically, of a distinctively philosophical character. Broad considerations of method and substance have to be explored and taken into account in trying to provide answers to them. Rival claims have to be adjudicated, each boasting the sanction of some strongly supported, and sometimes deeply entrenched institution or organon of scientific practice. Issues call for resolution which can be resolved only, if at all, when certain cognitive practices are viewed with others, and, sometimes further, are considered in relation to human activities and institutions which are not primarily of a cognitive character. Reference to these is sometimes helpful, as reference to our practices in dealing with the ordinary objects of daily life is helpful, when investigating the capacity of our language to reveal the existence and character of objects beyond us, to understanding what is at stake in the question of whether what we are discriminating are real objects, independent of our discriminations, and similarly whether the characters we attribute to such objects are not artifacts of our own invention, but ones to which differences in the objects do correspond.

The twentieth century of the Christian era did not begin the concern about truth and the responsive activities to it which have been explored here; nor, D.V., will it end them. Philosophers of differing persuasions and temperaments, recognizing this concern, may view the relation of their own vocation to those activities in differing ways. Some may recognize in the vocation no requirement of aptitude for or devotion to these activities. But surely, *pace* Marx, part of the vocation is to understand them.[1]

[1] I wish to acknowledge gratefully comments on an earlier version of this chapter by Jack W. Meiland, Thomas M. Robertson, Richard M. Rorty, David S. Shwayder, and Craig E. Taylor.

4

The Rational Governance of Practice

1   Throughout modern philosophy, and especially after the brief confident upsurge of early rationalism, there have been questions and controversies about the capacities and limits of rational processes in the governance of practice. More recently, in the past two decades, developments in a variety of fields, and particularly in the philosophy of science, have brought to the forefront of attention the social determinants of a variety of processes hitherto presumed to be paradigmatically rational ones. These developments have given to the questions and controversies about rational governance a new turn. To the extent that the processes of observation, reasoning, criticism, judgment, evaluation, and so on, traditionally associated with rational governance, are recognized to be thoroughly determined by, thoroughly rooted in, social practice, it has seemed to many philosophically sensitive writers increasingly difficult to continue to maintain for them their claims to rationality. The question, then, to which this paper is addressed is, Can a view of reason that recognizes and indeed emphasizes its determinants in social practice adequately account for the function that reason is commonly conceived capable of performing in the governance of practice?

2   As is illustrated in the preceding paragraph, the terms "reason," "rationality," and similar ones are, in one accepted philosophical usage, employed to cover a very broad set of forms of procedure, departures from which by relevant activities would correspondingly justify their classification as

arational or irrational. In this broad usage reason is not contrasted with, but rather embraces, a vast variety of procedures in the cognitive disciplines, the practical arts, and everyday life. It *includes*, for example, observation, experimentation, the collection and processing of data, and attending to and assessing testimony, as in a court of law.

Another common usage of these same terms is much narrower than this. In it the main contrast signified by "reason" and "rational" is with other cognitive activities, such as observation and the others just mentioned. Here the terms are reserved for activities closely associated with *reasoning*: with inferring, deducing, calculating, and similar activities that fit easily into the rubric of rational *thought*. In the question posed above, whether certain processes of governance can properly be viewed as rational, it is the former, broader sense of this key term that is intended. A consequence of the impulse in the classic modern rationalist philosophers to identify reason with rational thought was that for them the question of the rational governance of practice tended to become translated into the question of the competence in this regard of the reflective processes that fall under this rubric.

The term "governance" is used here in a very broad way to cover all the processes by which, in both individuals and groups, social practices are developed and regulated; strengthened or weakened; changed or preserved against change; and sometimes extinguished. These processes may be gradual and slow, or rapid and abrupt; and there are great variations among them in the degree to which they are conscious, intentional, or deliberate. The more conscious, reflective forms of these processes are of special but not exclusive relevance to the topic of rational governance. That there are rational processes that at times affect the character of practices does not of course imply that at these times the effect has, as it were, its sole ontological source in these processes, that they stand to the effect in the relation of a quite sufficient condition. As in the case of what are discriminated as the causes of physical states or events, what we discriminate as rational determinants of social practice produce their effects, not as solitary creators, but as joint producers in conjunction with a set of background conditions which for the purpose of the attribution of effectiveness and responsibility in this situation normally may be neglected.

The term "practice" likewise is used here very broadly. It applies to modes of procedure of both thought and action, and in all fields of thought and action: in morals, politics, and law; in intellectual disciplines such as mathematics, the physical sciences, and the social studies; in art, religion, and in philosophy itself. Commonly the singular term "practice" carries the connotation of actual modes of procedure, practices actually followed in some community; and that usage is generally followed here. It is sometimes necessary to refer to accepted modes of procedure plurally. In such cases the plural form will be used with some qualifying term like "accepted," except where such a reading is already sufficiently indicated by the context.

"Practice" and "practices" are not usual ways of referring to modes of thought in the theory of knowledge. In that field important broad patterns of thought are for a variety of reasons more commonly referred to by means of such expressions as "concepts," "ideas," or "conceptual schemes." These terms have the serious disadvantage of suggesting, almost irresistibly to many, that the items whose criticism or governance is under examination are features, components, or states of one or more private minds. If one uses the popular language of "concepts," for example, one needs to take special pains to emphasize and issue reminders that what are being referred to under this title are in a very real and profound sense social.[1] There may be important disanalogies, but there are also strong analogies which support the proposals of such diverse recent writers as Ernest Gellner and Stephen Toulmin to assimilate them to social institutions.[2] Concepts are connected with linguistic signs of a certain sort. But they are not internal mental correlates of these signs. They represent ways of proceeding that entail, that require in order to be what they are, their generation and preservation in the rich matrix of communal and social living. In order to give emphasis to this aspect of our intellectual resources the terms "practice" and "practices" have been preferred here.

3   The thought that the processes of governance of practice could be both rational and deeply rooted in practice has not been much favored in modern philosophy, which has in the main followed a contrary view forcefully advanced by Descartes in the *Discourse on Method* and the *Rules for the Direction of the Mind.* The extreme divorcement maintained between reason and accepted practice in the dominant tradition of modern philosophy was a

---

[1] The objective but nonsocial components of ideas or concepts were elaborated upon by this writer in "Thoughts and Things" [ch. 1 above.—*Ed.*]. These, and also the social components, were treated in Chapters 7 and 9 of his *Induction and Justification* (Ithaca, N.Y.: Cornell University Press, 1974).

[2] S. Toulmin, *Human Understanding*, vol. I (Princeton: Princeton University Press, 1974), 158–66; E. Gellner, "Concepts and Society" (1962), rpt. in *Rationality*, B. R. Wilson, ed. (Oxford: Blackwell, 1970), 18–49.

consequence of a presumption that since reason, as a resource in the governance of practice, must be granted to have the capacity to transcend and oppose practice, it must be conceived, as an authority and agent of governance, to be independent of practice. The passage from condition to consequence in this conviction excluded the possibility, little contemplated in this philosophical tradition, that rational governance of practice represented a capacity in accepted practice to transcend, oppose, and in other ways modify itself. Adhering to this conviction, a long line of modern philosophers through the years persevered in the search for resources in the governance of practice that are identifiable as rational and independent of all established institutions and accepted practices.[1] The plausible general loci of such resources were clearly *experience* and *reason*, employing the latter term now in its more narrow common usage to signify rational *thought*. But these familiar resources, as they are normally employed, are thoroughly permeated by social practices. It was therefore proposed that by careful intellectual analysis we might eliminate from them their conceived unessential and invalidating social elements, arriving at, as a purified form of experience, pure sensation, and a purified form of thought engaged solely with the relations of what were conceived to be certain very intimate, personal intellectual resources, namely, our own "ideas."

This general conception of rational governance, whether fleshed out in the general rationalist way exemplified by Descartes or in the empiricist way pioneered by Bacon and later refined by Hume, was riven by a fundamental contradiction. The more that philosophical analysis succeeded in eliminating the social components from these apparently competent resources, the less competent were the resultant forms for the purpose for which they were sought. By the time of Locke confidence in what in the way of knowledge could be achieved by "the perception of the connexion and agreement, or disagreement and repugnancy, of any of our ideas" was beginning seriously to fade. Fifty years later the incapacity of both the would-be pure surrogates of experience and thought were exposed by Hume. Neither of these, Hume convincingly demonstrated, could provide the sought-for governance separately; nor could they do it in conjunction. As governors of practice,

---

[1] The story of the appeal of this quest and the reasons why it was and is doomed to fail cannot be detailed here. A detailed examination of the appeal, and of the frustrations encountered in that version of the quest that sought to explicate everyday and scientific knowledge as the product of inductive inferences erected upon sensory intuitions, is given in Part II of *Induction and Justification*.

experience and thought, in their impure and socially infected forms, were competent but fundamentally illegitimate; in their pure and asocial forms, they were legitimate but utterly incompetent. Striking examples of this incompetence cited by Hume were, in knowledge, the incapacity of rational thought, joined with experience, to validate *any* conclusions from that experience (induction), and in ethical inquiry, the incapacity of these to discern any differences in value, even so gigantic a one as that between the scratching of a finger and "the destruction of the whole world." Rational governance of practice Hume therefore judged to be a myth, concluding that something altogether different, which he called "custom," not only is but must be the great guide of life. A true child of the Enlightenment, operating within a thoroughly Cartesian divorcement of reason and practice, he was constitutionally incapable of recognizing, what sometimes seems to be obtruding into his reflections, that rational governance of practice and life is to be found, not external to these, but resident in them, in custom-guided life itself.

The historical trial of the claims of independent sense and thought was recently reenacted in a shortened form in the rise and subsidence of logical positivism, and indeed in the life of one philosopher namely, Wittgenstein. After having formulated in the *Tractatus* a constitution for logical positivism, in his later philosophy he advanced most profound arguments against the claims of those two classical resources, sensory and rational intuition, to constitute sources of governance altogether external to and independent of practice. His criticism of putative independent sense is illustrated in his discussion of a private language and of "seeing as" in the *Philosophical Investigations*. His criticism of independent a priori thought, rational intuition, is illustrated in his discussions of logical necessity in the same book and in the *Remarks on the Foundations of Mathematics*.

The views of Wittgenstein on reason that are implicit in his writings on mathematics, perception, and knowledge generally are recent examples of an opposed tradition that goes back now about a hundred and fifty years. The pioneering expositor in this tradition, occupying the position in it that Descartes occupied in the more dominant tradition, was Hegel. Other, more recent expositors have been the two giant figures in American pragmatism, Peirce and Dewey. One most important point upon which this newer tradition opposed the older one was the relation between reason, as a governor of practice, and practice itself. Where the older view, following the divorcement of reason from practice to a logical conclusion, conceived of reason as a resource accessible to individuals independently of their relations with other individuals, independently of their membership in communities, the newer view has maintained that reason, and rational governance with it, can only be understood when they are conceived to be themselves fundamentally social.

4   Among the considerations that must count favorably for a social view of rational governance are the striking reversals encountered by advocates of the older individualist view in their efforts to locate a rational touchstone for thought and action in some resource quite independent of social life and practice. Some of these reversals were briefly noted in the preceding section. More positive considerations for regarding rational governance as immanent in social life and practice lie in the capacity of such a view to perform more satisfactorily with respect to rational governance in the two chief ways that any theory of governance must perform with respect to its subject matter. Such a theory must, first, account satisfactorily for what, independently of these rival theories, are recognized to be clear cases of rational governance. And, second, on the basis of success in performing the first function, it must apply illuminatingly to the unclear and controversial cases in such a way as to give guidance concerning how individuals and groups should act in those situations in which rational governance is called for and in which alternative paths of thought or action open to them affect the way in which governance shall proceed.

Rational governance is not some strange exotic plant that we need to visit intellectual conservatories to see. We are acquainted with it from our earliest years. And its ancestry in our individual personal lives includes aspects of our lives and experience that are features of our original nature. If we conceive of practices on the model of the habits, the recurring patterns of response that we as individuals display in our behavior, there is no doubt that to some extent our behavioral patterns are determined by our physical and psychological inheritance, and not exclusively by our physical and social environment. Once developed from whatever original physical and other determinants they have, a primary feature of human habits, and likewise practices, is their flexibility, their capacity, as dispositions to act, to adapt to and be modified by a great variety of conditions in the contexts in which they are translated from dispositions into actual performances. Included under the wide term "conditions of performance" are both personal aspects of those engaged in the performances and aspects of the impersonal environment in which they are performing. In this terminology the personal environment of any particular performance will include, as a most important component, many and varied other dispositions to act with which any given disposition is related and which may inhibit, intensify, or otherwise modify its realization.

In respect to their relations with such conditions of performance, the habits of individuals and the social practices with which they greatly intersect are very much alike. When habits are learned, when practices are mastered, more is acquired by the individuals engaged in the process than a simple connection in action between some specific occasion and some equally specific response. The driver follows a practice when, upon seeing the green arrow on the traffic signal, he moves the car in the direction of the arrow; or when, hearing a rapidly approaching siren, he moves the car out of the main traffic lanes. But this description by no means includes all he has learned to do, if he is a competent driver, in these and similar circumstances. The forms of action exemplified here extend far beyond the sequences of these immediate occasions and responses. They include a capacity to adjust one's way of proceeding to an array of wider conditions of performance. These will include in these cases other aspects of the present driving and traffic situation, and also other habits or practices with which the driver is equipped and which likewise help to determine what is proper procedure in situations like these.

We miss an aspect of practices that is vital for philosophical understanding if we restrict ourselves to those features that may be thought of as molecules composed of atomic bits of behavior, themselves thought of as fixed responses to limited sensory cues. Three-quarters of a century ago, John Dewey, a prominent psychologist of the day as well as philosopher, emphasized this point in an important paper on reflex theory, arguing that we thoroughly misunderstand learned human behavior when we think of it as a congeries or collection of bits of responses to bits of stimulation.[1] One who learns a practice as if he were a beginning soldier being imprinted with elements of close-order drill learns to behave in a way so odd and eccentric that Bergson could make it an important element in his theory of laughter. One essential thing missing from such learning is an understanding of how the more obvious, immediate responses that exemplify the practices are determined in character by features of the conditions of performance, includ-

---

[1] "The Reflex Arc Concept in Psychology," *Psychological Review* 3 (1896), rpt. in *John Dewey: The Early Works* (Carbondale and Edwardsville: Southern Illinois University Press, 1972), vol. 5, 96–109. See also *Human Nature and Conduct* (New York: Holt, 1922), Pt. I, §1. Dewey served as president of the American Psychological Association for the year 1899–1900. His presidential address was entitled, "Psychology and Social Practice."

ing therewith other dispositions to act, other forms of procedure, in short, other practices. This means that in following practices one is performing in a way that is governed in a great degree and in a highly complex way. Action is suited to circumstances, with of course varying degrees of success; and an essential aspect of this suiting of action to circumstances is the coordinating with each other of dispositions to action represented by divergent practices. Practices do, so to speak, confront circumstances, but not as individuals. Rather, in the metaphor employed by W. V. Quine in speaking of the coordination of statements with sense experience, they do so as corporate bodies.

Some rational governance, according to the view taken here, is an integral part of our accepted practices, of practice itself. One cannot be trained in these practices without being in some degree infused with rational governance as it is entailed in the following of these practices, in the consequent coordination and adjustment of them with each other and with various other components of the conditions of performance. Neither of these two chief components of the coordinating conditions of practices may be neglected. That practices adjust in concert with other practices to the circumstances in which the performance of the practices takes place should not obscure from us that they do adjust; and that they do adjust should not obscure from us that they adjust to circumstances while adjusting to each other. Both these aspects of coordination are indispensable and interdependent components of that form of rational governance that is learned with practices, because it is incorporated in the practices learned. It is governance of this kind, among other things, that a soldier or sailor learns when he learns how to occupy a post to stand watch. It includes a kind of flexibility of response that the once celebrated boy on the burning deck in a signal degree did not display when he stood fixed amid the rolling flames and booming shots simply because there was no one to inform him that his duty to remain had under these circumstances been overridden. It is this, in a very fine and complex way, that the skilled surgeon is expected to learn, partly through instruction and partly through experience about what is possible, desirable, optional, and necessary, in his craft. And it is this, in a simpler, more homely way, that one learns when one learns to cook, do carpentry, make cabinets, paint houses, drive a motor car, pilot an airplane, play a game like tennis, or participate in a sport like fishing.

5   Thus far, emphasis has been upon the point that rational governance is learned by individuals in learning practices, because governance is integral to

the practices themselves. This kind of governance might be called "governance *in* practice." It is governance in application to actual instances of action, governance primarily engaged in the control of such instances, utilizing relations of coordination between practices and the conditions of their performance that are already instituted and implicit in accepted practices. This may be contrasted with another aspect of the governing process, the one that is the primary object of concern in this paper. It might be called "governance *of* practice," being those processes by which the relations of coordination utilized in the governance of action are instituted, annulled, or altered. Though these processes are contrasted here, what needs to be stressed is their common character and close relations. They may be viewed as complementary phases of one fundamental process. To varying extents, depending upon circumstances, they commonly go together, since ordinarily one effect of the employment of practices in the governance of action is some alteration, which in some cases may be minute, in the practices themselves, and since ordinarily, as is exemplified in the case of such instances of governance as are represented in legal decisions defining laws, the occasion for governance *of* practice is ordinarily some difficulty encountered by governance *in* practice. Grasping the close relations between these two phases of the governantial process is a most important step toward answering the chief question to which this paper is addressed.[1] Taking advantage of this distinction, one may say that when an individual learns practices, he learns governance in both these respects. Part of what is instilled in the learner is what is accepted in the community in the way of an achieved coordination or governance of these practices. The culture provides for its continuance by, among other things, reproducing this aspect of itself, more or less adequately, and with some attendant variation, in the learning individual. But the individual who learns does so, not just as passive matter being given form by a cultural mold, but as, in this respect, a reproduction in miniature of the teaching community. Reproduced in him is not merely the product achieved, but also

---

[1] This emphasis upon continuity is fundamentally opposed to the emphasis upon discontinuity at a corresponding point in the well-known account of scientific revolutions advanced by T. S. Kuhn, *The Structure of Scientific Revolutions* (Chicago: University of Chicago Press, 1962; cited as "*Structure*"). The view of governance advanced here provides a more general epistemological ground for a criticism that was frequently made of Kuhn's account on historical grounds, namely, that in it the distinction drawn between "normal" and "revolutionary" science is unrealistically sharp.

in some degree the process. In acting as a member of the community in accordance with these practices he replicates naturally in some degree the process by which the community has achieved and repeatedly continues to re-achieve composition among these practices.

Some proficiency in the skill or art of rational governance is thus in an obvious way inherent in accepted practices, and, in addition to whatever of this skill or art is transmitted to new members of the community by physical or psychological inheritance, is transmitted with these practices in the processes of enculturation. In a less obvious way, inherent in the practices is some proficiency in the skill or art of altering this governance from the state already achieved. This likewise is an endowment of the individual, and likewise partly from nature and partly from nurture. This proficiency varies widely as a community endowment from one community to another. There appears to be wide divergence in this respect in the education of the young between mainland China and, say, Israel, and, by and large, between the Catholic and the Protestant churches in the United States. The proficiency also varies widely, in the same community, from individual to individual. The practices with which he is launched upon the world, like the laws which at any given time have to be interpreted in government by the judiciary and administered by the executive, are components of systems of governance that are designed to achieve coordination of practices in two main respects: with each other and with further conditions of performance, including those of neither a psychological nor a social nature. Governance may fail in its coordination of practices with each or, more typically, jointly with both of these components of the conditions of performance.

Each individual, in the governance of his own conduct, is thus in some degree in the position of a judge in the legal system when the latter is called upon to make decisions effecting determinations in case law or in constitutional provision that are similarly called for by some serious lack of coordination of what is manifest, recognized law either with other similarly manifest laws or with nonlegal aspects of the conditions to which these laws apply. To some extent the settled governance that came to the individual largely from his community, but which, as he matures, becomes in further degrees of his own making, needs to be further determined, refined, redefined, rectified, even reconstituted.

6   The very fact that the rational governance of social practice effected by the social processes just described can and does change has appeared to many to lead to a most serious skeptical consequence. This has been the subject of

much discussion during the past two decades. The elements of the apparent problem are simple. If rational governance, as a product, is identified with the result achieved by these processes, and if that result is subject to change —sometimes striking and rapid change—has not the identification of governance with these changeable and changing products excluded from rational governance the processes by which changes in these products occur? This has seemed to many to lead to a view of rational governance that applies only to and within systems of governed practices, that does not therefore apply to the processes by which one system is replaced by another, and which therefore has the result that these changes of governance—"revolutions" when the changes are large and abrupt—must be conceived to be effected by other than rational means. Rational governance of social practice, on this reading of the matter, is restricted to governance within such systems of practices as have been referred to in recent philosophy of science as paradigms, conceptual frameworks, systems of categories, or conceptual schemes.

It should now begin to be apparent that this difficulty, urged repeatedly against a social view of rational governance, does not necessarily accompany such a view. In particular, it is not a difficulty for the version of the view advanced here, but arises rather from a view of practices and their governance that the preceding pages have been careful to reject. This is a view which logically separates governance from practices, or what amounts to much the same thing, separates governance *in* practices from governance *of* practices and then identifies rational governance with the former, with the consequence that the processes by which the latter are effected are rendered intractable to rational governance. The roots of such a view lie in a tendency in much thought about social practices to think of them in the way that was criticized in detail in §4, that is, exclusively as templates for limited segments of action.[1] When practices are thought of in this abstract way, detached from life, there is no dynamism in them, no fundamental internal ground of change. And the same holds for any changes of governance that can be regarded as normal features of the functioning of practices in individual and social life. Fundamental change in governance is then thought to entail processes of a kind radically different from those of rational governance. On the other hand, when practices are looked upon more concretely, and the radical separation between them and their rational governance eliminated, fundamental changes in governance need no longer be regarded as beyond the

---

[1] [Cf. below, chs. 7–9.—*Ed.*]

capacities of rational governance itself. Such changes may be produced, though assuredly they are not always produced, by processes that differ greatly not in kind, but in dimension, from those adjustments of practices to the conditions of procedure that are in some degree constant features of living practice and that have been identified here as defining characteristics of the kind of governance that is rational.

Indeed the very changes that for some views of rational governance are surds or anomalies, are for the view sketched here prime, paradigm examples of rationality itself. That there are such changes is an immediate corollary of this view in its application to both individuals and social groups. Changes of governance are sometimes stimulated by perceived or somehow dimly felt inadequacies in governance as it has been achieved and is in place at any given time. The impulse to change in this manner need not be attributed to some mystic urge toward fulfillment present throughout individual and social life. Some change in governance is a natural consequence of governance, of life lived in accordance with practices coordinated in achieved governance. For not only do the conditions under which life is lived and practices engaged in change, generating inadequacies in previously achieved arrangements; so that present inadequacies may be attributed simply to failure of old governance to meet intervening new conditions. It is also the case that the success of previous arrangements may alter life in such a way as to lead to the modification or rejection of some of the very arrangements of practices and governance that have made this state of life possible; so that in these instances the inadequacy of old arrangements to meet new conditions, their failure, is a consequence of their preceding success. As it is characteristic of life lived through certain practices to undergo change that in some degree, sometimes small and sometimes great, renders the conditions of life, including the achieved governance of practices, inadequate, it is the soberest of truths that change is endemic to governance. Though some changes in governance, both large and small, are imposed upon governance from without, some are in some degree the natural products of governance itself. And however widely these latter changes may vary in dimensions, they are natural extensions of the homely day-to-day processes by which individuals and groups adapt general modes of action, within accepted parameters, to each other and to specific conditions of application.

What those parameters are, how strictly or how loosely particular action is determined by accepted practices, varies widely among practices and, even for the same practices, from one set of circumstances to another. Similarly, with respect to governance of the practices themselves, there is wide variation in the amount of indeterminacy that various systems of governance permit. Indeterminacy of governance in itself represents no failure in governance, since governance is not needed at every point at which practices impinge upon one another. It is needed at those points at which indeterminacy leads to conflict in action or incipient action, to either intrapersonal or interpersonal conflict, or, as commonly, a complex combination of both. Significant changes in large-scale governance of social practice are for the most part made by community action. And this, again for the most part, is not by referenda, or legislation, or judicial decision, but by direct changes taking place in modes of action as a natural consequence of living according to these forms. These changes take place, both in individuals and in communities, by far mostly in alterations in modes of action made by agents who have no clear understanding or appreciation of the process in which they are engaged. They are aware principally that they are responding to difficulties in accepted routines, accepted ways of acting and thinking. But in so doing, from time to time, more or less unknowingly, they make minor changes in the design of the governance which cumulatively they eventually realize, sometimes with a sharp shock of surprise, have produced a grand change in the *Gestalt*, in the grand design of the whole. The individual awakes one morning, as it were, to discover, what perhaps others understood long before, that he is no longer an agnostic but a believer, just as Pascal ("*Celà vous fera croire*") predicted, or no longer a believer but an infidel, as Pascal with equal logic, in different circumstances, might have expected. The community similarly awakes to find that it no longer believes that its kings rule by divine right, or, to take a striking historical example, now believes that the mother of Jesus Christ, though not fully divine like her son, was indeed a demigoddess. What these examples exhibit in changes in practices of belief can easily be exhibited as replicated in changes in practices of overt action. The individual more or less unwittingly has become a drunkard, or a teetotaler; the nation has become imperial rather than republican, the community hedonistic rather than moralistic in its attitude toward sexual practices.

The more conscious, deliberate forms of rational governance exemplified in philosophic judgment in science, morals, history, law, or whatever, whether these judgments are made by individuals or by groups, are all of a piece with the less conscious and less deliberate forms from which they take their rise. The story of the development leads back in individuals and the race through a regression of generally simpler forms to kindred primitive resources for response that are now part of our native endowment as members of this biological species and that perhaps have their material basis in us, not in the pineal gland, but in the central nervous system. What the more conscious, deliberate forms of governance are capable of contributing to the governance process in a special measure is understanding of the process (Hegel would have described it as reason becoming aware of itself) and, with that understanding, also in special measure, some sense of the present movement of governance, some vision of the character that this governance, if permitted to move according to its own inner logic, will have in its immediately next stages. To adapt to this situation the metaphor employed by Plato in the *Crito*, philosophical thought, in whatever field it is generated and nurtured by "the Laws," has some capacity, the Laws having been assimilated in it, and itself assimilated to the Laws, to perform a service for the Laws. As a portion of the photosensitive tissue of the Laws, developed into a kind of intellectual eye, it is capable of looking with special depth and breadth into some aspects of life lived according to and through the practices and institutions of the Laws. On the basis of a capacity for discernment somewhat broader and deeper than that commonly generated in the conduct of the affairs of ordinary life, philosophical thought—be it in doctor, lawyer, merchant, prince, teacher, preacher, or whatever—can offer to the Laws informed judgment and advice (often disguised as categorical imperatives) concerning the nurture of the practices and institutions with which it is concerned. Embraced under the term "nurture" here are both the strengthening and the weakening, the cherishing and the depreciating, the invigorating and the debilitating, in whole or in part, of individual items in the complex of practices and institutions. The availability of this specially informed judgment and advice may in some cases be decisive in determining in a substantial way the course that the practices and institutions will take; but ordinarily the effect is much more modest. Even where not decisive it may, if well-founded, be helpful—in an intermediary way analogous to that of Socrates with the knowing slave boy—in facilitating a course of development already substantially determined by other grounds. By rendering the determination of certain developments more patent, it may also render their realization easier, less generally disruptive, less costly in harmful sideeffects than they would otherwise be. Thus philosophic judgment based upon the Laws, speaks for the Laws. It attempts to say, in however tentative and fallible a way, what the Laws, yet inarticulate upon the point, would say, if they could speak upon it now: what, if the anticipated developments should be realized, the Laws will say when in the idiom of concrete historical reality they eventually do speak.

So speaks the court, when, performing this philosophical function in its own domain, it makes a *juridical* judgment upon a contested point of law, as distinguished from a judgment of fact. So speaks the judge when he supports such a judgment with a corresponding juridical opinion. So he speaks when the interpretation of the law, as he engages in it, is the kind that it is his vocation to make, when the term "interpretation" is not a misnomer for a form of covert, oligarchical legislation. Much of current discussion of activism versus strict interpretation of the law, particularly of constitutional law, would be helpfully illumined by a recognition of the implications of this point upon the seemingly obvious but greatly deceptive familiar distinction between the operations of making new law and discovering what the law already is. Here, as at many other places, a neat, well-worn distinction may serve to distort, rather than clarify the reality in which it is drawn. A decision speaking for the law, interpreting the law as it is, does not necessarily pronounce old law, since the law changes; and a pronouncement of *old* law, does not necessarily pronounce recognized law, since what needs to be explored in old law, and what is recognized or understood therein, is likewise subject to change. If we do suppose that interpretation of the law, as thus construed, is an example of a process that can be fully rational, and its results legitimate or valid, we can then begin to understand how a process that is fundamentally social in its basis and dynamics, can itself be a fully rational, legitimating one: and, furthermore, rational and legitimating, not in spite of but because of its being thus fundamentally social. Those whose vision has not been obscured by the blinding clarity of the distinction between "is" and "ought" will be in a position to recognize how, in this particular way in this context, "is" itself established "ought." Others further off the present beaten path in their philosophical tuition may recognize here a kernel of truths in those seemingly perverse pronouncements of Hegel, already misinterpreted in his own day, assimilating the rational to the real (the actual: *das Wirkliche*).

7 Two remaining points about the general process of rational governance call for attention here. First, having come to the point of recognizing the relations of mutual dependence and corrigibility that hold among those segments of social practice that we mark off and identify as individual practices, it is important that one not overestimate the degree of changeability at any one time in the whole system of practices that these relations entail. The philosophical skepticism that has haunted modern philosophy since its beginnings in the seventeenth century no doubt has something to do with the fact that up to the present time the changeability and hence instability of practices has tended to be exaggerated. It is as if without some firm center of un-

changeable practices, the totality must resolve into flux; as if the only alternative to Plato or Kant on these matters is Heraclitus; as if once pried loose
from the fixity of the forms or the categories, there are no elements whatever
of ballast making for stability in the system.

Some remedy for the intellectual vertigo that such thoughts as these are
capable of generating lies in the emphasis, implicit in the term, upon the
social character of practices. This is by no means sufficient, however. Typically it leads to a displacement of the relativism from a relation between
individuals to one between communities, often speech communities, and we
are invited, then, to consider the contingency of our practices in relation to
those of Eskimos, exotic aborigines, the inmates of the closed society of
George Orwell's *1984*, strangers from outer space, or even porpoises. There
is no one specific remedy that can be invoked at this point. But it is some
help to emphasize a further character of practices which is much more readily
apparent than when one employs the idiom of concepts, namely, that practices
are rooted in and depend for their continuance, not only upon the common
native components of human nature, but also upon a nonhuman, extra-
personal and extra-social environment in which life is carried on in accordance with the practices.[1] With these materials and upon this stage the
dramas of life are played, and the nature of the materials and the character
of the stage are most important determinants—representing both opportunities
and hindrances—of the kind of plays that may be performed. Over the
millennia of biological evolution nature, in the process of forming us, has
implanted in us physical and psychic structures that now constitute native
internal determinants, which may nevertheless tolerate a wide range of
parameters in the practices we engage in. Through our activities in these
practices in manifold ways we learn more and more about the determinants
of practice, both the external and the internal ones. Much of this learning is
embedded in common sense. Since the sixteenth century there has been an
increasingly rapid explosion of learning about certain facets of the material
world. But not all that we learn about ourselves or our environment comes to
us in the form of explicit statements, judgments, hypotheses, or theories *about*
the world. Nature, in and beyond ourselves, makes its presence and character
known not only in our scientific and other broadly scientific practices, but in
other practices as well, such as, for example, in politics, law, and morals. It
was the limitations imposed upon us and opportunities offered to us by

---

[1] [Cf. chs. 1 and 5 in this volume.—*Ed.*]

external and internal nature, and the revelations of nature itself effected by these limitations, that were grasped and stressed by the adherents of natural law in the long tradition of that name in the above fields of study. While their positivist opponents were surely in the right in stressing that the learning in these fields begins with the specific, limited modes of response with which we are indoctrinated, the adherents of natural law were equally right and have performed a great service in stressing something that now especially needs to be stressed, namely, that in external and internal nature there are, as well as opportunities for the development of practices, limitations upon the kinds of practices which may be developed, and that these limitations we ignore at the risk of the health and well-being of the system of practices and the quality of the life that is lived through them. All these limitations upon the variability of practices and governance, not least of which is that independent character of the objects of investigation with which in scientific and other cognitive practices we are directly concerned, represent sources of stability greatly counterbalancing any tendency there may be in governance and practices toward general, unmanageable instability. If, having given up the thought of fixed sources of governance residing in some Platonic reserve altogether external to practices, we are prone to think ourselves cast adrift rudderless upon the sea of practice, we need to remind ourselves that we never do, because we never can, face so desperate a predicament. And this, not only for physical, psychological, or social reasons, but also for firm logical ones. The primary reason why the incapacitating consequences of extreme conceptual relativism are not to be feared is that the predicament contemplated as threatening in that doctrine and from which these consequences are supposed to follow is one the very thought of which is logically incoherent in an extreme degree. To suppose an individual or a community to be in a situation in which all practices have, as it were, become unstuck, is in the first place to suppose a being that only remotely, if at all, resembles an individual, and likewise something, perhaps a collection of totally asocial animals, that is not a community. But, waiving that point, and supposing there to be such an individual or community, for either of them there would be no residue of practices which at the time are unquestioned and which form the critical mass of accepted practices necessary in order for a problem about governance to arise. There is, in short, no way in which we, either as individuals or as communities, can so saturate ourselves in skepticism about practices that we can divorce ourselves, even in thought, from all of them. And, were this possible, there would in consequence be insufficient logical material with which to construct a problem concerning the rationality of governance and governantial change. That there is always a residual mass of more or less well-governed accepted practices available, when questions about rational changes of governance arise, and that, further, this residual mass is our fundamental resource for devising answers to these questions, does not, as has already been indicated, mean that this residue is always adequate for the purpose. It means, rather there is a resource that is no more always and in principle sufficient for the purpose than it is always and in principle insufficient. The sober truth, much less philosophically exciting than either of those extreme alternatives, is that sometimes this resource is sufficient and sometimes it is not.

8   The second and final general point that needs to be emphasized about rational governance follows hard upon the first. The first point concerned the stability of governance and practices, and the limits that this stability imposes upon the extent to which at any given time these practices, and governance with it, are subject to change and challenge. The second point also concerns limits, this time limits upon rational governance itself.

However the notion of rational governance of practice is explicated, there is little doubt that limits must be recognized in the capacity of the processes of this governance to achieve their ends. There have been, are, and will continue to be numerous situations in which, for one reason or another, these processes falter in a variety of ways. They may falter in the maintenance or invention of needed features of governance, or in the divestiture of established or arising forms of governance of seriously deleterious features. And there is no guarantee that every time established governance falters, there is an adequate restorative, that for every disease of governance there is a remedy. First, granting that such restoratives or remedies are possible, there is no guarantee that available rational processes, in either their communal or individual forms, will be sufficiently sensitive to detect their needs; or that responding to the need they will be sufficiently clever and wise to devise them, that the measures they do devise may not be ones that, if taken, would exacerbate the very difficulties they were intended to reduce, or would generate difficulties as serious as, or more serious than, those that they were devised to meet. And if these incapacities must be recognized in rational processes generally, they may be expected in those more reflective, more conscious, more provisionally endowed forms of the processes that have been identified as those of rational reflection. In contrast with the attitude of unqualified confidence which is common among the philosophical toward something discerned by them in the more conscious, more deliberate forms of governance and identified with reason, the attitude toward rational processes that issues from the view set forth here is, without denigration, more sober and, it is hoped, more realistic. One consequence of the view is that there are occasions in which the residual mass of unquestioned practice is sufficient to demonstrate to philosophical reflection the need for criticism and change in practices and governance, but is yet insufficient to provide reflection with adequate guides either for that criticism or for the discovery of means by which amelioration may be achieved.

Nothing that has been said so far about the processes of rational governance provides any guarantee that what these processes yield at one time in the form of changes of governance may not at other times and from other points of view be rightly judged to have been deficient in rationality. There are some who readily concede the possibility of reversal in steps taken by individuals in the governance of habits in their own lives, but would demur in some degree concerning governance viewed on the broad stage of world history, where individuals, as agents of governance, are to a considerable extent replaced by social groups or institutions. Yet the hard facts of social life and proximate history count heavily against placing unqualified trust in any social agent of governance, however grand and impressive, whether it be a universal church, a dominant nation-state, or a rising economic class. A device commonly employed at this point to avoid the conclusion that rational governance, reason itself in its communal large-scale forms, may falter, is the advancement of some ground intended to guarantee that in the long run the proximate discrepant facts will be canceled, that in the long sweep of history episodes of weakness or fault will be minor, minor ripples or eddies in some irresistible progressive tide. Grounds—of various degrees of respectability: logical, mathematical, historical, or theological—are sought for demonstrating that somehow in the main, regardless of supersessions or because of them, the course is upward through improved versions of itself, toward rationality in some absolute form, which it may either eventually in some cases reach (Hegel), or progressively approximate (Peirce).[1]

----

[1] For Peirce's views see *Collected Papers*, "Three Logical Sentiments" (1878), 2:652–55; "The Social Theory of Logic" (1868), 5:341–57; "How to Make Our Ideas Clear" (1878), 5:388–410; "Definitions of Truth" (1910), 5:565–73. Perhaps the best brief, though typically obscure, statement on this matter by Hegel himself is in his own Introduction to the *Phenomenology of Spirit*. Much more of Hegel's thought in the *Phenomenology* or elsewhere needs to be assimilated before one can appreciate what he took to be grounds for that famous proclamation early in the *Lectures on the Philosophy of History*: "The only thought which philosophy brings to the treatment of

That there has been progress in approximation to truth in some domains of inquiry seems, as it seemed to Peirce, undeniable. That the process must continue, as Peirce thought it must in the community of investigators, is much more questionable. The divergence of the present view from that of Hegel is at this point wide. A judgment of the course of practices and governance in the world, reflecting and depending upon what we have been able to learn through these practices and their governance, will have to be much less bold and unqualifiedly optimistic than his. What we are acquainted with as reason in our lives and can further define in our deepest, most careful thought, what we can discern as reason in the world and in some degree attain in ourselves, has neither of the attributes of an omniscient and omnipotent God, striding triumphantly through the world or speaking infallibly to us. It is not the function of reason, as we thus know it, to ensure that the human journey of this world will terminate in some Promised Land, as did the fabled pillars of cloud and of fire in the Wilderness. Nor is its function to give infallible instructions, written in stone, of how we should conduct ourselves on this journey, like the fabled injunctions delivered to Moses on Sinai. The function of reason is much more homely, modest, mundane and, to change the myth, less Promethean than this. Drawing upon the most pertinent features of practices and governance we are able to say that, with these as with other things, new revised versions are not necessarily better; new manifestations of reason itself, are not necessarily improved ones; though they sometimes are. And who, or what, is to say? Who, but us? And upon what basis than these practices and what rational governance we have at any time achieved in them: not these in general, but those that are most pertinent, this too being a matter susceptible of judgment only by practices and their governance, though of course not the same ones that are the objects of question when a question of pertinence itself arises. Peirce was speaking of this aspect of rational governance when in his 1905 essay on pragmatism he emphasized that although it is plain that what we do not at any time doubt is not thereby established as true, nevertheless what we do not at all doubt, we must and do regard as truth—or as he actually put it, with some exaggeration and perhaps exasperation with "Mr. Make Believe" and his

---

history is the simple concept of reason: that reason is the law of the world and that therefore, in world history, things have come about rationally." *Reason in History*, R. S. Hartman, tran. (Indianapolis: Bobbs-Merrill, 1953), 11.

would-be doubts—we "must and do regard as infallible, absolute truth."[1] What holds for truth here seems to hold generally. On the other hand, those determinations which our practices enable us to make at any one time, and for which, judged by the pertinent arrangement of governance, there is no positive basis for doubt, no ground for singling out this rather than any other accepted item for doubt except that it is an accepted matter—those determinations we may, as we must, accept, as true, and without any twinges of Cartesian guilt. In this respect, as Justice Oliver Wendell Holmes wrote over fifty years ago, "imitation of the past, until we have a clear reason for change, no more needs justification than appetite."[2] One perhaps expresses only what is implicit in this striking remark when one closes with the reminder that, just as there are circumstances in which it is manifestly in accordance with rational governance to conform to accepted practices in our individual and collective actions, there are others in which it is manifestly in accordance with the same governance to act differently and in such a manner that, in a deeper sense than Hamlet intended by this phrase, we do honor the custom more in the breach than in the observance.

---

[1] *Collected Papers*, "What Pragmatism Is," 5:416.

[2] "Holdsworth's English Law," *Collected Legal Papers* (New York: Harcourt, Brace, and Co., 1920), 285–90. Quotation from Herbert Wechsler, *Principles, Politics and Fundamental Law* (Cambridge, Mass.: Harvard University Press, 1961), 23.

5

Reason, Social Practice, and Scientific Realism

ABSTRACT. Accompanying the decline of empiricism in the theory of knowledge has been an increased interest in the social determinants of knowledge and an increased recognition of the fundamental place in the constitution of knowledge occupied by accepted cognitive practices. The principal aim of this paper is to show how a view of knowledge that fully recognizes the role of these practices can adequately treat a topic that is widely considered to be an insuperable obstacle to such a view. The topic is that of scientific realism, of the independence with respect to cognitive practices of certain objects of knowledge.

1   The recent subsidence of empiricism in the theory of knowledge has resulted in some substantial displacement of problems in this subject. Various topics for which empiricist theory, if otherwise successful, seemed capable of providing fairly satisfactory treatment now seem to have become highly problematical. One of the most important of these topics is that of scientific realism, embracing the general question of the possibility of access in knowledge to objects that are independent of any practices of thought and action through which knowledge of them may be achieved. This topic takes on a very different aspect when it is looked at apart from the suppositions about

access that were central features and for a long time central attractions of empiricist theory.

Empiricism is a highly individualistic philosophical view, though like most individualistic views in contemporary social philosophy it has not been much aware of itself as individualistic and hence as one of the *possible* alternative views. It has seemed, rather, in this respect, the obviously right view.

Accompanying the subsidence of empiricism—indeed a primary cause of it—has been an increasing emphasis upon the social aspects of knowledge, upon knowledge as essentially a communal institution. Testifying to the extent of this influence has been the penetration of what had hitherto been seemingly impregnable redoubts of individualism as opposed to socialism on these matters, namely, physical science and mathematics, by paradigm theory and other revolution theory, by social evolution theory, and by what may be called *"Lebensformen* theory."

Foundational theory, of which empiricism is one species, has been thoroughly individualistic since its manifesto in the epistemological and metaphysical works of Descartes, an aspect that received hyperbolic expression in the famous *Cogito*. Both the empiricist and rationalist versions of Cartesianism sought to demonstrate that there are certain human resources capable of serving as firm bases for the criticism of social phenomena because they are quite independent of these phenomena. And both professed to find these resources in special acts of intuition that individuals are capable of performing quite independently of social influences, independently of any resources that are theirs only because they are members of communities. What distinguished the empiricists from other adherents of this individualist and foundational philosophy was the special trust invested by them in that sub-set of intuitions that was regarded as being furnished by inner and outer sense. It was primarily through a recourse to these, and what conclusions could be drawn from them by intuitions of the more rationalist kind, that the adherents of empiricist foundationalism proposed to follow the ringing injunction of Descartes, that we direct our inquiries "not to what others have thought," but to what the "unclouded and attentive [individual] mind [...] can clearly and perspicuously behold and with certainty deduce."[1]

---

[1] Descartes, "Rules for the Direction of the Mind," in *The Philosophical Works of Descartes*, Haldane and Ross, trans. (Cambridge: Cambridge University Press, 1911, 1967), Rule III.

For generations the empiricist program, which was to account for knowledge by showing that it could be assimilated to this model, had been stalled by the problem of demonstrating how the needed conclusions could be drawn in this manner from the stipulated premises (the so-called Problem of Induction). Now, in consequence of the recognition of the social aspects of knowledge, and indeed, of experience itself, the putative data of sense, hitherto thought to exemplify primitive independent objects of knowledge, were discovered to be in a variety of ways dependent upon, subject to determination by, the very kinds of social artifacts, opinion and practice, of which they were required by the theory to be independent. In American philosophy assimilation of this discovery and the drawing of what seemed to be some profound skeptical consequences of it were accomplished in one short philosophical generation from C. I. Lewis to W. V. Quine and vigorously exemplified by the latter in a variety of writings, including, among the more recent, *Ontological Relativity*.[1]

A recent writer who has been most effective in drawing attention to the social determinants of knowledge has been, of course, T. S. Kuhn. In his very widely read and influential book on scientific revolutions he supported the thesis of the social determination of what actually function in scientific work as observational data with a persuasive array of examples from the history of these disciplines. And one of the conclusions that he tentatively suggested we might draw is that in the domain of science something like ontological relativity, or at least physical relativity, does hold. Granted that there is something in the career of science that can rightly be termed progress, it may be a serious mistake to think that in this progress, in contrast with progress in other fields, say, art, political theory, or philosophy, large-scale changes of patterns of thought (Ptolemy to Copernicus; Newton to Einstein) "carry scientists and those who learn from them closer to the truth."[2] It was thus not incautious exposition but philosophical considerations of an important and unsettling kind that impelled Kuhn, while wishing to maintain that after one of these so-called scientific revolutions, "the scientist is still looking at the same world," also to say that the large-scale patterns of thought that he called paradigms "are constitutive of nature," that "after discovering oxygen Lavoisier worked in a different world," and that "pendu-

[1] New York: Columbia University Press, 1969.
[2] *Structure*, 169.

lums were brought into existence by something like a paradigm-induced gestalt switch."[1]

2   A philosophy of science committed to the view that it is possible to succeed in our quest for truth about the physical world is required to provide some acceptable account of how knowledge of this truth can be achieved. It was the distinctive way in which, according to the empiricist philosophy, this is accomplished—in particular, the way in which a coordination between our thoughts and their objects is achieved by an "unclouded and attentive mind" —that was increasingly discredited by the increasing emphasis upon the social determinants of our language, our ways of thinking, our "conceptual schemes." The abandonment of the very feature of the philosophy in which the union of thought and object is to be consummated independently of these determinants resulted in a philosophy unable to talk about the objects with which thought is supposed to be coordinated in exactly the same way that in Kant's theory of knowledge the scientist was held to be unable to speak consistently about things-in-themselves.

It is, furthermore, of great importance for philosophical understanding here that one grasp that the problem of realism in physical science and elsewhere is one particular phase of a much more general problem about the revision and reconstruction of social practice. The more recognition there is of the social aspects of language and thought, the more the roots of our patterns of thought and inquiry are exposed in the forms of life, in social practice, the more pressing becomes the need to understand how thought and inquiry rooted in practice itself can yield valid criticisms and properly grounded clues for the reconstruction of this practice.[2] And when the specific practices concerned are practices of scientific inquiry, one particular, most important matter needing clarification is how and in what circumstances the criticisms and clues for reconstruction yielded by those practices may be taken as proper guides to the truth or falsity of claims concerning the objects with which the practices are employed.

Three essential pieces of the puzzle posed by these matters have now emerged. There is, first, the important shift from individualism to what, were not the term already pre-empted for other uses, might properly be referred to as "socialism" in the theory of knowledge. Incorporated in this shift is a

---

[1] *Structure*, 128, 109, 117, 119.
[2] [Cf. chs. 4, 6, 9.—*Ed.*]

recognition, second, of the extent to which knowledge, as a human institution, is not merely rooted in, but is constituted by social practices. Though not the only ingredient, so thoroughly essential and determinative are these practices that what at any given time we have achieved as knowledge is quite inconceivable without them. Third, in consequence of this shift and recognition the focus of the traditional philosophical questions about the criticism, appraisal, etc., of putative items of knowledge likewise shifts. The concerns represented in these questions become largely concerns about the performance of these functions in connection with the practices which these items incorporate.

And given that on such a view, criticism, appraisal, and the other similar functions are recognized to be themselves informed, directed, and, indeed, in good part constituted by social practices, there are now present all the materials for the generation of a philosophical difficulty that has been urged against such a social theory of knowledge in a variety of forms in recent discussion. How can one view the criticism, appraisal, and so on, of practices as being always performed in thorough and essential dependence upon social practices themselves, without entrapping oneself in some sociocentric and in the end fatally skeptical predicament? How, if one views in this way the processes of criticism, appraisal, and so on, including fundamental philosophical forms of these functions, can the results attained be viewed as legitimate or valid ones?[1]

If we now encapsule in the term "governance" all the functions of criticism, appraisal, reform, and reconstruction referred to, and use the more common philosophical term "rational" to express the question about the

---

[1] Asks Q. Skinner in his review of R. Bernstein's *The Restructuring of Social and Political Theory* (1978): "How can we possibly hope, by using (as we are bound to) our own local assumptions and canons of evidence, to construct a theory which is then employed to criticize these precise assumptions and canons of evidence? Doesn't it begin to look as if the project of 'critical theory' amounts to little more than a version of the Indian rope-trick?" ("The Flight from Positivism," *New York Review of Books* [June 15 1978]: 26–28; p. 28.)

Over seventy-five years ago Peirce gave this answer: "In studying logic, you hope to correct your present ideas of what reasoning is good, what bad. This, of course, must be done by reasoning.... Some writers fancy that they see some absurdity in this.... They say it would be a *petitio principii*.... Let us rather state the case thus. At present you are in possession of a *logica utens* which seems to be unsatisfactory. The question is whether, using this unsatisfactory *logica utens* you can make out wherein it must be modified, and can attain to a better system. This is a truer way of stating the question; and so stated, it appears to present no such insuperable difficulty, as is pretended" (*Collected Papers*, 2:191).

legitimacy or validity of these processes, we may formulate the central question summarily as a question about the rationality of the governance of social practices. Can the governance of practices be performed in thorough dependence upon practices?[1] When the governance of social practices is conceived to be carried out always and necessarily in this practice-informed and hence practice-dependent way, can the processes and the results ever be regarded as rational? These general questions may then be applied to distinctively cognitive practices, to practices in domains like those of the physical sciences, in which the validity or rationality of the practices entails a capacity on the part of the practices to yield reliable information concerning objects of some sort with which they are engaged. So applied, the general questions yield, among others, the question of *realism*.

3   In partial answer to the question of realism a few examples will presently be given of the establishment of the existence and character of independent objects through the practice-informed, practice-directed governance of practices. By themselves, however, such examples are insufficient for elucidating the matter. They meet the questions about the possibility of such establishment only obliquely. For these questions are philosophical questions about possibility, asking not so much for proofs that a certain kind of achievement occurs as for an explanation of how it occurs. Typically in such situations the questions are the expressions of a difficulty encountered in assimilating the facts of occurrence, however patent they may be, into a background of presumption according to which what seems to be demonstrated to have occurred is by some strongly held principles precluded. One can imagine a skeptical observer at Kitty Hawk being puzzled about how it is possible for such a contraption to fly and needing to have the strong yet controvertible evidence from observation that it did fly vindicated in relation to some deeply entrenched principles ensuring that it could not. Similarly, many philosophical observers of the effectiveness of governance need, for the satisfactory assimilation of their own observation, to have it vindicated in the face of some profound philosophical preconceptions that obstruct its being recognized as what it is.

The philosophical difficulties addressed here about governance and realism concerns not governance as it may be conceived in general, but governance as conceived in a social theory of knowledge and of reason, that

---

[1] [Cf. ch. 4 above.—*Ed.*]

is, governance that is itself viewed as carried on in thorough dependence upon practices themselves. Such governance was characterized above as dependent upon practices for its constitution, form, and direction. Henceforth in this essay, purely for reasons of stylistic convenience, these qualifications of the term "governance" will ordinarily not be repeated when the context indicates sufficiently clearly that governance of this kind is intended. Exceptions will be made in those cases in which some special emphasis or reminder seems desirable.

In thinking of such governance one must guard against a pair of related intellectual stereotypes, powerful but illusory Idols of the Theater. Both of these misleadingly neglect features of practices and their governance that are essential to them. The first of these, which may be called the "Relativist Illusion," seriously underestimates the plurality of types of practice and the liberating effect of this upon the process of governance. The second, which may be called the "Coherence Illusion," seriously underestimates other external components of the existential situations in which practices are engaged in.

It is characteristic of practices that they cohere with other related practices in systems, wholes, *Gestalten*, "conceptual schemes," or "frameworks." These vary widely in both magnitude and in the tightness with which the components are bound together. The recognition of the capacity of large and tightly organized collectives of practices in everyday life, science, and other domains to determine the character of thought and action, and therewith the consciousness, experience, and life of the individuals who participate in them, has had the effect of intellectual shock upon those whose philosophical expectations were molded by individualistic empiricism. The momentum of a sharp reversal in the estimation of the effect of social practice in the development of knowledge has led many of these mistakenly to overestimate the monopolistic effect in methodology, judgment, and opinion that a single system of practices may have. Viewing the thought and action of an individual brought up in and participating in such a system as determined exclusively by that one system, they have concluded that what can be effected by thought and action guided by practices, and hence also what can be effected by similarly guided governance of practices, is necessarily restricted to internal refinements in this system, fleshing out its details, leaving the essential character of the system unaltered. By means of the kind of governance of practices that is under examination here, applied to practices assumed to cohere in one overarching and dominating system, it appears that it is possible to produce only effects that are in conformity with accepted practices, and thus of course never effects the cumulative consequence of which would be the displacement of one system of practices by another. Changes of the latter sort, changes of systems themselves, when they occur, must be effected by other means, by some other form, or forms, of determination, which, if the term "rational" is reserved for practice-informed and hence practice-dependent governance, must be judged to be other than rational.

This view is provocative, but extremely unrealistic in its totalitarian model of the way in which systems of practices influence, direct, and give form to the thought and action of those who participate in them. The relation between a system of practices and participants in it is conceived to be like that between an absolute sovereign and a community of subjects, subjects who can be released from their servitude to one sovereign only when some-how that one is overthrown by another, whose utter subjects they in turn now become. But systems of practices in science, politics, religion, education, or other domains need not be and are not ordinarily, if ever, like this in their determining effects in the communities that participate in them. Rather they coexist in these communities with other systems, with which they both cooperate and compete in their effects upon their participants. These other systems are part of the existential situation in which any system of practices occurs: no less a part than the nature of the human beings engaged in the practices or the physical environment in which the practices are followed.

There are, to be sure, great differences from individual to individual, from group to group, and from one system of practices to another, in respect to the dominance exerted by a given system of practices in the determination of the thought and action of the members of the group. But what one does not find, even in extreme cases, is a state of complete hegemony maintained over a group of individuals by one all-embracing system of practices. A feature of any moderately civilized society that helps to dissipate the danger that the members of the society will become the captives of one such system is that they are simultaneously the participants in many: of many and various frameworks, conceptual schemes, linguistic and thought structures, systems of categories. As a plurality of communities has been one source of freedom in modern democratic states; as checks and balances, despite their logical untidi-ness, have proved to be elements of a workable system of political self-governance; so to some considerable extent the possibility of rational governance of practice, in individuals and groups, lies in the plurality of accepted systems of practices.[1]

The strength of the totalitarian view of the determination of thought and action by accepted systems of practice derives in good measure from the confluence of two streams of thought. One of these is the increasing recognition of the social determinants of thought and action; the other a highly restrictive, narrow view of human reason. Without the latter, without certain preconceptions about the limited processes which could be recognized as being rational, what might have emerged from the recognition of the social determinants of thought and action was a view of the social character of reason itself.[2] Athwart this avenue of philosophical development lay a deeply entrenched view of the processes of reason as essentially calculative ones participated in by individuals in their capacity as individuals; thus as essentially individual processes rather than as group or communal ones. Rational results, upon such a view, are only those which can be shown to be derivable by a process that begins with grounds having a certain form, namely, that of symbolic formulae, and proceeds by performing similarly symbolic transformations upon these grounds, transformations sometimes discriminated into two subspecies, deduction and induction.

Little reflection is required to see that what can be achieved by rational processes as so conceived is severely limited. There is no provision, in this conception, for procedures for the revision, radical or moderate, of the canonical forms of formulation of grounds or the canonical procedures of eliciting consequences. And, equally striking, there is no provision in what are conceived to be rational processes for the revisionary effect, both with respect to grounds and the processes of proceeding from them to consequences, of communal, interpersonal relations. All those real processes by which our grasp of grounds and recognition of consequences are molded and remolded by communal life and thought proceeding from generation to generation are extruded from the conception of rational processes. It is a strange prejudice that precludes the classification as rational of any processes of development, in science, morals or whatever, that cannot be managed in one single generation and therefore require transgenerational mutational processes of intellectual reproduction. It is a strange prejudice that restricts the dimension of rational results to those that could be encompassed, begin-

---

[1] [Cf. ch. 2 above, esp. §§42–44, and chs. 4, 6.—*Ed.*]

[2] [Cf. chs. 4, 6–9.—*Ed.*]

ning with accepted procedures, by one person in one lifetime. The transitions from introspectionism to a more functional psychology, from absolute space and time to relativity, or from deterministic to statistical mechanics, are not proved to have been nonrational by the fact that they required too great a reconstruction of settled habits of thought to be managed by many, especially in the older generations of investigators in these domains, to whom they were offered. Similar comments apply to the reconstruction of habits of thought with respect to the Commerce Clause of the Constitution signaled by the historic decisions of the Supreme Court expanding the scope of constitutional federal regulation of interstate commerce at the end of the fourth decade in this century. They apply also to the similar historic decisions concerning de jure segregation handed down in the sixth decade, and, to add but one further example from a very different domain, to the transition in the interpretation of the Scriptures slowly made in Protestant Christian thought in the past hundred years.[1]

4   In the Relativist Illusion the predicament seen to be confronting the participant in a system of practices is one of incapacity of governance. Systems of practices, or conglomerates of such systems, are conceived to determine the main features of a participant's thought and action so completely that he is rendered incapable of any fundamental criticism of or dissociation from the system or systems involved. Any activity pretending to be governance in any important, constitutional respect is a sham. The predicament contemplated in the Coherence Illusion is of a different kind. It is not that effective criticism and judgment is in general impossible, but rather that in one cardinal respect it is inutile. Whatever discriminable differences there may be between systems of cognitive practices, in one respect they are all the same. This is in respect to their preclusion of the access of participants in systems of practices to independent objects of knowledge. One and all, in an irremediable way, systems of practices deceptively interpose themselves between objects and aspiring knowers, proffering to the latter artifacts of practice in place of the aspired-to independent objects.[2]

There is indeed a danger that in emphasizing the role of systems of practices, frameworks, or institutions in the pursuit of knowledge one will generate this illusion. For in spite of great efforts to forestall this effect, it

---

[1] [Cf. below, chs. 6, 8.—*Ed.*]
[2] [Cf. above, ch. 3.—*Ed.*]

remains difficult to prevent many who are stimulated to think of these matters from neglecting one of the very things that the terms "practice" and "practices" were intended to emphasize, which is that the modes of proceeding denoted by these terms are in a variety of ways affected by, controlled by, or more exactly, constituted in part by determinants external to, independent of, the individuals engaged in them.[1] Practices are modes of proceeding, forms of activity, that are themselves realized in certain kinds of existential situations. They require certain kinds of situations for their realization, and are guided by features of these situations in the specific manner in which they are realized. A human practice thus incorporates within itself, besides the human beings engaged in the practices, other components of the existential situation. The determining or constitutive effect in this regard that is of special relevance to the topic of realism is that produced in our cognitive practices by the objects of investigation: objects which, if revealed with sufficient clarity and certainty by the investigation, become objects of knowledge. Keeping this effect firmly in mind is most helpful in devising an acceptable answer to the primary question about realism that is posed by a view of rational governance as necessarily practice-informed and practice-dependent, namely, of how it is possible by means of such governance to acquire knowledge of objects that are not dependent in their existence and character upon practices.

A good part of the deceptive power of the Coherence Illusion associated with this question lies in a neglect of the roots that practices have in independent objects. Recognizing the thoroughly social character of most of our practices, including our cognitive ones, but neglecting the independent roots or components of such practices, one seems to become again a captive of practices. Practices are thought of as having their existence and careers independent of objects; governance is correspondingly conceived to be a process that takes place quite independently of objects, and is thus incapable of yielding as a product genuine knowledge of such objects.

The obvious place to begin in dispelling such an illusion is at this metaphysical source. The case that governance is a process impotent with respect to objects stands or falls with whatever case there is that, conversely, objects are impotent with respect to governance itself. And this latter case, in turn, stands or falls with the case that practices and objects are impotent with respect to each other. If independent objects can affect thought and action in

---

[1] [Cf. above, chs. 1, 4.—*Ed.*]

and through cognitive practices, and if in consequence thought and action according to these practices are competent to acquire knowledge of such objects, then governance of these practices, itself a phase of this thought and action, is likewise competent with respect to knowledge.[1] One point central to the case about governance here deserves emphasis, though it cannot be dilated upon. It is that governance, as an activity directed to the control of practices, is continuous with activity according to practices directed primarily to more direct, nongovernantial ends. Control, modification of, as well as stabilizing of practices, is a natural concomitant of the conduct of the affairs of life according to these practices.[2] That is why, to use a piece of formal terminology, the competence of governance of practices to acquire knowledge of independent objects is but a lemma, once the proposition is established that activity in accordance with practices is competent for this purpose.

A major source of the Coherence Illusion, as it arises with respect to practices and their governance, is thus an unrealistic view of practices, a view of them that neglects the effects that objects independent of both practices and their governance have upon both of these. When these latter effects are neglected, talk about governance of practices by means of practices easily suggests a procedure that might be engaged in independently of the external existential situation in which practices are realized and by which they are in part controlled. One thinks of an individual or group arranging, re-ordering practices, much in the way that someone might in some private retreat sort out and compose his feelings after some disconcerting emotional episode. But practices are not private entities like feelings, and governance not such an autonomous procedure.

To the credit of the empiricists in modern philosophy was their recognition, which they tried to articulate in their theories of impressions, sense-data and the rest, of this limitation upon the autonomy of cognitive practices imposed both for individuals and groups by the existential situations in which the practices have their roots. Although these existential situations may be internal to the individuals following the practices as well as external to them, the empiricists, who in contrast with the rationalists emphasized the role of the environment in human knowledge, tended to neglect the internal determinants of cognitive practices. Implicit also in the empiricist program was a sound presupposition that there is a great deal of variation among our prac-

---

[1] [Cf. above, chs. 1, 4.—*Ed.*]

[2] [Cf. below, chs. 7–9.—*Ed.*]

tices in the degree of determination that external situations impose upon them, that in this respect there are levels of determination effected by the environment upon practices of a cognitive kind. At the basal levels of commonsense practices dealing with molar objects and with other living creatures, including our fellow human beings, the degree of determination in which features of the existential situations, both external and internal, limit the kind of practices that may be followed is very great. How much of the determination at this level is external, exerted by the objects, states, or whatever with which the practices are engaged, and how much is internal, itself the product of millions of years of evolutionary contrivance, it is difficult to say, or even to ask. So complex and ill-defined at the present time remain the factors whose effects have to be accounted for, that it is difficult for us to know, when we set out to ask, just what it is we are asking.

If it is true, as was said above, that activity in the governance of practices is continuous with activity in accordance with these practices, it is likewise true that the mixture of these activities at different levels varies widely. Those writers in the theory of knowledge and philosophy of science who have recently called attention to the effects of social determinants in the development of perceptual discriminations have helped us to discern aspects of tractability to governance at a level of practice in which determination of another kind, and hence intractability to governance, is a much more dominant feature. These variations of degree of determination by existential situations, and of consequent degrees of intractability to governance, added to the sometimes deeply entrenched effects of learning, help to make understandable the high degree of directness, obviousness, and determination *for us* exhibited by results obtained by cognitive practices at some levels, like those of ordinary perception and perceptual observation, in contrast with the equally high degree of indirectness, implicitness, and discrimination *by us*, exhibited at other levels, like those of the construction of models and the development of theories.

5   The history of scientific knowledge is rich with episodes illustrating in striking ways the efficacy of activities following practices in achieving knowledge of objects other than the practices themselves. One of the lessons to be learned from an exploration of this history is that in following the general

formula, *per uses ad astra*,[1] through these various new institutions, allowances must be made for the peculiar characteristics of the institutions. The practices of physical science, for example, are not to be assimilated to those of apothecaries or gardeners, as Hobbes rightly said while mistakenly deprecating Boyle's experiments with the air pump. For one thing, the goals of these contrasting activities are very different. The practices of science are practices developed for the exploration of nature; they are the gears and levers of a great engine that has been fashioned over the years for the purpose of expanding knowledge of a certain kind, of using achieved knowledge to generate further knowledge, much in the way in which in capital investment wealth is employed to produce more wealth. The primary crop that Mendel was interested in harvesting from his garden was not peas, but information about the transmission of inherited characters from one generation to another in these plants. This was a difference in practices that some of the more enthusiastic exponents of pragmatism, most notoriously William James, tended to neglect and were roundly rebuked by their critics for neglecting. Not all "working," to use one of the controversial terms in the disputes over pragmatism, is the same; not all practices are devoted to the same ends; "leading prosperously," to pick out another phrase, in the natural sciences is to be construed in science in the context of the problems and goals of these institutions. It is badly understood if it is construed in science primarily in ways that are appropriate to economic, moral, or even religious institutions. A similar lesson applies, though not so strikingly, to the relationship, so important in our own day, between the institutions of science and of technology. Close as this relationship is, understanding of technology is not well served when it is conceived to be merely the transplantation of scientific practices, the exploitation of these practices for wider human ends. It is this, but not merely this, if for no other reason than that in the transplantation of practices from one institution to another devoted to very different primary ends, mutations, sometimes small and sometimes great, must be expected in the practices themselves.[2]

All this may seem to be little more than redescribing certain obvious features of the development of knowledge in a special terminology, and to have little bearing upon the question of how knowledge about independent objects may be achieved by means of practice-informed, practice-directed

---

[1] ["By practice to the stars".—*Ed.*]
[2] [Cf. below, ch. 7.—*Ed.*]

governance. The terminology, however, is important, because what it is intended to convey, beyond the painfully familiar truism that our thoughts, opinions, hypotheses, etc., are altered by "experience," is that one of the ways in which experience influences the suppositions we make about the existence and character of independent objects of knowledge is through altering our practices. Recognizing this is a first step in dispelling whatever incredulity may be aroused in our minds by the suggestion that, in both individuals and groups, clarification or grasp of hitherto unappreciated or unrecognized relations of practices may yield new knowledge of objects.

6   Simple practical examples of objects of knowledge that were thoroughly independent of the practices through which they were discovered were various gross features of the earth that came to be known through the practices of navigation and exploration that were developed and followed in the fifteenth century. Columbus did not succeed in answering the chief question that motivated him in his western voyages, that of whether there was a practical direct route to the Orient across the Ocean Sea. After a long period of time, Western Europe, through various emissaries engaged in a variety of activities, military and naval, commercial, religious, and scientific, and following a corresponding variety of practices, did finally reach an answer to Columbus's question. By the time the answer was reached the question itself had undergone great change, chiefly as a result of activities engaged in and practices followed in arriving at an answer to it.

The effectiveness of activities following practices in achieving knowledge of objects other than and independent of the practices is illustrated in the early discovery by Galileo of four of the moons of Jupiter. Similarly illustrated, though to a lesser extent, is the effectiveness of the governance of practices in the same regard.

In that discovery, as we would say now, signals coming from Jupiter and those moons played an important role. How did they play this role? By impinging upon Galileo, who, in addition to having a telescope to help gather and transmit these signals, was a well-trained and experienced natural philosopher, or, as we should say now, scientist. As such this man at the small end of the telescope was expert in a complex set of cognitive practices designed to exploit effects like this in cognitively rewarding ways. Galileo did not simply stare at those oddly moving lights, never before reported, like a child marveling at the shifting sights in a kaleidoscope. He tried to understand these lights from the point of view of the astronomy and physics available at his time, following a complex set of technical practices of thought and action available in or appropriate to these branches of learning: practices of observation, calculation, and instrument construction, and practices embodied in a complex technical language. Proceeding thus he translated the signals into messages from Jupiter to the effect that it was not alone in its movements in the heavens, but was accompanied in both its retrograde and direct movements by other bodies or stars revolving about it. Since these stars, like Jupiter, Venus, and others, did shift their positions relative to the fixed stars, he classified them with the other long-recognized wandering stars or planets. There was not yet (Newton's *Principia* being still over fifty years away) an explanation in the Copernican "system of the world" of how the Earth could move in an orbit about the sun without losing its moon, and this, as Galileo commented in the *Sidereal Messenger*, was regarded by some people as a decisive objection to that system. That Jupiter, recognized in both the Ptolemaic and Copernican system to be moving in some kind of orbit, could do so without losing its own accompanying bodies now appeared to dissipate much of the force of this objection.

The transition from Ptolemaic to Copernican astronomy exemplifies more than the preceding example the acquisition of new knowledge by means of the governance of practices. In the end Copernican theory effectively supplanted Ptolemaic theory in spite of the fact that there were no crucial experiments to dictate the decision between the two theories, and in spite of the fact that, Kepler's ellipses having not yet been discovered, there remained in the Copernican view a large number of insuppressible epicycles. The Copernican theory was, as it is commonly said, a simpler theory than its older rival. More precisely, as Dudley Shapere has put the matter, although it had no distinct advantage over sophisticated versions of the Ptolemaic theory with respect to observational adequacy, predictive accuracy, or number of epicycles, "it did, in its details, provide a far more unified account of solar system astronomy." A variety of items that on the Ptolemaic view were arbitrary assumptions or mere coincidences followed naturally from the Copernican theory.

Yet, as Shapere emphasizes, these items of disunity were not problems recognized as existing for the Ptolemaic theories. So long as "astronomical theories were considered [as in much of the tradition they had been] as mere collections of devices, to be applied to different cases in different ways according to need, for the sake of prediction ... [as] mere predictive devices, constructed to 'save the phenomena'," the items cited were not and certainly did not need to be recognized as problems. However, these items were and did need to be recognized as problems when each of the rival astronomical theories was taken, as Copernicus seems to have taken his theory, as not merely an instrument of calculation or prediction, but "as a realistic representation of the structure of the solar system." It was indeed largely because of the high degree of unity achieved with respect to these items by the Copernican theory that it became easier at this time to view astronomical theory as realistic and representational, rather than merely a predictive, fictional device. But when the Copernican theory itself was so viewed, it came into conflict with certain portions of Aristotelian physics, so that the acceptance of this theory, realistically interpreted, was in turn a beginning, important step in the transition to the new physics that culminated in the next century in the work of Newton.[1]

One begins to appreciate some of the logical momentum at work in this rich and fascinating episode of theory-change in astronomy when one begins to look upon the rival theories in question, not as sentences to be parsed, or logical propositions to be analyzed, but more important, as rival programs for the governance of practices and of the intellectual institution of which these practices are features; when one thinks of what sort of institution astronomy had been in the centuries preceding Copernicus, and of what sort of institution, according to certain tendencies in it, it might become. If astronomy, hitherto primarily an institution for celestial calculation, was in the process of giving increased emphasis to another mission, that of developing an acceptable cosmology, and was therefore in the process achieving a new identity among the cognitive and other institutions of the time, then there was strong logical impetus to the change, rooted in the inner dynamics of the governance of practices in these institutions. "Simplicity," then, suggesting as it does, a somewhat subjective quality discriminated by a kind of refined logical taste, appears to be a questionable, pale misnomer for the kind of strong dynamic that is not peculiar to this case, but rather is characteristic of any large-scale scientific change.

Commenting upon the synthetic unity that is easier to recognize in the Copernican theory than to analyze, Shapere observes that "nothing is to be gained in illumination, and much is lost because of highly misleading associations, by referring to such considerations as 'aesthetic'."[2] Yet such was the

---

[1] Dudley Shapere, "Copernicism as a Scientific Revolution," in *Copernicus*, A. Beer and K. A. Strand, eds. (*Vistas in Astronomy* 17 [1975]: 97–104; cited as "Copernicism"), 101, 103.

[2] "Copernicism," 102 note 4.

kind of extremity to which the philosophy of science was driven when it set
out to understand this particular episode of scientific change, after having first
resolutely blinded itself to some of the aspects of these considerations that
are most important for their illumination.

A now familiar story from recent physics that exemplifies strikingly
discovery by means of governance deserves brief mention. Without changes
in the governance of practices of thought and action ("conceptual change")
in the field of atomic physics, the discovery of nuclear fission could not have
been achieved in the way it was. Indeed it now appears that it had already
been achieved earlier than its more celebrated discovery, for example, by
Fermi in Italy, but was not recognized as such. Similarly when Hahn and
Strassmann in Berlin during the fall of 1938 had bombarded uranium salts
with neutrons, producing nuclear disintegration and its products, they were
informed of this by one set of firmly entrenched practices that told them that
they had derived barium in this process, while another set led them as
strongly to suppose that such a result, by the means they had employed, was
not possible. So Hahn, an outstanding nuclear chemist, proceeding with the
greatest care in the identification of the materials produced in the experiment,
found his test declaring for barium but, with his assistant, Strassmann, in
reporting the results of their experiment to the German scientific periodical,
Naturwissenschaften, was led to say "as chemists we are bound to affirm that
the new bodies are barium ... [but] as nuclear physicists we cannot decide to
take this step in contradiction to all previous experience in nuclear physics."
It was left to Lisa Meitner, a longtime associate of Hahn, at the time a
fugitive of the Hitler government in Sweden, to see first the way to solve the
apparent dilemma. Within a few weeks of learning the results of the experiments in a letter from Hahn, she was able to suggest a way in which, by a
suitable alteration in the way the results of the experiments were construed,
they could be satisfactorily and very excitingly explained.[1]

These and a multitude of similar examples that may easily be drawn from
the history of knowledge, and particularly scientific knowledge, attest the
capacity of practice-directed governance of practices to make valid determinations of the existence and character of objects. Of the general effectiveness
of this procedure in generating valid determinations of objective matters, the
corporate project of theoretical physics is a paradigm exemplification, as are

---

[1] Robert Junk, *Brighter than a Thousand Suns*, J. Cleugh, tran. (New York: Harcourt, Brace and World, 1958), ch. 4; Junk quotes Hahn and Strassmann on 67–68.

to a lesser extent similar projects in other domains of the physical sciences. There is some irony in the present phenomenon in philosophy that at a time when such governance has most spectacularly demonstrated its effectiveness in this regard in scientific domains, among philosophers sensitive to developments in science this success has generated little confidence in the capacity of similar governance to achieve similarly valid results in corresponding projects in their own domains. Rather, some of the most acute and distinguished contemporary philosophical writers in the United States, when they don their ontology hats, or seat themselves in their ontology chairs, find themselves persuaded of profound skepticism concerning the capacity of governantial processes in this regard.[1]

In this connection it may be desirable here to append a few words upon a point that is implicit in the preceding pages but which it has not been possible to develop. It is that just as human practices are primarily social or communal features of our lives, generated and formed in us and engaged in by us as members of communities, so it is with practice-informed, practice-directed governance. This is not to deny that some valid determinations of governance are effected by private, individual conscious reflection. It is rather to emphasize that even these determinations are indirectly social in character, and, further, that the thesis of the competence of such governance to make valid determinations of existence and character leaves open the question of the relative effectiveness of these more individual modes of determination in comparison with the more overtly social and impersonal ones. Without doubt one effect of a transition from the traditional and received views of reason and knowledge to a more social view of these matters is a marked alteration in some very common though highly implicit presumptions in much contemporary philosophical thought concerning the capacity of individuals to make rational determinations and achieve knowledge on their own, without reliance upon group and institutional resources. Just how much in the way of valid determination by governance is possible by means of individual reflection, whether in the forms of calculation or armchair philosophizing, is another matter, and not something that can be discovered a priori by Cartesian meditation. Rather it remains a topic to be explored in the development of the social view of reason and knowledge, in conjunction with related inquiry

---

[1] In point are the doctrines advanced in W. V. O. Quine, *Ontological Relativity*; Richard Rorty, "The World Well Lost," *Journal of Philosophy* 69 (1972): 649–65; Nelson Goodman, *Ways of World-Making* (Indianapolis: Hackett, 1978); and Quine, Review of Goodman, *New York Review of Books* 25, no. 18 (Nov. 23, 1978): 25.

in a wide range of relevant fields of study, including psychology, sociology, anthropology, the history of science, and the philosophy of that history generally.

7   To recognize the role that practices and their governance play in the conduct of investigation is by no means to depreciate the role that the objects of investigation themselves play, in particular cases, in determining the course of investigation and, eventually, its results. It is to facilitate the effectiveness of objects in this regard that practices in the cognitive domains of our lives are developed, revised, and refined. Recognition that knowledge of objects is gained through practices has led some philosophers to conclude that objects thus known are produced by the practices and are thus artifacts somehow dependent for their existence and character upon the practices themselves. Judged in the context of the history of human knowledge, and in particular the fabulous development of physical science in the past four centuries, this is perverse. Cognitive practices are designed to discover and disclose objects, not to produce them, and not to obscure them by interposing between us and them surrogate objects, "phenomenal objects," objects-as-known, as distinguished from independently real ones. Of course not all cognitive practices are *well* designed for the purpose; but as is indeed obvious to us when we are not bemused by some potent philosophical illusion, they are not all *ill* designed. And the same may be said of the kind of governance of practice that is constitutionally dependent in existence and character upon practice, that does not need to be imported from without *for* practice, because it is, in varying degrees and various ways, a natural development of practice itself.[1]

---

[1] [Cf. above, ch. 4.—*Ed.*]

6

Reason and Tradition

What had he once written in his diary? "We have thrown overboard all conventions.... We are sailing without ethical ballast."
  −Koestler, *Darkness at Noon*

All democrats object to men being disqualified by the accident of birth; tradition objects to their being disqualified by the accident of death. Democracy tells us not to neglect a good man's opinion, even if he is our groom; tradition asks us not to neglect a good man's opinion, even if he is our father.
  −Chesterton, *Orthodoxy*

1   All of us members of civilized societies are, individually and collectively, the legatees of a vast and complex cultural heritage in which a great variety of strands—scientific, technological, religious, moral, political, artistic, and so on—are interwoven. A central component of this cultural heritage is a great body of customary, approved ways of thinking and acting that, whatever their basis in our genetic inheritance may be, cannot be accounted for simply or primarily by reference to that. This body we commonly call "tradition." The customary ways of thought and action comprising it operate as norms or standards for these activities, which, having been received, followed, preserved, and altered in varying degrees by each generation, are passed on more or less successfully to succeeding ones. In addition to these norms or standards there is another resource, the relationship of which to them is far less agreed upon. This is the resource which under the title of "reason" or

105

some such name we frequently appeal to when we are moved to examine, criticize, maintain, or emend some of these customary standards. Again and again proposals for the maintenance or alteration of features of accepted practice in thought and action are advanced with the claim that they are sanctioned and validated by reason. What kind of resource is this? In particular, how is it related to the body of customary ways of thinking and acting? In short, how is it related to tradition?

Upon one point in this general topic the early modern philosophers, and most of their latter-day successors, have spoken with remarkable agreement. The view of reason that most have held has been of a resource that is accessible to all of us and competent to effect criticism of tradition because, among other things, it is in some fundamental way independent of tradition. It is a radically different endowment that comes to us, not through cultural channels, but directly or indirectly through features of our genealogical inheritance, as part of our membership by birth in the great family of man.

Of the various points at which this prevailing view may be contested, one only is selected here for examination. This is the manner in which the view applies, or, rather, fails to apply, to the procedures we follow, and need to follow, when we set out to achieve rational scrutiny and control of customary ways of thinking and acting in situations of great indecision and controversy.

Diverse views of reason and its relation to tradition, whether explicitly held or more or less unknowingly acted upon, affect greatly the generation of these situations of indecision and controversy and the effectiveness of the steps we take to meet them. In times of great fragmentation of opinion and increasing faction—political, economic, religious, and ethnic—as exemplified strikingly in the United States and some of the other nations of the Atlantic Community, the prevalence of a theory of reason that obscures the character of doubts and disagreements about the rational authority of steps proposed or taken in the criticism and governance of traditional ways of thinking and acting, and that in consequence obscures also the ways in which such doubts and disagreements may be resolved, is an obstacle to philosophical enlightenment and to philosophically enlightened practical action. The obstacle is increasingly serious when the prevailing view in question, preached from thousands of pulpits, academic and other, becomes the common background, the very common sense of a large educated segment of the population that is the major medium through which intellectual movements of opinion in humanistic culture have their effects in the affairs of common life.

As C. S. Peirce observed a long time ago, one of the pillars of the modern philosophy that bears the general name "Cartesian" is the doctrine that "the ultimate test of certainty is to be found in the individual consciousness." The criterion it offers to the individual in the pursuit of knowledge is, he said, "whatever I am clearly convinced of is true," adding that "thus to make single individuals absolute judges of truth is most pernicious."[1]

Generations brought up to consider that what they are clearly convinced of is true are being encouraged to ignore the safeguards developed over millennia of civilized life against the very kind of narrow commitment to private prejudice that is now widely regarded as the only alternative to the uncritical acceptance of often outmoded and even corrupt tradition. The employment of the principle that killing is wrong, *tout court*, without the balancing considerations of other principles and values, is then considered to expose, in one brilliant flash of reason, the unacceptability of *pare bellum* in all cases and the inequity in all but possibly the most extreme cases of the termination of pregnancies by the techniques of abortion. Similarly, without balancing consideration, an admitted emerging right to privacy, and even to freedom of "lifestyle," is held to ensure the moral impropriety and constitutional illegality of actions of society to limit what may or may not be done to and through one's body affecting reproduction, or what modes of sexual practice, this side of physical violence, consenting adults may follow when they are secluded from actual public observation.[2] What then pass as exemplifications of reason are what generations of treatises on logic have isolated, warned, and striven against under the title of the Fallacy of Accident.

2   An early exponent of the prevailing view of reason was the philosopher from whose name the term "Cartesian" derives and whose influence was so great that he is sometimes referred to as the father of modern philosophy. Descartes' program for the rational reconstruction of the tradition in the physical science of his day incorporated a paradigm form of a conception of the relation between reason and tradition that was extended by his followers

---

[1] C. S. Peirce, "Some Consequences of Four Incapacities," (1868); *Collected Papers*, 5:264–317.

[2] "Finally it must be emphasized that even though a constitutional right to private sexuality may exist, it still must be weighed, as in *Doe v. Commonwealth's Attorney*, against countervailing state interests. Adultery is one type of sexual activity in which seclusion and autonomy rights may combine, but which the state may still regulate to further its interest in the preservation of the traditional family." G. Edward White and J. Harvie Wilkinson, III, "Constitutional Protection for Personal Lifestyles," *Cornell Law Review* 62, no. 3 (1977), rpt. in G. E. White, *Patterns of American Legal Thought* (Charlottesville, Va.: Michie; Indianapolis: Bobbs-Merrill, 1978), 351.

to a variety of fields, for example, to morals, law, and politics and to philosophical inquiry itself.

In a remarkable passage beginning the *Discourse on Method* Descartes proclaims that "the power of judging well and of distinguishing between the true and the false, which, properly speaking, is what is called good sense or reason, is by nature equal in all men." While one may reject the extravagant intellectual equality proclaimed here, it is undeniable that the resource of reason is a widely shared one. Judging well and distinguishing between the true and the false are capacities that we all have to some extent and to some extent realize in our daily and professional lives, whether or not we are engaged in scientific and scholarly pursuits. Descartes regarded this capacity and achievement as deriving from a common gift, a natural light, which regardless of the inequalities of health, and strength of special talents, of wealth and station, that prevail among us is, in a striking example of distributive justice, bestowed upon all of us in equal portions.[1]

Philosophically, the distributive aspect of reason conveyed in this proclamation is by far more significant than the alleged equality. Those who followed Descartes in this matter were committed, often without realizing the presence or depth of that commitment, to an extremely individualistic view of what might be called "rational man," man as exhibiting reason in thought and action. Rationality, as it is expressed more or less well in various areas of human life and thought, is on this view the product of an identical resource residing in individuals. The realization of this character in life and thought may be encouraged or discouraged by the relations between individuals, by the practices and institutions that are social. But it is a character that arises in individuals, a character that in a primary and fundamental way is a character of individuals. It is through them, and secondarily, that it may be attributed to communities.

Two individuals, four individuals, a tribe, a city-state, a nation—two scholars, four scholars, a research group, a larger community of scholars— may achieve much more than one individual; but what these larger groups produce is something more rather than something different. Or, it may be said, there is a difference of quantity rather than quality, as two individuals

---

[1] Norman Kemp Smith remarks that in formulating his doctrine about "good sense or reason" Descartes borrowed from Montaigne's *Essays* (Bk. 2, ch. 17), and that Hobbes likewise was presumably borrowing from the same author when in *Leviathan* (Pt. 1, ch. 13), he advanced a similar argument concerning the distribution of wisdom (*New Studies in the Philosophy of Descartes*, 72 note 2).

can lift a larger stone than one, or two pianists playing the same piece in unison on two instruments produce a greater volume of fundamentally the same sound and a not strikingly different one, as they might were they playing in harmony or in discord. As social life can merely augment the force and effect of the resource of reason with which we are all individually endowed, if we are to understand this resource and use it more knowingly, we need to understand only what is accessible to us in this individual way, which is to say, quite independently of our relations with each other contemporaneously, and equally independently of our relations with our predecessors and the effect that they have upon us through the medium of social tradition. It is by means of a resource like this that we must proceed, if we accept the task of determining whether some features of actual tradition, or some proposed revision of traditional arrangements, is a rational one.

The agreed-upon individualism of the theories of reason developed by Descartes' empiricist and rationalist successors was much more important than the much advertised differentia that divided them over the relative importance of what are widely conceived to be two chief components of reason, namely, experience and reflection. The rationalists, championing the claims of intellectual analysis, the elaboration and refinement of basic ideas, were led by their individualist preconceptions to give a similarly individualistic account of this analysis and of the entities with which, under the title of "ideas," it was taken to be employed. Experience, as a component of reason, underwent a similar striking transmutation at the hands of the empiricists. What could be counted as experience was only whatever could be conceived of as a quite personal resource, accessible to each individual in his own person, independent of his communal associations with other individuals, living or dead. Paradigm examples of experience, so conceived, were Locke's "sensations," Berkeley's "ideas of sense," and Hume's "impressions." It is difficult to leave this brief account of the career in philosophical thought of the individualist view of reason without mentioning the congruence of this view with a few other views, in such diverse domains as religion, economics, and politics, with which it has been closely associated. Among other things the doctrines of Protestant Christianity embodied a more individualist view of divine faith, grace, and salvation than its Roman Catholic parent and rival. There were similar individualist analogues, Marx would hasten to point out, in the view of what are natural, normal relations of the production and distribution of commodities that was arising contemporaneously with this philosophical theory and was given classic and influential formulation in the *Wealth of Nations*. And the same may be said of that model or metaphor that lies at the base of much Western political philosophy to this date: namely, the general contractarian view that regards political and other institutions as the constructions of individuals, which may be regarded as sound only to the extent that their features are grounded in the characters that these individuals have or would have prior to or independent of the construction.

3   To the extent that criticisms and measures of control are rational, they claim the acceptance of the members of the community to whose norms they are directed. What is the link here between rational and acceptable, between reason and acceptance, or more exactly, between being rational and being worthy of, even requiring acceptance? How does reason command interpersonal respect?

The answer to these questions given by the individualist, distributive view of reason stresses the harmonious result of a ground of thought and action that is the same in each individual. One person, say Smith, in the course of critically examining accepted norms in some areas, advances revisions of or replacements for some of these. To the extent that the proposed norms have the sanction of reason, are rational, they qualify for the acceptance of Jones (and Murphy, Cohen, Schulz, and Lopez), because the sanctioning authority in Smith is the same in all the others. Hence the norms that Smith, acting in accordance with reason, advances for thought or action in certain circumstances coincide with what Jones and the others would themselves advance, if they should similarly engage in the criticism and reformation of the original norms and follow reason in so doing. The projected effect in thought and action is analogous to the celebrated preestablished harmony of Leibniz's monadology. Each individual, in the rational governance of thought and action, harmonizes with other individuals. Reason unfolding in each, though quite independently, nevertheless reflects reason unfolding in the thought and action, and the dispositions to think and act, of others. A more common example of the same effect is the explanation offered by the intuitionists in moral philosophy for the fact that, though the fundamental arbiter of right and wrong is the conscience of the individual, there are nevertheless principles and maxims common for all.

That this aspect of acceptability cannot be adequately accounted for on the extremely individualistic view of reason was already beginning to emerge at one point in Descartes' own reflections, when he addressed the topic of the guides that need to be followed and the warnings that need to be heeded by one setting out to conduct reason rightly and seek truth in science. Having summarized the method in the familiar formulae of "clear and distinct ideas," or equivalently, intuition and deduction, Descartes had to deal with the danger, all too obviously prevalent, of individuals mistaking ideas that are in varying degrees unclear or confused for those that are requisitely clear and distinct, mistaking as intuitions of the understanding elements of consciousness whose genesis lies in other sources. Among the various methodological steps and cautions by which Descartes proposed to reduce this danger were: the employment of systematic doubt to counter the effects of parents, teachers, hearsay, example, and custom; the reduction of complex matters to their simple elements and the beginning of the quest for intuitions with the latter; and warnings concerning the deceptive capacity of perceptions of sense and constructions of imagination to pass as genuine apprehensions of the understanding.

Connoisseurs of the Cartesian philosophy have not widely recognized how considerable a qualification, when their significance is realized, these needed steps and warnings constitute to the view that knowledge consists in nothing but intuitions (singly, and linked together in fruitful, deductive chains) of "a pure and attentive [individual] mind."[1] For the methodological guides preliminary to and contemporary with intuition and deduction that are referred to in the mention of these resources are those that must be followed when there is indecision in one individual mind or among several minds as to whether an ostensible deliverance of the natural light of reason is what it purports to be. Granted, to take the simplest case, that a genuine intuition is never wrong, there are at least some occasions when ancillary means need to be employed in order to determine that some proposed truth is a properly intuitive one.

The ancillary means are significant for the question of the authority of reason because, though they are not commonly recognized as such, they amount to serious divergences from the extreme individualism of the doctrine to which they are appended. These divergences are, one and all, forced and distorted recognitions of the thorough dependence of the rational activity of any individual, as it is conceived in this individual-oriented theory, upon tradition, custom, and the other determining resources of common life.

For how indeed could any individual, however private and detached he strives to be from social life and the traditions it embodies—how could such an individual follow these recommended guides and warnings? How is such an innocent, "born-again" mind to follow the instruction to analyze complexes

[1] My appreciation of this point has been enhanced by some unpublished writing of Craig E. Taylor.

into their simple components? What are "complexes," and "components," and "simples" to him? After centuries of acute and learned minds having, in certain contexts, encountered great perplexity in determining what shall be counted as components of larger wholes, are we to suppose now that all will be made obvious to an innocent mind, so that now an intellectual little child shall lead us? Can this child-mind, unencumbered by "what others have thought," and stripped of "all opinions and beliefs formerly received," be conceived to have the analytic acuteness and subtlety required to make the kind of distinction between genuinely clear and distinct ideas and ideas that are only apparently so that, according to Descartes' own account, is required in order to derive rational knowledge from the perception of so simple an object as a piece of wax?

In short, the actions that a pure and attentive mind need to be able to perform in this philosophy are ones of considerable subtlety and complexity, ones that require a mind carefully critical and highly disciplined. And it could not succeed in taking care and adhering to discipline solely on the basis of innate resources. These would require the kind of development, tempering, refinement, constant exercise, and monitoring that logically implies a background of social practice that extends through time and is accessible to individuals through tradition. By now many have learned from Wittgenstein what a century and a half of more foreign voices have been proclaiming to deaf ears, namely, that the discrimination in ourselves of even the most private feelings and sensations, requires the resources of a public practice or institution. If the most rudimentary language of sensation has its roots, its logically indispensable bases, in the social forms of life of those who employ it, the same is true with even more clarity of the kinds of refined and sometimes extremely subtle discriminations that a pure and attentive mind, on Descartes' own accounting, must be presumed capable of making in rightly following the path of intuition and deduction.

What has just been elaborated with reference to one version of the general individualistic philosophy of reason seems readily to apply to others. This philosophy fails to satisfy one major test of a theory of reason, which is that it provide an adequate answer to the question of interindividual, social acceptability, the question of how a judgment issued by the reason of one individual in a community commands the respect and acceptance of others. The answer that reason is a common mental endowment of all human beings, coupled with the doctrine that derives common acceptability from the dispositions of numerically different rational faculties to proceed in identical ways, guarantees that the rulings of individuals on the same matters, when they are made by these faculties, will coincide. But in applying such a view to specific cases one immediately confronts the need, since ostensible judgments of reason do commonly diverge, of means for determining which, if any, in the contests of opposing judgments represents a rational faculty. At this juncture the appeal to common native endowments needs to be supplemented by other resources, resources capable of rendering critical judgments in this domain, and ones patently accessible to us only because we are individuals living in communities, and as such, the legatees, custodians, and users of a vast store of resources that are communal in character. Furthermore, employment of and reliance upon these resources are, and necessarily are, so thorough, widespread, and constant, that providing a place for them effects a radical change in the theory to which they are appended. The contribution of our native endowments to the constitution of reason cannot be isolated from the contribution of individual experience, practice, and custom, and the communal versions of these in tradition. So that tradition, we now see, is not an influence on us separate from or opposed to reason. It is rather a necessary component of it.

4   Striving, as we frequently do in the criticism, fixation, or emendation of tradition, to proceed according to reason, we are naturally influenced in our proceeding by how we view this latter resource. If we take our touchstone to be what we are clearly convinced of, and if we take clear conviction to be an achievement of an individual mind, as it pays attention to its experiences or its ideas, then it is on this basis that we have to take account of and deal with the notorious fact that apparently clear individual convictions do often differ in contradictory ways. Yet if reason itself is one, if it is not itself riven with contradictory elements, some disposition of the conflict of clear convictions, or ostensible clear convictions, needs to be made.

The response of the prevailing view is that at least some of the ostensible clear convictions are not clear; not really, but only apparently so. The charge against the view at this point is that it seriously distorts, obscures, and renders less tractable the situations of doubt and controversy over rational results and procedures. The picture it presents of contesting opinions and the contestants who advance these opinions is extremely unrealistic, and even less realistic than it would be if contestants were not influenced by their own acceptance of the view to comport themselves in ways more in conformity with it. In consequence the view obscures the resources and ways by which rational criticism, fixation, and emendation of tradition in such situations proceed in the sciences and other cognitive disciplines, as well as in morals, law, politics, religion, and other areas of thought and action. Its concentration upon the decisive effect of the clear convictions of individuals encourages a disposition among adherents to neglect the resources of rational criticism, emendation, and the rest that reside within conflicts of thought and action, and, neglecting these, to regard the conflicts as terminal obstacles to rational procedures.[1] And the effect of this is that a view, one principal aim of which was to expand the area of rational decision and agreement, has in such situations the contrary effects of reenforcing indecision and intensifying faction.

For if conflicts are due to the circumstances that some unclear convictions are passing for clear ones, if the fault lies in acts of apprehension, judgment, or decision that can be performed and are performed properly by the individual mind itself, isolated from the influence of custom and tradition, then there has been some faltering in individual performance which calls for equally individual reexamination and correction. The conflicts are a sign that the case is to be returned for retrial to the lower court, or courts, which issued the conflicting opinions. The remedy for poor individual performance is better performance by the same agencies. And, for assistance in this regard, in detecting where and how the intention to secure genuine intuitions previously miscarried, individuals are called upon to perform a peculiar and especially difficult examination of their previous performances. Although we commonly recognize that in many of the actions of everyday life we need much assistance from our fellows, both present and past, and the vast cultural resources they provide for our purpose, to understand ourselves, to see ourselves and our actions as they really are, in this essay into self-knowledge and knowledge of performance we are curiously counseled to dispense with such assistance. Difficult as this examination may be, in it the individual may trust no outside help. In the pursuit of genuine intuitions, and the exposure of plausible counterfeit ones, trusting only himself in this trial, he must, though the defendant in the trial, also discharge the functions of judge and jury.

So bizarre a method can only in the rarest instances effect a genuine trial; the normal defendant, especially in such circumstances, is ill prepared to ensure the conditions of a fair trial, and at the conclusion to render a fair verdict. If indecision within one individual was the precipitating cause of the trial, the indecision is apt to remain. And if the conflict took the form of a divergence of opinion and controversy between individuals, the divergence

---

[1] [Cf. below, ch. 9, regarding the "latent" aspects of norms.—*Ed.*]

will likely persist, and the controversy, now that each individual has confirmed himself in the rightness of his own judgment, will likely be
exacerbated. And when otherwise percipient individuals persist in reporting
clear perceptions that greatly diverge from one's own, one's disposition will
be stronger to judge them perverse.

5   A view of reason that corresponds more closely with rational practice in
situations of indecision and controversy needs to depart sharply from the
prevailing one upon the two closely related points that have been most
prominent in the preceding discussion, namely, the extreme individualism of
that view, and its false opposition of reason and tradition. This departure
enables it to recognize the close relation between these two human resources,
and to take advantage of this recognition to illumine the way reason is
employed in such situations to effect the criticism, fixation, and emendation
of tradition itself.

A first step toward such a view is recognition of the large role that
tradition plays in determining for all of us at any given time what we clearly
conceive or otherwise find intuitively obvious. The question is not whether
we all have such clear conceptions or intuitions. It is rather a question
whether we take their incandescent clarity as a sign that they are the revelations, the apocalypses, of a reason that is capable, in its incorporation in
individuals, of determinations that are quite immune to the influence, and
hence also to the criticism, of public experience, custom, and tradition. It is
whether in situations of indecision and conflict among apparently clear conceptions, for example, we are entitled to conclude that the logical opposition
among them demonstrates that some, at least, are entirely bereft of the force
of reason; or whether, in consequence of the generative influence of tradition
upon our clear conceptions, these opposing ones are both clear and persuasive
because they represent important elements of a by no means univocal tradition, all of which must be accommodated in a resolution of the indecision
and conflict that itself qualifies as rational. In short, apparently clear
intuitions may be divergent, not because some of them are only apparently
clear, but because they are all clear, though deriving their clarity from an
internally divergent tradition that employs these situations of indecision and
conflict as one means of meeting these conditions and striving to alleviate
them.[1]

---

[1] [Cf. ch. 9 below.—*Ed.*]

The generation of contrary intuitions concerning whether some basic feature of our traditional ways of thinking and acting should be altered is in many cases a natural consequence of divergences in the broad cultural grounds from which these intuitions spring. In cases of this kind, partisans of opposed positions naturally appreciate the clarity with which their respective intuitions come to them. And in this, of course, they are not wrong. What the situation suffers from is not too little but too much of this partial, one-sided clarity, since the clarity on one side of the controversy may be matched by an equal degree on the other. A view of reason in its relation to tradition that is obliged to find merely specious clarity on at least one side of such a dispute is destined to misunderstand it and to obscure the features of the situation upon which the resolution of the dispute depends.

When we put ourselves into the situation of the ancient mathematicians confronting the demonstration of the incommensurability of the diagonal of a square, we can appreciate the force with which two brilliantly clear but opposed intuitions collided at that crucial point in the development of the theory of numbers: one to the effect that because the square root of two cannot be expressed as a relation between two whole numbers, it cannot be a number; the other that it had to be, since it expressed a relation of magnitude between two indisputable geometrical distances. Though a rich supply of similar episodes is furnished us by the history of modern and recent science, including the social sciences, it is perhaps more helpful at this point to think instead briefly of their analogues in the fields of education, morals, laws, and politics. Some of these were cited earlier in this paper (§2) and need not be rehearsed. For others we need not look far back in our educational and widely social tradition. We are struck there, for example, by the clash of clear conceptions about the idea and hence the social mission of a university that was precipitated by the rise of modern physical science and the ordeal of controversy that was aroused by its introduction into the university curriculum. Similarly, differing conceptions, deriving from different components of our traditions, clashed in the past hundred years over the issue whether it was or was not part of the mission of a universal institution of higher learning, born in religious congregations in the Middle Ages, to minister to the needs of the mechanical and agricultural arts in our society, and not merely to those of so-called learned professions. Some of the atmosphere of this controversy, especially the appeal to alleged obvious truths deriving from ideas deeply entrenched in tradition and polished like gems in it, was revived a few decades ago in the educational counterrevolution emanating from the Chicago of Robert M. Hutchins and Mortimer J. Adler.

A vivid illustration of a conflict between sets of clear conceptions in morals, law, and politics was the extended controversy about secession that erupted in civil war in the United States in the last century. Partisans on both sides of this controversy could advance strong moral, legal, and political grounds for their respective positions. To the extent that the constitutional tradition, to which each side appealed, looked upon the federal government as a union of sovereign states, it implied a right to dissolve the union that was analogous to the right to dissolve their own union with Great Britain that the thirteen colonies had maintained in the Declaration of Independence. Opposed to this was the right and duty of a government-in-being to preserve itself. What kind of government could one conceive had been formed by the Constitution of 1787, if its duly authorized actions could be nullified by dissenting states, and if among the rights reserved to the several states was the right, in self-judged extremity, to secede? Illustrative of the persuasive power of each of these two opposed moral, legal, and political traditions bearing on secession was the way in which each of them in the space of little more than a decade won the endorsement of the greatest political figure of that period, Abraham Lincoln. At the time of the Mexican War Lincoln had urged that the right of any people, or portion of such people, "to rise up and shake off the existing government and form a new one that suits them better ... is a most valuable, a most sacred right." Later as President, confronted by the secession of the Confederate States, he urged with equal force the right of a constitutionally elected government to suppress rebellion. So in May 1861, he said, "We must settle this question now, whether in a free government the minority have the right to break up the government whenever they choose." And two months later, addressing Congress in phrases that were to become more familiar after Gettysburg, he said, "The issue embraces more than the fate of the United States. It presents to the whole family of man the question whether ... a government of the people, by the same people, can or cannot maintain its territorial integrity against its own domestic foes."[1]

There is space to mention but two more recent situations in which there has been large-scale indecision and controversy about the preservation or alteration of deeply entrenched ways of thinking and acting in social affairs in the United States. The economic depression in the 1930s and the election of an administration that found itself, not very self-consciously, more and

---

[1] Quotations from Shelby Foote, *The Civil War*, vol. 1 (New York: Random House, 1968), 66–68.

more committed to federal regulation of economic activity and intervention in the distribution of the wealth issuing from that activity, precipitated a division of opinion, expressing itself in clear intuitions on both sides, of what is required in a complex industrial society by a commitment to freedom for its members. Thirty years later division over this matter has been joined and complicated by a division over what is legally, morally, and politically required to erase the effects of invidious racial discrimination in education, employment, and housing, and latterly, over whether discriminatory treatment on racial grounds, both by private parties and governmental agencies, is now not only not necessarily invidious, but in some cases benign and even morally and legally mandatory. The opposition of clear intuitions on these matters that is exhibited by discussions in the local tavern, and duplicated in somewhat more elevated language and considerably more logical refinement in the division between the majority and minority members of the Supreme Court, exemplifies again that in such situations clear intuitions do not suffice for rational criticism, control, and rectification of traditional forms of thought and action.

6   In every great divisive controversy, within academic disciplines and in wider communities, there are basic generating causes in our tradition. Communities of scholars and scientists, and moral, political, and religious communities, find themselves collectively at a loss as to how to think and act; and individuals in their more private lives find themselves similarly at a loss because for a variety of reasons in different cases their tradition provides them with no one single clear guide. In many situations different components of their tradition point in different and contrary directions.

A most serious defect of the prevailing individualist view of what constitutes rational criticism and control of tradition is the way it obscures our understanding of ourselves and reduces our capacity to act with understanding in such situations. It is very inspiriting for us, when we are engaged in controversy over rational standards of thought and action, to picture ourselves on the model that Thomas Jefferson, with the editorial assistance of Benjamin Franklin, has made familiar to us, as the champions of self-evident truths. This is especially deleterious—remember that Peirce said "pernicious"—when our philosophical doctrine leads us to disregard the fact that what may be self-evident to ourselves may be opposed by the equally clear intuitions of others, and that there is in consequence something both intellectually and socially unresponsive in the appeal to self-evidence upon controverted issues. Appeals by opposing advocates then begin to fulfill the extreme condition set down by Ambrose Bierce when he mordantly defined the self-evident as that which is evident only to oneself.

When one's opponent has become one's enemy, it may be too late to rely upon procedures of rational adjudication to settle one's dispute with him. But it is of assistance in understanding what we are about when we engage in civil disputes over ways of thinking and acting, and in preserving civility in disputes that otherwise would not remain so, to recognize that the rational resources that we appeal to in such situations do not only not prevent such disputes, but do indeed generate them. The abrasion of conflicting elements in our tradition is one of the chief ways in which tradition changes, as it must, to meet new circumstances. The various forms of conflict and dispute in which this abrasion takes place, though signs of failure of elements of tradition in such circumstances, are also the normal accompaniments and means of a rationally adjusting tradition moving to retrieve that failure. Agents in such disputes, engaged in the adjusting processes, misconceive their situation and objectives to the extent that they think of themselves as engaged in the task of divining, in quite personal intuitions, what must be imposed in the resolution of these disputes, rather than engaging as members of a community in the kind of processes in which perennially, sometimes blunderingly and sometimes well, they resolve differences together.

These processes of adjusting, adapting, and the rest, which on the prevailing, individualistic view seem to be defections from the straight and narrow path of reason, are, then, prime examples of what rational procedure in the criticism and emendation of tradition is. To depreciate these processes as those of compromise, of trimming, of bending rational principle to necessity, is to mistake as mere expedients in individual and social life the very processes by which rational changes are achieved. Our failure, because of the false preconceptions of what rational processes in these situations must be, will not, of course, relieve us of the need to engage in them. It may, however, make some difference in the effectiveness of our engagement if we consider ourselves in these cases as making-do with resources that are not the best available; if overhanging our efforts is the haunting suspicion—generated by the preconceptions—that we are compromising our rational consciences, accepting inferior substitutes for genuinely rational processes and results.

Some readers may initially regard the charge of extreme individualism advanced against the prevailing view of reason, in its relation to tradition, as an intrusion into domains of logic and the theory of knowledge of foreign matter that is better confined to its proper home in political philosophy. Those familiar with Peirce's emphasis upon the community in various parts of his philosophy, including logic, may be less disposed to regard such criticism as eccentric. Over a hundred years ago, discussing some issues posed by Berkeley's idealism, Peirce commented upon the way in which views about the relation between the individual and the community, in knowledge and in other pursuits, reflect issues of great human significance that had been debated in earlier philosophy in the controversy over nominalism and realism in the theory of universals. The question whether the community is to be considered as more than a collection of individuals, and if so, what is the relative value of each of these two polar features, Peirce went on to say, should not be viewed as a merely abstract logical, epistemological, or metaphysical puzzle. In its practical bearing in regard to every public institution which we have it in our power to influence, he said, this question is the most fundamental.[1]

[1] Peirce, review of A. C. Fraser's edition of Berkeley (1881), *Collected Papers*, 8:7–38. This chapter developed from a lecture (the Humanities Lecture of 1980) given at the University of Illinois at Urbana-Champaign on April 15. I am indebted to my colleague James D. Wallace for reading an earlier draft and suggesting lines of revision.

7

Rules and Subsumption:
Mutative Aspects of Logical Processes

1   A central object of concern and puzzlement in modern philosophy, accounting in some considerable degree for the dominance of epistemology in this period, has been the processes of critical appraisal of accepted practices of thought and action. Though these processes are by no means concerned only with the identification of loci and forms of desirable change of practices, during these centuries of accelerating change and reformist spirit the employment of the processes of appraisal in relation to questions of change has dominated the investigation. Upon this employment attention will be concentrated in the present paper. It is worth noting at the outset that the legitimate purpose and result of the scrutiny of the warrant for change of any item of practice are not necessarily to reveal the need for change in that practice nor to discover the form that possibly needed changes should take. The legitimate purpose, or the legitimate result, in many cases may be the elaboration of a judgment confirming the warrant of an item of practice as it stands, thus contributing to stability at this point rather than change. Moreover, the motive of philosophic investigation of the appraisal processes, in spite of the demurrers of Marx and others, has been not so much to participate directly in the processes of appraisal and change as to understand them. The distinctive philosophical task has been the identification and illumination of the general

character of warranted changes, and, with that, the general character of the
warrant that such changes are able to produce under investigation.

2   In general the present situation in the investigation is as follows: one long
dominant view of the warrant of change has been seriously discredited, while
its main contestant, in spite of almost two centuries of intermittent development, has yet to establish its right to succession. The defining characters of
the former view, articulated early in modern philosophy in two different ways
by the empiricists and rationalists, have been its extreme individualism and
the hierarchic or foundational model through which it has sought to understand the warrant of items of practice, both accepted and proposed. This view
has been, as much of modern Western philosophy has been, thoroughly
Cartesian in its conception of the warrant. It has conceived it as residing
ultimately and exclusively in a source that every normal human being in his
right mind has necessarily, because he is a human being. He has it as an
endowment by birth, distributed in a remarkable exemplification of distributive justice among all men independently of race or creed, or of the richness
or meagerness of their social relations. This ultimate source of warrant is
conceived as providing warrant for accepted or proposed items of practice by
first providing warrant for a primitive, basic set of practices that are collectively capable of providing warrant for further practices, which are themselves
capable of providing warrant for further practices, and so on. The question of
the warrant of any accepted or proposed practice is thus construed as a
question whether it is connected by one or more of these umbilical conduits
of warrant to this primitive foundational set that is the ultimate logical
mother of all. Sometimes the source of this set is taken to be our capacity to
have sensory impressions and to construct ideas and connections of ideas
from them; and sometimes to be ideas already somehow embedded in our
human constitution. For present purposes these further specifications are less
important than the common conception of the warrant as ultimately deriving
from an original source in this progressive way.
    A deep presumption, closely related to the reigning psycho-physical
dualism of the period in which this view has flourished, is that what is
essential in practices may be abstracted from them, and the question of
warrant then translated into a question about these abstract entities. These,
through the centuries, have been referred to in a variety of idioms, for example as ideas, propositions, beliefs, or sentences, the varying terminology
reflecting in various degrees their fundamental quasi-linguistic or quasisymbolic character. Having made this abstraction, a natural model for con-

ceiving transmission of warrant among these entities lay close at hand in the axiomatic model so highly favored in the philosophy of mathematics in the seventeenth and eighteenth centuries. The warrant was thought of as transmitted from the primitive to the dependent entities through a complex of chains of warrant like those that hold between the axioms of a geometric system and the theorems, lemmas, and so on, that depend upon them.

3   Integral to the foundational view of the warrant that features of practice may be made to display under investigation is this abstract quasilinguistic, quasisymbolic view of the principal items that are the components of the body of practice. These items are conceived to be entities that have and retain identities that can be discriminated and treated independently of the matrix in human life in which they are found and which they serve to inform. This mode of conception was supported by the successful way it seemed to apply to the large segment of our actions that are routine. It is the practices embodied in highly routine action that for many purposes lend themselves to representation by symbolic formulae specifying by the proper descriptive expressions certain key features of an action following the practice. For these purposes the formulae specify adequately the conditions of the action conforming to the practice, and the action itself. It is possible to skim off these key features and through them represent action conforming to the practice, because in practices of an extremely routine character much, both in the background of the action and in the action itself, may be neglected.

But for some purposes what is neglected in this abstract representation is of great importance; and this applies eminently to the topic of subsumption, of following or employing a practice, of subsuming instances under a rule. Subsumption has a very different look, when one thinks of it concretely as exemplified in action, from the way it looks when one thinks of it symbolically as merely a matter of effecting concrete expansion of a general formula by the substitution in it of proper specifying expressions for the variables employed in signifying the conditions of application. The easy way with which, given the rule that the Achaians are proud, we manufacture the expression "Achilles [or Agamemnon, or Menelaus] is proud" masks some of the features of the more concrete process, not of substituting a name for a variable, but of applying in thought the rule about pride to individual Achaians. Thinking of the rule as merely the symbolic formula, and subsumption as merely symbolic expansion like the above, one is encouraged to conceive of following practices, of applying rules in concrete cases, as similarly an easy, automatic, and likewise all-or nothing procedure.

4   Action following a routine practice, routinely subsuming instances under the rules of the practice, whether the action is overt or is only an action of thought, may be called "routine" subsumption: this in contrast with that in which the application of rules is in some degree problematic. Routine subsumption is widespread, and unquestionably an essential part of human life. That it is widespread and essential does not justify the concentration upon it, indeed the almost exclusive preoccupation with it, that has prevailed in modern philosophy. One important reason for this concentration has been the success attained in the theoretical development of symbolic analogues of this process. So successful has been the collective analogue as a theoretical model of the process, that it has effectively graduated from its position as analogue to that of philosophic definition of the process itself. Just as among some enthusiastic psychologists the success of the model of the conditioned reflex led to the elevation of that model to the status of a definition of learning itself, so among many philosophers the admittedly valuable analogue of routine subsumption came to be taken for the process itself, and, in consequence whatever in the original process could not be reduced to the model was extruded from this refined philosophical conception of it.

Several things, be it noted, are being distinguished here: first, the general process of subsumption; second, two subspecies of the whole process denominated respectively "routine" and "problematic"; and, third, the symbolic analogue of the routine process. The thesis being developed here is that the great success of the symbolic model in illuminating the routine subspecies led to the mistaken identification of the subsumptive process with this model and with the routine processes of which it is a surrogate. In consequence of this the vast body of nonroutine, problematic, less symbolically tractable subsumptive processes was excluded from the philosophically oriented study of rules and practices, and the wealth of illumination that may be developed from the study of them was thereby lost. In particular, the consequence of this for the understanding of the warrant for change of practice has been that one of the major sources of change, and of the warrants for such change, has been on principle excluded from the consideration of practices in use and the sources of change and warrant in that use. An example of this in the area of cognitive practices has been the development of a theory of inference that concentrates upon determinate validating relations holding between premises and conclusions—the kind of relations that are characteristic of routine subsumption—and neglects the rich store of much less definite relations that hold between practices and conclusions drawn through them when following the practice is not routine, but requires in the following a kind of crafting of the practices themselves.

5   Applied to the simpler, more elementary components of practices, namely, rules, the point concerns the character of rules and of action following rules, concerns the problematic, as well as the routine forms of this activity, and the function performed by the problematic forms in generating change and developing warrants for change. Valuable as it is for certain purposes for us to distinguish sharply our action in following a rule from our action in discerning the need for change in the rule and in moving to effect change, for other purposes the distinction is extremely unrealistic and the source of much theoretical as well as practical difficulty. For one of the most important sources of change of rules and of detection of warrant for change in them is our action in following them, and our coordination, while engaged, of the action with the ends that the rule is employed to serve.[1]

It is important, then, to recognize the largeness of the role played in our lives by the mutant-producing capacity of problematic subsumption, to recognize the prevalence, proximity, and normality of this mutational effect. This effect pervades all domains of thought and action, from the most homely situations in daily life to corresponding ones in the physical and social sciences, including both the abstract mathematical ones and, of course, such extremely concrete ones as law, politics, religion, and morals. But it may be quickly observed that this recognition is not enough. Granted the prevalence, etc., of these mutational processes, what shall we make of them? Where shall they fit in our view of practices and rules, and of action guided by these? Upon what has in general been the majority view, these aspects of subsumption are not essential to it, are to be conceived rather as perturbations of the process due to imperfections of the practices or rules involved. When subsumption is viewed through the paradigm of symbolic expansion there is no place for, no need for recognizing these aspects of the process. Concretely, when applied to action governed by rules, this means that there is no place in the conception of rule-governed action for these same aspects, no place for the adaptive, adjustive, redefining, reconstructive processes that commonly in many areas of life are essential features of such action. It will be helpful in exploring these matters to have available a short characterizing label for the view criticized here. There being no established usage in this matter, the

---

[1] [Cf. below, ch. 8.—*Ed.*]

relatively less misleading term "logistic" will be employed to refer to it.
Should a label be needed for the view advanced as an alternative to it, the
much abused term "pragmatic" will perhaps suffice.

6   At the heart of the logistic view lies a conception of a process that has
been described as a symbolic analogue of routine subsumption. When this
analogue is taken to be a criterial paradigm of subsumptive processes generally, it is misleading in two important and closely related respects. One of
these is its neglect of the problematic kind of subsumption, and its mutant-
producing capacity. The other is its disregard of the wider, holistic aspects of
rules and of action following rules. This is a further serious obstacle to the
understanding of subsumption generally, both the problematic and also the
routine varieties.

Both these topics bear directly and fundamentally upon our conception of
rules and of action following them. First, how are mutant effects to be
understood? Are they, when they occur, something foreign to the subsumptive
process, perturbations of a process that can be conceived without them? Or
are they one form of a more general effect—call it a "reactive" effect—that
is itself an essential feature of the process, so that what needs to be
accounted for is not the presence of such effects in some cases but their
apparent absence in others?

There is on the one hand a conception of following a rule as essentially
replicating a mode of action stipulated by the rule. The rule says, "Slow
Traffic Keep Right," and the slow driver replicates this in his response. The
rule is an archetype. A person following the rule conforms to the archetype,
exhibits in behavior an instantiation of it. Following is conforming. This view
may be contrasted with one in which a rule is seen, not as an archetype to
be replicated, but as one of a variety of components out of which the action
governed by the rule is formed. For rules do not govern individuals in a
vacuum. They do so in company with other and often competing rules, and
in a great variety of circumstances that can and do affect the action that is a
response to the rule. The slow driver does not respond to but one rule, but
to others that take into account the condition of the road, the state of the
traffic, and so on. This latter view of action following a rule differs from the
former archetypal-replicative one in being, rather, compositive or organic.

If the subsumptive process is regarded as a purely replicative one, the
mutational effects that sometimes are generated in applying a rule to instances
will be regarded as external to the process itself. But if the heart of the
process is not replication-in-act of a character already present and predeter-

mined in the rule, but is rather the generation, creation, or composition of a character of which the rule is one major, but not the sole component, then an access otherwise lost to understanding these effects is provided. The reconception of rules and of action according to them that is implicated in the assimilation of mutant effects to the subsumptive process is a considerable one. Having included these effects in the process and begun to understand the generation of them in individual actions, one is prepared to begin similarly to understand, upon this somewhat Lamarckian model, how, over extended time, these effects may be accumulated and stabilized. One who is most interested in the matter of change of practice, and in the warrant for change, will naturally be most interested in those effects that serve this end. But as the evolutionary model reminds us, the effects of use, of application, need not be mutational in character. The same forces that in some circumstances work for change of practice, in others further stability. The latter effect is especially pronounced in the forms of subsumption that have been called routine. In them the effect, over time, is to stabilize practices, and forms of action governed by them, so that altogether some practices are modified by the reactive effects of use; some are stabilized; some are eventually extinguished; and in the processes new ones are generated and refined. Routine subsumption, it now appears, should be viewed, not as a form of subsumption from which the general reactive effects of use are utterly absent, but rather as a form in which these effects are stabilizing, not mutational, and much less prominent than mutational ones.

7   Consider, for example, that subsumption to which J. S. Mill devoted much valuable if inconclusive effort in his discussion of the syllogism.[1] The application of the rule of human mortality to even so redoubtable a figure as the Duke of Wellington, is routine, as it would be if the subject were George IV, or that king's valet. Nothing in the circumstances of drawing a conclusion about the mortality of these men is problematic; nothing suggests a question about whether each is an individual to which the rule of mortality properly applies, or similarly whether the termination of the mortal career of each properly qualifies as death. Nothing adaptive, accommodative, or generative in the way of reactive effects upon the rule is entailed by the application of the rule to the Duke.

---

[1] [A System of Logic, 2 vols. (London: 1843), vol. I Bk. 2 chs. 2, 3.—Ed.]

Contrast with this our situation if we set out to apply the rule to such extraordinary individuals as, say, Elijah of Old Testament theology (remember the chariot of fire), the mother of Jesus in modern Roman Catholic theology (think of her Assumption), or King Arthur ("I pass, but shall not die"). These eccentric examples illustrate the possibility of difficulty arising in the application of so routine a rule as that concerning human mortality. For such out-of-the-way difficulties we have a ready supply of means that render them tractable without denying the reality of the instances from which they derive. A much richer supply of subsumptive difficulties would be required to lead to the revision of such a deeply entrenched rule as this. Such a supply might have seemed available to one of the early Christians of the first century expecting an imminent return of Jesus Christ, as it might now seem to a member of a Christian sect committed to some version of the millennial eschatology.

8   If all my large drill bits are in the black drill case, and if what I need to drill a hole for the bolt is one of my large bits, then the bit I need is in the black case. The rule, "for large bits, black case" tells me where to seek such bits among my tools. Is there any way in which the application of this rule to bit-seeking could lead to some warranted change of the rule? Obviously, if in following the rule in repeated practice I persistently do not find the large bit that I need. How could that occur? For one thing, my craft as a mechanic may develop in such a way that I use larger and larger bits, so that eventually a one-fourth inch bit, which once counted in my practice as a large one, and is normally the largest bit in an assorted pack, now counts as small, or perhaps intermediate.

A likely response to the portrayal of such a homely example of reactive change is that the proper employment of the subsumptive technique embodied in the example presupposes that descriptive expressions like "large" not undergo a shift in meaning in the process of delivering the intended conclusion. "All you need to do," it is commonly said, is to "define your terms," and proceed faithfully according to the definitions. The confidence of this remark is reminiscent of that of Achilles in Lewis Carroll's celebrated imaginary colloquy between Achilles and the tortoise.[1] For just as Achilles is revealed there to be reacting to a kind of supposed incompleteness of

---

[1] [Lewis Carroll, "What the Tortoise Said to Achilles," *Mind* N.S. 4 (1895): 278–80.—*Ed.*]

premises in a simple deduction that cannot be remedied by the adduction of
further premises, no matter how far this process proceeds, so anyone who
supposes that the reactive mutant-producing capacity of subsumption can be
altogether eliminated by a program of definition does not understand the
character and hence the necessary limits of this latter procedure. There is a
deep, basic reason why in the case of most, if not all the terms we employ
in subsumptive processes, we are not provided with rules ready for all
imaginable circumstances. Or, more accurately, there is a reason why our
rules of application for these terms do not provide answers to questions of
application in all circumstances. For that is the kind of extreme sufficiency
that rules of application alone are in principle unable to provide. This is what
the open texture of concepts teaches us. Rules of application of such concepts
achieve definition of them in contexts in which for a variety of reasons all
those disturbing imagined possibilities ("cats" that grow to the size of bears;
"goldfinches" that recite passages from Virginia Woolf) may be neglected.[1]
"Sufficient unto the day is the definition thereof" is a rough rule of parsi-
mony that is by no means limited to juridical practice.

9   The capacity of a rule to be remolded in subsumptive use was illustrated
in an extremely rudimentary and personal way in the example of the drill
bits. A less rudimentary and more social example would be that of a university senate, previously composed of all faculty of the rank of professor,
proceeding to interpret its own resolution to alter its composition to that of
a number of representatives elected in a scheme of proportional representation
from and by the full-time faculty members of the rank of instructor or above
in the various academic units of the institution. The general rule of proportional representation of faculty has already undergone some reactive definition
in the exclusion of staff members on part-time appointment and those below
the rank of instructor, for example, graduate assistants. Further definition will
be required when the rule of suffrage-cum-representation encounters units that
have hitherto been classified as academic, though members of them did not
participate directly in the great teaching and research functions of the university. For payroll purposes, for union membership, or similar reasons, it was
by and large more convenient to count them on the academic rather than the
nonacademic side of membership in the university family. An example of
such a unit would be a large staff of permanent professional workers required

---

[1] [Cf. ch. 1 above.—*Ed.*]

to operate a large library, or collection of libraries, and the supplementary information retrieval agencies that are naturally associated with such institutions. The *Porosität* of the term "faculty" begins to be apparent to the constitutional congress when subsumptive application of the proportional representation rule yields the result that the large staff of such a unit, most of whom have no formal teaching or research responsibilities, will now have a much larger voice in the determination of educational and research policy of the university than most of the academic departments that are directly engaged in performing these basic functions of the institution.

It is of course not inadvertently but by design that on the logistic view subsumption is isolated from cases in which mutational effects of the above sorts are realized. It is not competent, because it is not meant to be competent, to account for these effects. This design is reflected in a clear way in one aspect of the theory, namely, the translation in it of subsumption into a process of a completely symbolic kind, and the absorption of the question of the application of rules into an algebra of the permutation and combination of symbols.

10 The wider, holistic aspects of rules and of action following rules was mentioned in §6 as a second respect in which the logistic view, with its exclusive emphasis on the replicative aspects of action in accordance with rules, is inadequate.

In both the *Philosophical Investigations* and the *Remarks on the Foundations of Mathematics*, Wittgenstein posed some penetrating questions concerning action in accordance with a rule, as that topic bears on the nature of logical necessity.[1] How in following a rule is action determined to follow the course that we commonly think of as conforming to the rule, when, if we consider just an individual, his personal resources, and his subsequent action, there is apparently no end to the number of contrary possible courses of action that might be construed as action by him in following the rule? This question of Wittgenstein's was a kind of converse analogue of one commonly asked in the present century about the conformity between statements, propo-

---

[1] *Philosophical Investigations* I, §§143–243, etc.; *Remarks on the Foundations of Mathematics* (Cambridge, Mass.: MIT Press, 1956), Part I, §§1–5, 113–169, etc.. Interest in Wittgenstein's discussions has recently been revived by Saul A. Kripke's *Wittgenstein on Rules and Private Language* (Oxford: Blackwell, 1982).

sitions, or sentences, and their objects that is in some way implicated in the conception of truth.[1]

What is this relation that holds between the rule and the action of the individual, that picks out among possible courses of action, the one, or ones, that conform to the rule? Consider, for example, an individual who has been taught to produce a series of cardinal numbers according to the rule, "Add 2." Beginning at zero he proceeds under instruction to produce the series, 2, 4, 6, 8, 10.... How does this rule, "Add 2," determine for him that at some particular point, say at 96, the next number in the series is 98? What, if rounding the turn at 1000, he produces the numbers 1004, 1008, 1012, and so on? We naturally say that at this point he ceased to follow the rule. But suppose that to him it is natural to go on as he did, as natural as it would be for us to go on with 1002, 1004, 1006. How does the rule determine that our construction is right and his is wrong?

11 We may profitably consider Wittgenstein's example without entering into the controversial question of what exactly about logical necessity he wanted to teach with this and similar examples. A primary object of his criticism in these discussions was the notion of a private rule and, with that, of a private language. This bears directly on the topic of the present paper. If one thinks of a rule as a mental or even cerebral construct, as a template for action, it is difficult to see how the idea of such a template can be elaborated so as to provide an answer to the questions raised concerning the conformity or disconformity of actions with the rule. This conception of a rule, quite contrary to the intention with which it was developed, does not illuminate, but rather renders incomprehensible how rules do guide actions. Considered in this way the rule and the action conforming to it are estranged from each other. Too much has been eliminated from the larger situation; from the whole complex nexus of native responses, habits, rules, practices, and institutions individual and communal, that serve as the background for the action; and too much also from the complex existential situation in which the action takes place.

Apart from components of native and learned responses, and the rich complex of social tradition implicated in the latter, the symbol "Add 2" is not a rule. It is a mark, not even a notation. And the rule itself does not guide a being who, like a newly created Adam, is without tradition, company,

---

[1] [Cf. above, chs. 2, 3.—*Ed.*]

practices, and institutions, from which numerical rules are generated. The rule guides beings like us, with all these developed resources. It is these that perform the function of ballast, providing the steadiness that we expect in the performance, a curb to whatever impulse there might be to pass from 22 immediately to 44, from 1000 to 1004, or, perhaps sadly, thinking of history, from 1912 to 1920.

Barry Stroud, in a well-known paper on Wittgenstein, commented that the kind of persons supposed by Wittgenstein in examples like this would be "different sorts of beings from us, beings which we could not understand and with which we could not enter into meaningful communication."[1] Strong as this statement is, it appears that it could be stronger. For it appears that the more we try to understand in detail the supposed actions of such beings, the less we succeed. The same fundamental obstacle, namely logical incoherence, that would prevent our communication with such beings prevents our succeeding in imagining them to exist, when we are clear-headed enough to comprehend what we are trying to do. The lesson to be drawn from such illustrations is not skepticism about logical necessity, as some have thought, and not conventionalism. Part of the lesson is the essential soundness of the historical rationalist intuition that at the heart of logical necessity lies the inconceivability of the opposite.

12 The apparent indispensability of the wider aspects of rules to the understanding of subsumptive processes in such abstract and routine contexts, reenforces, to the extent that it is sound, the conclusion already drawn concerning this indispensability to understanding subsumption in contexts that are more concrete and problematic. Inclusion of the wider aspects of rules in the consideration of the more routine and abstract forms of subsumption serves to flesh out and clothe with great philosophical significance the distinction made earlier between the stabilizing and the mutant varieties of reactive effects. The absence of mutant effects in certain broad domains of subsumptive procedure has long served as a key support of the logistic view. And to someone inclined to this view the discrimination of reactive effects which are not mutant may at first seem a merely ad hoc proposal intended to weaken this support. What has been urged about the wider aspects of rules in the

---

[1] "Wittgenstein and Logical Necessity," *The Philosophical Review* 74 (1965): 504–18, rpt. in *Wittgenstein: The Philosophical Investigations*, G. Pitcher, ed. (Notre Dame, Ind.: Notre Dame University Press, 1966), 477–96.

more abstract and routine cases indicates that the stabilizing reactive effects are by no means palliatives invented to shore up a view of subsumption that is challenged by them. Rather, a more understanding view of these cases reveals that the view is not merely not challenged by these cases, but is positively supported by them. Recognition of these aspects, and of reactive effects generally, is no less, though more subtly, necessary to our understanding of what we are doing when we easily apply the rule of mortality to Socrates than it is when we stumble over its application to Elijah. It is no less necessary to our action in proceeding to draw conclusions by *modus ponens*, or through the transitivity of the if-then relation, or, as we often do, in balking at so doing in domains and situations, sometimes very concrete and sometimes highly theoretical, in which the conditions render these procedures seriously problematic.[1]

13 Indispensable to understanding both stability and change in practices, and the warrants for each that are discernible in philosophical reflection, is a recognition that practices are not the abstract inert symbolic entities into which they have often been transmuted by a resolutely linguistic philosophy. Rather, they are, concretely, aspects of life, forms of living thought and action. From the vantage point of a theory couched in these terms one can appreciate more easily the extent of the wider influences to which practices are constantly exposed in their employment, and further, how these same influences constitute resources for philosophical appraisal, when the liability of practices for maintenance or change comes under judgment.[2] A variety of related sources of puzzlement and controversy in modern philosophy change aspects and are illuminated under the inspection of such a theory. Among these are the noted polarities of "is" and "ought," given classic formulation in Hume's *Enquiry Concerning the Principles of Morals*, and the similar more recent polarities of "discovery" and "justification" in the philosophy of science, and of "cause" and "reason" in ethics.[3] Consideration here will be restricted to just one of these, the celebrated "is" and "ought."

---

[1] The converging views of R. Nozick and F. I. Dretske on the matter that Nozick refers to as the "failure of knowledge to be closed under known implication" is a striking example in recent theory of knowledge. See *Philosophical Explanations* (Cambridge, Mass.: Harvard University Press, 1981), 204–11, 869–90.

[2] [Cf. below, ch. 9.—*Ed.*]

[3] [Cf. below, ch. 8.—*Ed.*]

14 The heart of the problem represented by this polarity, put in terms of practices and their appraisal, is one about the relation between accepted practices and their actual or proposed revisions or replacements. This, in the theory of the succession of governmental forms in political science translates into a problem about legitimacy. There is patently some kind of logical gap, some logical disparateness, between what we do in the way of practice and what is set in contrast as what we ought to do instead. How, for example, is it ever possible for one, acting in accordance with a certain practice, and with the authority of that practice, to come to follow and exhibit a form of action that is contrary to the original from which, and on the basis of which, he has proceeded? Such is the Parmenidean conundrum.

15 Of course if we translate this into the favored idiom of logical foundations, of premises, and conclusions erected upon these, deriving their stability from them and therefore weakened by any instability in them, or worse, by any discrepancy between conclusions and them—if we try to rationalize in this manner the passage between premised practice and concluding practice— we shall not succeed. We shall not succeed if we try to assimilate this kind of process to logistic ones: and not because of any internal defect in these latter processes, for, considering the purposes they serve and the manner appropriate to the serving, they would, rather, be imperfect if they did permit the assimilation. The passage of developing practices can however be rationalized when the processes are transferred into another jurisdiction, one in which the purposes of the processes do not call for the suppression of mutative effects, but for a recognition and exploitation of them. Concrete nontechnical illustrations of such processes have been considered in the preceding sections. Here, by way of conclusion, a few brief citations may be made from one particular discipline in which processes of this kind are a major component of the methodology. That discipline is law.

16 Juridical interpretation, especially of items of constitutional law, provide some of the most striking of the readily available instances we have of the defining and mutative effects of reactive subsumption. From the time of John Marshall, for example, the subsumption by the United States Supreme Court of problematic instances under the famous commerce clause of the Federal Constitution giving Congress power "to regulate Commerce ... among the several States..." has repeatedly led to the refashioning of this grant of power. This reactive activity was most pronounced in the fourth and seventh decades of the present century. In the earlier of these periods, after some years of

increasing political friction, a Court that had been attempting to preserve a longtime precedent-honored distinction between "production" and "distribution" in the interpretation of the clause, moved, in a widely celebrated (and bitterly criticized) set of reversals to greatly dissolve this distinction, and with that to affirm the power of Congress to intervene widely and actively in the regulation of the economic life of the nation. A generation later a succeeding generation of judges on the Court effected a similar refashioning of the clause when the clause, as hitherto interpreted, abraded against a rising tide of sentiment in the nation to ensure to all persons, regardless of race certain fundamental rights in public accommodations, employment, and in the possession and use of real property. At the present time the best known of recent juridical reactive subsumptions is perhaps that in which the Court, in another celebrated reversal a decade earlier, employed the equal protection clause of the Fourteenth Amendment of the Constitution to invalidate the practice of regulating attendance of pupils to individual units of the public school system on the grounds of their race. This large quantum movement in the interpretation of this particular clause has so dislodged it from its traditional moorings in legal practice as to stimulate an avalanche of attempted expansion of its application that still continues, and in view of which it is impossible to say with any confidence what it will eventually be when legal interpretation and legislative attempts to influence that interpretation once more reach a state of relative quiescence.[1]

17 In the development of a broad view of ways in which philosophical reflection may be engaged in the criticism and judgment of accepted practices, attention must be paid to processes and effects like these, to the differential effects of success and failure, satisfaction and dissatisfaction in the employment of practices themselves. So long as inattention to these prevails, it will continue to be a serious impediment to the development of an adequate philosophical theory.

[1] [Cf. below, ch. 8.—*Ed.*]

8

Pragmatic Rationality

1   It comes with remarkable regularity in a class at the end of the examination of a piece of legal reasoning, say, a lawyer's brief or a judge's opinion in which the issue addressed is one of law rather than fact and the conclusion seeks to determine what the law actually is in some problematic, debatable case. With care the issues have been identified, likewise the conclusions and the grounds adduced for them. All seems to lie open. And then someone raises a hand to ask, "But *where* is the reasoning?" He (or she, if you prefer) is well aware of all the above-mentioned components in the examined instance. He sees where this argument began, what grounds were adduced for the conclusions drawn, and so on. What he doesn't see is the reasoning itself by which the conclusion is supposed to be elicited from the grounds. How, by *reasoning*, is one supposed to go from the premises of this argument to its conclusion?

What leads the questioner to suppose that the reasoning is yet to be discovered is commonly a preconception, formed by previous philosophical instruction, of what genuine reasoning is. Indeed, the inquirer is here replicating in miniature a large philosophical quandary that has been generated in Western philosophy for centuries by an extensive version of this preconception. The preconception has permeated our language in the form of conventions about what in our performances and achievements we may properly refer to under such names as "reason," "reasoning," "rational," "logic," "logical," and so on.

Before positively characterizing this preconception, one recent feature sometimes attached to it may be briefly noted. This is the requirement of formalizability, namely, that proper reasoning be a procedure assimilable to formal elucidation. Hence the determination of the rationality of any procedure is thought to consist in the demonstration, perhaps by some judicious translation, that it is an instance of a formal rule of logic. These rules, in turn, are normally thought to be ones that stipulate what are and are not proper combinations of certain kinds of linguistic or quasilinguistic entities: predicates, logical particles, sentences (or propositions), and the like. Although in recent years this requirement has been accepted by a considerable number of those attached to the central preconception, that acceptance has been by no means universal. Furthermore, historically and even at the present time, this requirement is of less significance for the broad study of rationality than others.

Perhaps the most important of these requirements is the substantial identification of rational processes with those of argument, of proof. Rational processes are conceived to be forensic or *probative*, not in the sense that they are necessarily directed to achieving certainty, but rather in the sense that they are directed to producing conviction or assent. In the sense that is commonly used in much contemporary philosophy, the processes are justificatory or establishing ones. Implicit in them is the presumption that there are available proper ways of proceeding to determine the adequacy of proposed answers to a variety of questions, and that the task of the reasoner in appraising such an answer is to show to himself and others how, following these ways, it can or cannot be reached.

A second important feature, essential to achievement of their probative aim, is that with respect to accepted practices these processes are essentially *applicative* or subsumptive, rather than generative or defining. The tasks performed in them are ones for which accepted procedures are themselves sufficient, and deviation from them counts as violation. If it can be shown that a proposed result requires such deviation, the result, as arrived at in this process, is invalidated, just as a result in ordinary arithmetic would be invalidated if it required for its production a violation of the rules of multiplication. This applicative employment of accepted means is exhibited strikingly in the kinds of scientific research to which T. S. Kuhn gave the name of "puzzle-solving," that is, research carried on in periods in which what he called "paradigms" of theory and practice are deeply entrenched.[1] As in a puzzle, the pieces out of which the solution of the problem is to be formed are already given. What counts as a piece in the puzzle or a proper step in the solution is not contingent upon what solution is reached. The solution is validated by the pieces and the steps, its validity flows from them, not vice versa. The term "puzzle-solving" is not to be taken as minimizing the difficulty that may be encountered in producing a solution from the given materials. In many cases the task may be very difficult. Great effort and ingenuity may be required to devise a solution from the materials, just as, in a limited way, these are sometimes required to solve the harder problems at the end of the chapter in a textbook of mathematics or physics.

The third and fourth closely related features characterize the central paradigm of argumental reason. The activity in question is conceived primarily to be one *engaged in by individuals*, in their capacity as individuals, and also primarily as one that is *conscious* and intentional. Reason, whether largely a native endowment, as the rationalists conceived it, or an exclusively acquired character, as the more extreme empiricists maintained, is regarded as a feature that is developed in and manifested by individuals, in commerce with other individuals and with themselves. Reasoning of the forensic, probative kind is an activity of individual minds or persons. It is primarily individuals who engage in argument, set out to achieve conviction or settle disputed issues, just as it is primarily individuals who inform, teach, advise, praise and blame themselves and each other. And again, fully developed, model examples of these are activities carried on between individuals knowingly engaged in them, just as it is knowing individuals who make and receive promises, make contracts, put questions, receive answers, make calculations, and so on.

2   It is widely recognized now that intimately related to these argumental processes are others that contrast with them on each of the features just noticed. The processes are ones which in most important ways help to determine the character of the procedures that at any time are accepted as legitimate in the argumental forms. Interest in these processes has been in good part a consequence of the increased acceptance of the view that the first and greatest source of proper procedure in dealing with tasks of the puzzle-solving kind at any given time and in any particular domain of life is a vast store of practices of thought and action, of which individuals arc the benefici-

---

[1] *Structure*, ch. 4.

ary legatees through all the processes of inheritance, both biological and cultural.[1] The collective body of practices is in widespread ways, in various degrees at various places, subject to change, revision, and reconstruction, results characteristically produced in it by discrepancies arising *internally* between component practices, or *externally* between various practices and the conditions of their application.

The philosophical understanding of the processes by which human practices are and may be modified seems to have suffered seriously as a consequence of the philosophical abstraction of the forms of practice embodying rationality from their matrix in life and action, from the isolation and identification of them in some universe of discourse as *universales ante rem*.[2] Whether one views these as ontological, psychological, or linguistic entities is less important than the attempt to understand them as objects having a status independent of the activities they inform and the functions performed by these activities in human life. For example, the shift of attention from the body of forms of practice to more or less successful symbolic transcriptions of them has had the following distorting effects: The components of a calculus or other highly organized symbolic system have a kind of fixity both of individual character and of relation with each other that renders such a system a poor model for investigating certain questions about so loosely organized, untidy, and internally dynamic entity as a body of accepted practices. The components of such a symbolic system, by being organized in the way they are and having the kind of identity conferred upon them in this organization—in short, by being well designed for their primary purpose—are not well designed to represent the kind of modification that forms of activity undergo naturally in use. In particular, as models, they do not illuminate, but rather obscure, both the important *direct* local effect in the control of the character of individual and closely related groups of practices that activity informed by these practices may have, and also the *indirect* effect that modifications produced in this way may have upon more remote components of the total body.[3] Likewise such a model does not represent well the great variety in degrees of inertia and mobility that is one of the striking features of the components of a body of procedures. The effect of viewing systems of practice through the lenses of systems of linguistic and other syntactic entities

---

[1] [Cf. above, chs. 4–6.—*Ed.*]

[2] [Cf. above, chs. 4, 7.—*Ed.*]

[3] [Cf. chs. 4, 5, 7, 9.—*Ed.*]

is a strong reenforcement of a tendency among philosophical observers, springing from a variety of sources, to conceive of these as bound together in a highly totalitarian organization.[1] And when, while viewing these systems in this fashion, one wishes to take account of the effect of practice in the determination of their character, one will naturally be led to conceive this effect in a similarly totalitarian manner.

The consequences of overemphasis upon the effects of use in producing global changes, and of neglect of the local but less dramatic ones, are pronounced in recent philosophy. Global modifications—changes of "logical frameworks," of whole "conceptual schemes" or systems of practice—viewed as single steps, or as massive alternatives confronting human choice, are, in an extreme way, whether in individuals or in groups, resistant to direct reflective, deliberate determination. Concentration upon these global modifications, and neglect of those of a more modest kind, has helped to segregate *generally* the processes by which procedures are determined by use, and to ascribe to them all generally, as thus segregated, the kind of insusceptibility to reflective scrutiny and control that would be ascribable only if that scrutiny and control were attempted always and necessarily on some extremely massive scale, only if the processes were those effecting in single, giant, revolutionary steps the displacement of whole systematic codes of procedure.[2]

3   Some very different, more modest processes of modification come into view when one concentrates upon concrete human practices as they are realized in human thought and action, where they are generated and through which from time to time they are in various degrees modified. Rather than primarily probative and, in consequence, applicative, these modifying processes are primarily *generative* and *definitive* (the latter term being used, of course, in the sense of "defining" that does not imply finality).

---

[1] [Cf. above, ch. 5, regarding the "Coherence Illusion."—*Ed.*]

[2] Such was the effect of three influential recent writers whose exploration of the pragmatic aspects of knowledge came in connection with interest in and exploration of large-scale, abstract symbolic systems. C. I. Lewis, *Mind and the World Order* (1929; 2d rev. ed. New York: Dover, 1956); Rudolf Carnap, "Empiricism, Semantics, and Ontology," *Revue International de Philosophie* 4 (1950): 20–40, *The Continuum of Inductive Methods* (Chicago: University of Chicago Press, 1952), "Replies and Systematic Expositions," in *The Philosophy of Rudolf Carnap*, P. A. Schilpp, ed. (Library of Living Philosophers: 1963), 859–1013; W. V. Quine, *Word and Object* (Cambridge, Mass.: MIT Press, 1960), *Ontological Relativity*.

However ill-designed were the methods with which a variety of post-Humean philosophers tried to deal with them, it was these processes that they had to deal with in that part of their philosophy commonly referred to as dealing with "induction." Similarly it is the processes fitting the model of argumentation that during this same period have commonly been referred to under the title of "deduction." By this time, however, centuries of usage under empiricist presumptions have so strongly marked the term "induction" as to render it unsuitable as a general name for the processes in question. Over the years since Bacon, through Hume and Mill, a particular way of conceiving the generative, definitive processes has come to displace the more general ones in the connotation of this term.

The confining and distorting presuppositions about the character of these processes which the term "inductive" now commonly conveys have prompted the substitution for it in this paper of the term "pragmatic."[1] This latter term, introduced into general use by C. S. Peirce, serves better to mark off the generally generative and definitive processes that are of primary interest here from the fundamentally applicative ones to which the term "deductive" still seems fairly adequately to apply.

Pragmatic processes employ practices in such a way as not only to derive certain results through their application, but also, in deriving these results, to mold and accredit the practices, and, of course, sometimes to *dis*credit them. Here these processes diverge widely from the puzzle-solving deductive ones. Not all the pieces of *this* "puzzle" are given antecedent to the process. Rather it is only when this kind of puzzle is solved, and as a consequence of the solution, that what are the pieces and what are the rules of their employment are for this particular puzzle finally determined.

The processes by which both the habits of individuals and the customs of groups are modified are of course *by no means always, nor even paradigmatically*, conscious, deliberate, or knowing ones. These processes are constantly on-going, and though sometimes the changes are effected under careful scrutiny and direction, sometimes they occur at or beyond the penumbra of consciousness. Both individuals and groups may be taken by surprise at ways, sometimes considerable ways, in which their modes of proceeding have altered without their notice. With some shock a man who was once a model of scrupulous personal grooming may be led to discover that he now pays

---

[1] The character and sources of these presuppositions were elaborated by the present writer in ch. 2, "The Shaping of the Problem," of *Induction and Justification*.

much less attention to such concerns than he recently did and had continued to suppose that he did. Similarly a religious congregation once adamant concerning points of dogmatic theology may be surprised by a recognition that in a relatively uneventful and inconspicuous way the position of these traditional goods in its order of values has been substantially altered. Furthermore, as the above comments already indicate, these processes of modification, especially those that occur outside the reaches of consciousness, are primarily *social* ones, that is, ones that occur primarily in groups, and occur in individuals primarily because and in so far as they are members of communities sharing these practices and the effects of communal change in them.[1] Because the practices followed by individuals vary widely in their social character, the processes by which practices are modified likewise vary widely in this respect. The social character of these processes is especially prominent in the cognitive practices that are constitutive of modern science and modern scientific technology, and also in the domains of moral, political, and legal thought and action, as well as in the subdomains of religious practice that are commonly referred to as "organized religion."[2]

A realistic view comprehending both these two kinds of process must reflect prominently that there is no sharp line dividing these two kinds from each other. Normally they occur together. Normally pragmatic modification of practices occurs in conjunction with their employment in broadly deductive ways, in consequence of results derived in this employment. The guides to pragmatic modifications of the accepted modes of procedure that we constantly exploit in deductive practice emerge from that practice.[3] Pragmatic processes may be thought of as ones through which the broad organon of deductive practice alters itself. Yet, since an essential part of this process by which pragmatic modifications are produced lies in the generation through them, under deductive exploitation, of certain results, it may likewise be said that deductive processes are ones through which these modifications are produced. Rather than quite independent kinds of process, these two contrasting ones are in actual thought and action closely intertwined in many complex as well as simple ways. They ordinarily represent two aspects of

---

[1] [Cf. ch. 6 above.—*Ed.*]

[2] Further exposition of the positive character of the pragmatic processes is given by the present writer [above, in ch. 4—*Ed.*]. The topic of realism in connection with these processes is treated in [ch. 5 above—*Ed.*].

[3] [Cf. above, ch. 7.—*Ed.*]

what we do as we live, think, and act according to accepted practices, rather than two altogether ways of different doing.

4   In use, practices from time to time, for a variety of reasons, and in various degrees, falter and fail, providing stimulus and grounds for change. And as a result of their corporate character, changes generated or coming to be generated in one set have impacts upon others, including sometimes responsive changes and sometimes defensive dispositions to resist change. Sets of practices have to be accommodated to each other. Stress, abrasion, and confusion generated among them provide motives for this accommodation, the kind of motive which Hegel referred to as the "tremendous power [*ungeheure Macht*] of the negative."[1] What may appear in its local environment as merely faltering, failure, or confusion in certain readily formalizable procedures, in a larger context may be revealed to play a most important positive role. The faltering, failing, and confusion may provide not only motivation for revision of these procedures, but also indications of the general location where revision is called for and the general direction the revision should take. Some of the perplexity in the debate that flourished briefly a short time ago on the question whether there is a logic of discovery was due to the fact that, on the affirmative side, there was an intuitive recognition that the activities in which new views in science and elsewhere are generated and formed abundantly exhibit responses to reasons, grounds, considerations, and are hence of a generally rational character. Yet, on the negative side, it seemed clear that these activities cannot be made to fit into the model which the term "logic" suggests to many, namely, a theory of reason constructed exclusively on the model of deductive processes.

The processes by which practices are modified on a wide social and historical scale, which extend far beyond the activities of one individual and often embrace generations of those who employ these practices, are also replicated to some extent in miniature in the lives and activities of single individuals. There, *in fore interno*, individuals who are reflective may become intimately aware of the processes in which, out of the abrasion, conflict, and confusion of competing modes of activity—all of them settled features of one's character—modifications, adjustments, accommodations of these are effected, some of them highly rational and some much less so, and some of

---

[1] *Phenomenology of Spirit*, A. V. Miller, tran. (Oxford: Clarendon, 1977), Preface, ¶38.

such magnitude as to amount to Gestalt-shifts in the characters in which they occur. A familiar example of pragmatic processes operating at an individual level is that by which in elementary mathematics we lead a student to recapitulate the evolution, accomplished by our ancestors with extreme travail, of the concept of number from that of whole numbers, to those supplemented by zero, then fractions, then roots, including the irrationals and the imaginary numbers, and so on. Each of the large steps just referred to in the development of the theory were made in history, and are recapitulated in the indoctrination of individuals, by a procedure that entails some change in the basic concept of number itself and hence in basic premises employed in reasoning about numbers. At each stage in the historical development there were reasons both for and against these changes, though some obliviousness to the latter is a natural and normally serviceable consequence of custom to the deeply entrenched theory. Likewise in physics, it was not by thinking restricted to employing mechanical models of the sort favored and effectively used by Lord Kelvin that we have come or could have come to understand the partly particulate and partly undulatory behavior of what we discriminate as photons, protons, and electrons, in response to which, over time, there has been an alteration in the concept of a particle and in premises employing this term in reasoning in the subatomic domain. Closely similar pragmatic processes are exemplified in various activities directed to the determination of the law in types of ease in which significant indeterminacy at some point needs to be reduced. Examples would be the various processes of thought and action, of individuals and other agencies, through which a corporate body like that of the modern nation-state continually defines key provisions of its constitutional law, such as the provision of the United States Constitution that no state "shall deny to any person within its jurisdiction the equal protection of the laws." Does or does not this clause, as the courts of the United States have been called upon to determine during the past decade, forbid racially discriminatory entrance qualifications at a medical college (University of California), tolerate similar qualifications for promotion among employees of a large industrial corporation (Kaiser Aluminum), and require racially determined assignment of pupils and teachers in the public schools of large cities like Boston, Chicago, and St. Louis? Deductive elaboration of legal formulae is without question an important facet of the whole process of legal determination in such eases. But it is no more sufficient by itself in these than it is to determine whether birth control or abortion (even in cases of rape or incest) violates the Mosaic commandment "Thou shalt not kill." What can be soundly based on the key formula in these constitutional cases depends upon the significance of the formula in United States constitutional law. And this is itself something dependent upon, that reflects in its own character, complex social processes through which over time—sometimes slowly and sometimes rapidly, sometimes reflectively and sometimes with remarkably little conscious thought—the very conceptions of equal protection of the law, and of persons entitled to this protection, undergo revision.[1]

5   To an audience less captivated by the deductive forms of rationality Hume's proclamation that custom is the great guide of life could have been taken as a signal for the expansion of the study of "human understanding" to include the processes by which, in both individuals and groups, custom is preserved and altered, reformed, refined, and of course also weakened and corrupted. But with most philosophers of Hume's and later centuries the increasing prominence of these processes has had an altogether contrary effect. Repeatedly, because these processes are not tractable to the same kind of investigation and analysis as the deductive ones, they have been judged to be intractable generally to rational reconstruction and reformation. And because the processes do play central roles at various places in vast domains of life and thought, these domains have themselves been concluded to be at these places of impingement on principle and hence necessarily beyond the reach of rational criticism and control.

Philosophers against whose vocation the tyranny of particular methods is a cardinal sin, have in this connection displayed an outstanding susceptibility to this very intellectual weakness, and to the narrowness in investigation which it promotes. Commenting upon this weakness in investigation in the philosophy of mathematics, I. Lakatos in 1963 drew a satirical analogy that can easily be applied more generally. Opposing the limitation of investigation in the philosophy of mathematics to what can be achieved by formal techniques carried on in metamathematics, and objecting to the contention of A. Tarski that only those deductive systems which are strictly formalized are suitable as objects of scientific investigation, Lakatos wrote:

> Nobody will doubt that some problems about a mathematical theory can only be approached after it has been formalised, just as some problems about human beings (say concerning their anatomy) can only be approached after their death. But few will infer from this that human beings are "suitable for scientific investigation" only when they are "presented in 'dead' form," and

---

[1] [Cf. below, ch. 9.—*Ed.*]

that biological investigations are confined in consequence to the discussion of dead human beings—although I should not be surprised if some enthusiastic pupil of Vesalius in those glorious days of early anatomy, when the powerful new method of dissection emerged, had identified biology with the analysis of dead bodies.[1]

So strong is the general deductivist predisposition in Western philosophy, particularly in its English and American branches, that little is accomplished by securing abstract, general assent on the part of those affected by it that the philosophical study of rational processes must be expanded to include the pragmatic processes by which deductive practices are modified. Those who by teaching and long intellectual habit are prepared to recognize as rational only those processes having the general form of argument, of ratiocination, naturally interpret their assent as directed to processes that may plausibly be conceived as exemplifying this form, however rudimentary, imperfect, or covert these exemplifications must be conceded to be. Preconceptions about form and method prevent their recognition of the very processes to which their assent should lead them. Thus, as the analogy of Lakatos suggests, a general, abstract endorsement of the study of pragmatic processes is quickly transformed into a study of deductive ones. What is studied is not pragmatic processes as they are, but such as they would be if they were a variant, hitherto little understood form of deductive process, hence ones that with some nonessential alterations can be made to fit the model of deductive (i.e., argumental, applicative, deliberative, and individual) reasoning. Standing in the way of a rectification of the situation are methodological commitments arising from deep philosophical preconceptions about what rational procedure in general must be, preconceptions that effectively obscure the possibility that the source of failure lies less in the processes under investigation than in the means by which the investigation is carried out. In concluding this paper, the next three sections will endeavor to support this assessment by briefly considering some closely related quandaries generated by these preconceptions in three different areas of contemporary philosophical study. The light shed upon these and similar quandaries is one of the major dividends and supports of the general philosophical view from which the assessment springs.

---

[1] "Proofs and Refutations," *British Journal for the Philosophy of Science* 14 (1963), (rpt. Cambridge: Cambridge University Press 1976), 3 note 3.

6   *Agnosticism in science.* The well-worn quandary bequeathed to us by Hume concerning cause, uniformity, and induction surely needs no elaboration here. In both the *Treatise* and the first *Enquiry* Hume first leads us to follow him in adopting that celebrated persuasive definition that identifies rational processes with deductive ones (fitting the Descartes-Locke formula of intuition and demonstration), then easily springs the trap binding us to the admission that an entire class of processes that we previously had regarded as reasoning from experience can no longer be so regarded. Many in the present day who would be unmoved by so simple a version of deductivist agnosticism are susceptible to other versions that in essentials, though not in stark simplicity, replicate the familiar Humean moves.

By far the most notable contemporary version of this scientific agnosticism is that generated by Kuhn out of a comparable distinction between normal and revolutionary forms of science. Much more important than the rejection of Hume's simple deductivism, in Kuhn's view of the scientific enterprise, is the more complex and subtle deductivism embodied in the fairly standard midcentury positivist view of rational processes as being exhaustively "logic and experiment."[1] By this formula, sometimes also put as "logic and neutral experience," are excluded from the domain of normal science and of scientific "proof" all the many and various unruly processes by which the forms of thought and action, including broad categories of thought and paradigmatic scientific procedures, are molded and modified through time, by individuals and groups, and under great variations of degrees of reflective consciousness.

When, in setting out to appraise the claims to acceptance of any pattern of scientific procedure, one first excludes all these processes from consideration and seeks a form of "proof" altogether separate and independent of them, one has surely set for oneself another trap. From the confines of this trap one will eventually be obliged to report that "proof" in such matters is impossible, that custom—smoothly in some cases, turbulently in others—is the great guide of life. When experience, or experiment, as a component of scientific reason is conceived to be pure in the sense that it functions quite independently of these processes, it will be possible to show quickly that, whether a state of quite virgin purity can ever be attained, the closer that state is approximated, as Kant taught long ago, the less capable the experience, or experiment, in question becomes to perform any proving function

---

[1] *Structure*, 93, 149.

with respect either to already accepted practices or to proposed candidates for such acceptance. In relation to such experience or experiment, linguistic practices will be in principle "underdetermined," and fundamental indeterminacy of "logical frameworks" and "conceptual schemes" irreducible. More insidiously, within logical frameworks and conceptual schemes themselves the links of logical necessity will be loosened in a disturbing way. Though we may have thought that it is by freeing logical forms from dependence upon broad social practices that pure, absolutely binding logical necessity in them may be discussed, we have now strong reasons, uncovered by Wittgenstein, to suppose that utter separation from these forms ensures not a strengthening and clarification of them, but their dissolution.[1]

Many years ago, in their general program of bringing Hegel to the masses, Marx and Engels called upon their readers to recognize the great extent to which our ideas are molded by the complex social processes through which our lives are lived. Although their own elaboration of this point was distorted by various influences, among them a reaction against some features of the original Hegelian philosophy, the central point remains a sound one. And one who has absorbed it will be aided greatly in understanding some of the philosophical quandaries concerning the irreducible indeterminacy of conceptual frameworks, conceptual schemes, linguistic systems, and cognitive paradigms that have proved so vexatious to many in contemporary philosophy of science and in the philosophy of knowledge generally. At the heart of these quandaries careful inspection reveals again an abstraction of intellectual forms from their roots in human life, and a correlated propensity to raise questions about the possible governance of modifications of these forms in isolation from, in a studied lack of consideration of, the ways in which they are actually generated in human practice and modified in use.

7   *Legal Realism.* There are many areas of life and thought in which agnosticism of the sort that levels in one deflationary sweep whatever does not fit the deduction paradigm, has little practical effect. In such cases, to use Hume's words, our nature is "too strong for principle," and whatever doubts might have been generated in us by the skeptical arguments are dissipated by "the first and most trivial event in life."

---

[1] [Cf. above, ch. 7.—*Ed.*]

Our nature's being too strong to be completely overborne by "principle," however, does not prevent its being affected by that principle, and sometimes in very serious ways. Thus philosophical doctrines that on principle exclude from the study of rational processes those by which ideas, and procedures implementing these ideas, are modified in practice have seriously affected both the study of juridical interpretation and the juridical decisions in which these interpretations are applied. Years ago, in the opening pages of his *Introduction to Legal Reasoning*, E. H. Levi briefly struggled with the quandary of how the processes of legal interpretation to which his monograph was directed and which deviate so markedly from deductive models could be legitimately given the title of "reasoning." Putting aside the "pretense" that "the law is a system of known rules applied by a judge," Levi argued that in legal interpretation the rules are not so much known and then applied, as coming to be known as they are applied. A most important kind of legal interpretation is one in which the rule that is interpreted is forged and hence modified in the interpretation, in which the classification system employed in the rule undergoes change as the interpretation proceeds. The prominence of this aspect of some forms of legal interpretation suggested the question whether they qualify as reasoning at all. A negative answer to this suggestion Levi reflectively rejected. "Reasoning appears to be involved," he wrote. "The conclusion is arrived at through a process and was not immediately apparent. It seems better to say there is reasoning, but it is imperfect."[1]

The major question is not whether "there is reasoning" of some sort, somewhere in the juridical process in which laws are interpreted and applied to particular and sometimes very puzzling cases. Much more sharply defined than this, it is a question raised by the features of this juridical process that deviate from the deductive model of reasoning. It is essentially a question about those cases in which, in order to make a definite determination whether some putative instance does or does not fall under the rule, the rule has to be further defined in such a way as to undergo definite modification.

Consider, for example, one question to which the United States Supreme Court addressed itself in 1954 concerning the equal protection clause of the constitution mentioned above. Does the rule that no state shall deny to any person within its jurisdiction equal protection of the laws forbid public school authorities in the states assigning pupils to their schools in such a way as

---

[1] E. H. Levi, *Introduction to Legal Reasoning* (Chicago: University of Chicago Press, 1948), 1–4, 8.

intentionally to preserve racial segregation in these schools? Of course, if the prescription of equal protection is taken in a certain way, if equality is measured in such a way that the "separate" of segregation entails "inequality," then a valid deductive conclusion will be that the segregation in question violates the prescription. But this interpretation of equality could be and was contested on constitutional grounds, just as it could be and was advocated on such grounds. The situation in constitutional law in the United States at mid-century was that either decision on the separate-entails-unequal issue would itself entail some alteration in the law, if for no other reason, because the law was seriously equivocal and contradictory on the matter. Reduction of the indeterminacy and contradiction in what may be called the law of equality embodied in the Fourteenth Amendment of the Constitution required a thorough consideration of the significance of the key provisions of this Amendment in American law, the function that these provisions had come to perform in the law of the country, and the grounds for this in American life: in morals and politics as well as in strictly legal practice.

As reflective activity of this kind, effecting modification and adjustment, does not fit the model of deduction, those exclusively preoccupied with this model do not find in this activity an exemplification of rationality, and judge those who urge otherwise to be possible victims of, and certainly propagators of, an illusion. When deviations from the deductive model are seen to be deviations from the path of reason, and yet such deviations in the form of responses to moral, political, and economic considerations are seen to be inevitable, the main tenets are available for a view that legal interpretation in such controversial cases is determined necessarily and fundamentally by processes that cannot be defended as rational. Such a view of necessary direct action on the part of judges in their function of defining the law was widely propounded in the fourth decade of this century in the United States under the name of "legal realism," and has remained an important strand of American jurisprudence to this day.

As the effect of deductivism in Hume was to erase the line between science and superstition in matters of fact, so the effect in legal realism was to erase the line between legitimate and illegitimate practice in all those cases of juridical judgment in which the definition of the law was made on political, moral, economic, and other wide social grounds. If any interpretation that is determined in any substantial degree by political or moral considerations *of any sort* has thereby forfeited its claims to be a reasoned interpretation, then scruples about such considerations may be forgotten. If the distinction between a wise, informed response to moral considerations, and the blindest subservience to personal, partisan, or class moral imperatives is thought to be dissolved upon the basis of profound philosophical theory, dissolved also is the obligation and motivation in juridical practice to keep arduously to the former and resist the often great seduction of the latter. The record through the years of all too many juridical decisions traceable to political, economic, racial, and religious prejudice counsels caution in the acceptance of a philosophical view which has among others this effect upon its adherents: that the barriers against juridical prejudice, often enough difficult to discern, are rendered quite invisible.

In a recent comment upon the jurisprudence of W. O. Douglas, Ronald Dworkin dealt in a somewhat different way from that followed here with the narrow view of reason employed by the adherents of legal realism in deprecating the rational pretensions of juridical decisions.[1] A decision guided by reason, as the realists used this term, was, as Dworkin puts it, one "logically compelled by prior legal doctrine whose content all reasonable men must recognize on pain of contradiction and which was, in that sense, there for reason to discover." Quite rightly the realists insisted that "few, if any, important judicial decisions could be said to be entirely guided by reason in that sense." Rather, important juridical decisions such as those in which the Supreme Court moves to interpret the broad and abstract provisions of the Bill of Rights, require for their justification appeals "to some consideration of justice or fairness or policy which ... [is] not a matter of logic and with which all competent lawyers would not in fact agree." With "based on reason" given so narrow a construal as to exclude such appeals, the legal realists, in the manner of Hume, assigned these appeals to categories that this exclusion seemed to require, namely, "emotion" and "inclination." Even at the hands of so masterful a philosopher as Hume, dichotomies like this, between reason and emotion (Hume's term was "the passions") turned out to be seriously misleading and, in the end, mischief-making. All the processes that in this present paper have been marked off and emphasized under the title of "pragmatic" now appear under the curious title of "emotive." "Most rules of law," Dworkin continues, "are to some degree indeterminate in their application, and often require 'interpretation' that ... [according to this inapt terminology] depends upon emotion." Incautious use of such terminology,

---

[1] "Dissent on Douglas," *The New York Review of Books* (February 19, 1981): 3–8.

with which it was most difficult to preserve caution, easily led to such disastrous results as the suggestion

> that no important distinctions needed to be drawn within the large class of reasons that judges might have for a judicial decision that clearly went beyond binding legal precedents. There was no important difference, for example, between the argument that a decision was right because it was required by some general theory about fundamental political rights that could be defended both in the abstract and as tested against hypothetical counter-examples, and the cruder argument that the decision was right because it seemed appealing either to the community as a whole or to the judge in particular. The choice of such arguments was an "emotional" one and not much more needed to be said.
>
> That refusal to countenance obvious distinctions suggested, in turn, a particularly deadening form of moral skepticism—dark, unexamined, but carried in the vocabulary of legal realism as that apparently enlightened philosophy spread through American law schools. It was, I am afraid, left behind there, in the walls, even when later generations of law teachers and students finally and decisively rejected the less dangerous because more patently absurd idea that law is a matter of what the judge had for breakfast.

The effects of such doctrine upon the jurisprudence embodied in the opinions of Justice W. O. Douglas were in Dworkin's judgment serious and debilitating. During his career on the Supreme Court Douglas came, as Dworkin portrays him, to believe with some intensity and act upon "the idea of moral rights distinct from and often opposed to the will of the majority." This commitment to moral rights presupposes that a certain degree of objectivity is attainable in moral and legal judgment that is incompatible with the view, central to legal realism, that such commitments in legal matters on the part of any judge have "no more independent objective validity than his tastes in food and drink." Maintaining a commitment to moral rights that could not be squared with his "realist" philosophy, Douglas was rendered incapable by the lingering effects of this philosophy of providing a clear and coherent defense of the commitment in his legal opinions.

In a brief published comment upon this article, Warren Lehman of the University of Wisconsin Law School echoed and confirmed Dworkin's fears of the skepticism and cynicism about the juridical process that a philosophy of this kind generates. "It would be hard, I suspect," wrote Lehman, "to get through an American law school today without getting the impression that the law is merely an excuse for policy. The law is how policy is mystified. That kind of cynicism is ... only the latest of the bad consequences of realism."[1]

During its flourishing years of the late forties and the fifties this realism was accompanied by a view in moral philosophy that drew analogous skeptical conclusions about moral judgment. As with legal realism, the popular "emotivism" of this period seemed to gain considerable illicit plausibility from an indiscriminate use of the category of *emotion* to cover whatever forms of judgment could not be assimilated to a narrow paradigm of what rational or "cognitive" judgments must be. And, as with legal realism, a great part of this plausibility seemed to ebb when it became obvious to its twentieth-century advocates that the conflation of such extremely diverse elements under the title of "emotion" would have to be supplemented with a recognition of the highly diverse character of the elements that were being referred to under the common title. By the sixth decade of this century, when moral advocacy in both the courts and the academy was in flood, a skeptical view of moral judgment, however titillating it had been to an earlier generation and however useful as an instrument of attack against features of established morals that present generations wished to oppose, quickly displayed its essential incapacity to serve as a platform upon which moral advocacy of any kind could be consistently, successfully rationalized. Throngs of youths loudly proclaiming the moral sovereignty of their self-described "gut feelings" were possibly a stimulus to some academic observers to reexamine the claims of that moral reasoning of which they had hitherto on philosophical principle been deeply suspicious.

8   *Moral Intuitionism.* Throughout this century a somewhat less skeptical, but still uneasy view of moral judgment has been taken by various writers in whose moral philosophy intuition has come to play a role somewhat similar to that of emotion in legal realism. In two papers on intuitionism presented to the Aristotelian Society a few years ago by D. O. Raphael and J. O. Urmson, these two noted and able British philosophers found themselves somewhat unhappily driven to accept the fundamental thesis of intuitionism concerning the considerable degree to which the irreducible plurality of moral principles generates moral conflict in practice, conflicts which in spite of the contrary claims of a variety of writers, we cannot hope to settle merely by

---

[1] *New York Review of Books* (May 28, 1981): 52.

the application of some rule or set of rules.[1] It appears that the existentialists are right, Raphael held, as against views like that of the utilitarians and
Rawls, that in many cases of deep moral conflict between two contending
courses of action on the part of individuals or social groups, "it cannot be
correct to say that one policy is objectively right and the other objectively
wrong" (12E). Nevertheless, contrary to the arbitrariness emphasized by the
existentialists, there must be some rationale applicable to such decisions. For
often in them there is an appeal to reasons; the decision is preceded by
deliberation; and, it is possible sometimes, looking back upon former decisions of this kind to say that they were mistaken (12A–12B). These processes
fit the categories of neither deduction nor induction; they "cannot be fitted to
a precise formula"; perhaps they should be classified as forms "of 'rhetorical'
reasoning, such as goes on in debate, and notably in juridical debate ...
[since] it is notorious that one cannot give a precise form to the alleged logic
of rhetorical reasoning," nor can one say of such debate and deliberation that
they are "altogether irrational or non-rational" (12D).

On the same topic Urmson wrote that while it is "theoretically possible
to have a set of first principles, or primary reasons, with the decision-proced-
ure which intuitionism lacks," and while he would rejoice if such a procedure
were discovered, he is inclined to believe that the discovery of such a
procedure is effectively precluded by the recurring strain and disharmony
which one must acknowledge among moral principles (116, 119). There is in
moral decision making an unavoidable need for an intuitive weighing and
judgment of reasons for and against competing alternatives. Yet, far from
anomalous is our situation in this respect. It is "our ordinary predicament
with regard to reasons in most fields," readily exemplified in the normal
procedures by which we weigh evidence in issues of rational belief, or
appraise the relative prudence of alternative courses of practical action (119,
117). In view of this, Urmson found the conclusion of the intuitionist moral
philosophers that there is no substitute for the intuitive weighing up of
reasons in situations of moral conflict to be "neither surprising nor unduly
distressing" (119).

There is some coincidence between Raphael's insistence that certain
processes sometimes pejoratively characterized as "intuitive" are not thereby

---

[1] D. D. Raphael, "The Standard of Morals" and "Appendix" to "The Standard
of Morals," and J. O. Urmson, "A Defense of Intuitionism," both in *Proceedings of
the Aristotelian Society* 75 (1975): 1–12, 12A–12E, 111–19.

excluded from the scope of rationality, and the insistence in the present paper upon the inclusion in the investigation of processes relevant to rationality, not merely those exemplifying accepted practices, but also those less ruly ones by which these practices are modified. All these have been included here under the broad character of pragmatic. There is likewise some coincidence with Urmson's insistence upon the recognition of situations of conflict in morals, as widely in other fields, for which there are no available more or less routine means of decision making and which, if they are to be handled reflectively, require recourse to some kind of intuitive weighing up of reasons.

There is, nevertheless, a great difference between a defensive, grudging admission of the insufficiency of routine application of accepted practices to provide guidance for thought and action, in certain situations, and a positive recognition of the distinctive functions in life and thought that alternative pragmatic processes perform. The concession that these processes can have some rationality about them, perhaps of a rhetorical kind such as is exemplified in debate, and hence "are not altogether irrational or non-rational" (Raphael), seems to testify by its meagerness to the strength of the deductivist model of rationality from which it represents a small divergence. Similar lingering effects of a deductivist model of rationality are apparently discernible in Urmson's comments, despite the eminent realism of his judgment that the need to employ nondeductive procedures in moral decision making should not be regarded as "scandalous" or an "irrational" anomaly, since this is "our ordinary predicament with regard to reasons in most fields." But if ordinary, why regard our situation in this regard as a predicament? And why view the conceivable though unlikely discovery of a credible decision procedure for moral questions as an occasion for joy? Thus, gratified at first by this much divergence from the general deductive model, one is struck upon reflection by the distance by which it falls short of a thorough-going recognition of the vital testing, controlling, modifying, and reconstructive functions performed generally in life and thought by indispensable nondeductive processes.

9 This chapter began with a notice of a difficulty encountered by students with minds so captured by the paradigm of deduction that they cannot discern reasoning in nondeductive processes of thought and action, though it is before them in plain sight. It ends with a notice of some of their teachers manfully struggling to extricate themselves from the grip of the same paradigm.

In the present philosophical climate of opinion the distinctive character, contributions, and virtues of pragmatic processes need to be more widely and explicitly, and less regretfully recognized. The disposition to recognize as rational only those forms of activity that are distinctively probative, applicative, individual, and deliberate is strong among those whose business it is to illuminate rational activity in its various manifestations, with the natural result that the predominantly generative, definitive, social, and nondeliberate forms suffer philosophical neglect. Furthermore, since these latter forms are implicated in the constitution and regulation of deductive processes themselves, a result of the neglect is that the processes of constitution and regulation are, on a wide scale, less examined and enlightened than they might otherwise be.

It has been emphasized that pragmatic processes are by no means contrary to deductive ones, are rather supplementary to them, as conversely the deductive ones are likewise supplementary to pragmatic ones. Better understanding of this situation and greater capacity to take advantage of it wait upon, as a first step, a far broader and deeper understanding of pragmatic processes than we have so far achieved, an understanding embracing both their distinctive characteristics and their characteristic virtues and failings.[1]

Again and again, in the philosophical scrutiny of various domains of human life and thought—scientific, political, legal, moral, and religious—we face situations in which what is needed is not finer, more assiduous application of accepted practices, but some critical examination and revision of practices themselves. In such situations philosophical preoccupation with applicative or subsumptive processes tends to shield these practices from the modifying ones, to significantly obscure their effect.[2] In extreme cases this preoccupation may serve to entrench practices toward which sharp skepticism is needed, to harden into dogma principles of thought and action that may be ripe for intellectual solution, to promote inflexibility where flexibility instead is imperative. A philosophical theory like any other theory may miscarry. So, one designed with the purpose of illuminating and improving performance in the rational scrutiny and governance of individual and social practices, may, in serious ways, through neglect of some important facets of this practice, defeat the ends it was designed to serve.[3]

---

[1] [Cf. chs. 7, 9.—*Ed.*]

[2] [Cf. above, chs. 4, 5.—*Ed.*]

[3] I wish here to acknowledge my indebtedness to my colleagues David S. Shwayder and Robert G. Wengert, who gave me valuable comments upon an earlier attempt to deal with this subject.

9

Philosophic Governance of Norms

ABSTRACT. Norms are widely regarded as kinds of templates (mental, physical, or otherwise) of performance, resident in agents. As such they are thought to determine unilaterally what kinds of thought or action accord with them. Under philosophical elaboration this view has led to multiple perplexities: among them the question of how there can be evaluation, justification, and rectification of such unilaterally determining entities. Sometimes one can appeal to other, supervening norms; but the need to terminate the regressive procedure typically leads to appeals to dubious "foundations," to conventions, to "intuitions," or to sheer prejudice.

In a feat of surpassing acuity Wittgenstein exposed this view of norms to be inadequate in the apparently paradigm contexts to which traditionally it seemed best suited, these being those of mathematical rules and principles. An alternative general view of norms is one with important congruences with the view taken by the Critical *cum* Pragmatic philosophy concerning the constitutive role played by norms in creating the texture of human life and thought. This view is that norms are intrinsically socio-psychological entities that interlock with each other and are rooted deeply in the practices of individuals and their communities. Embedded in these practices, norms are in principle open-textured: open to further definition and revision when serious anomalies in their extant forms are encountered.

This article explores certain features of the alternative view, concentrating upon the illumination it sheds and the guidance it provides in the conduct of the fundamental philosophical activities of assessment, criticism, and revision of broad and deep personal and communal norms.

TOPICAL OUTLINE

§§1–6   Rules and norms. Acting in accordance with a norm. The occasion-response connection view of what a norm is. This identifies the norm with what may be called its "manifest aspect." How the view is incorporated in the template view of the relation between the norm and action according to it.

§§7–11   Wittgenstein's exposure of serious weaknesses in the template view of a domain in which its application has seemed apt and secure, namely, mathematics. Implicit in Wittgenstein's criticisms is the suggestion of the importance of the "latent" aspect of norms. This aspect is indispensable for understanding logical necessity.

§§12–14   In a similar way appreciation of the latent aspect of norms is indispensable for understanding philosophical scrutiny of them. With a radical alteration of our view of norms themselves comes a similar and illuminating alteration of our view of their scrutiny.

§§15–17   Conceived as sociopsychological entities norms are *active* rather than inert: alive in relation to other norms and to those aspects of life that they together more or less collectively inform. Correspondingly, in relation both to the conditions of their application and to their prescriptions of response, norms are intrinsically to some degree *open*, rather than closed.

          With respect to the degree that either one of these two characters (liveness; openness) is realized in them, there are wide differences among norms.

§18   There are also wide differences in the degrees of tightness in which norms are *bound together* in Gestalten, in consequence of which these more or less coherent bodies of them may be said to articulate some large or small sphere of human activity, practice, life.

          In the process of articulating spheres of human life norms *undergo alteration*, singly and in groups, as the bodies of life that they themselves have helped to make possible themselves undergo change.

§19   The four features of the aspect of norms just specified are important for understanding the critical scrutiny of them that philosophical understanding can provide. For these features, in combination with the manifest content, largely provide the motives and resources for the determination of norms.

§20   The basis of an evaluative judgment concerning a norm lies in the norm evaluated, in its combined manifest and latent aspects.

§21   The view advanced here is a version of naturalism, but—and this is most important to note—it is very different from scientific or positivist versions of this general view.

§22   Also worth noting is the influence of these latter versions in generating with respect to norms the great Problem of Evaluation.

§23   The avoidance of this familiar philosophic quandary requires no minor revision, but rather thorough reconstruction of our conception of norms.

§24   A norm, comprising both its manifest and its latent aspects, is a part of the fabric of life of the individual or community that accepts or follows it.

Commonly the occasion for critical scrutiny of these components of our lives is some serious faltering in the responses dictated by their manifest aspects. These aspects, which have hitherto served readily as expressions of the latent contents in this type of situation, no longer will serve this purpose.

One way of describing the task of reflective reconstruction of norms is that of devising means for restoring the articulation between the manifest and the latent aspects. This ordinarily entails some significant alteration in both.

§25   The ever-present possibility of disarticulation between the manifest and latent aspects of norms is both a source of dysfunction of them and a source of change, be that on the whole beneficial or the contrary.

§26   The latent aspects of norms of any important institution extend widely throughout the societies in which they reside. On some occasions scrutiny of norms may need to reach far into this extension, on others a restricted, proximate scrutiny may suffice.

The development of geocentric astronomy, and its subsequent transformation into heliocentric, exemplifies in turn first a more restricted and later a greatly extended involvement of the latent aspects of the norms of such a cognitive institution.

§28   Present controversy in the United States centering upon proper activities directly affecting fertilized human egg cells, embryos, fetuses, etc., exemplifies in an extreme degree the depth and breadth to which the latent aspects of norms may extend. Beyond the more obvious moral, religious, and legal facets of the controversy are many less obvious social, political, and economic ones that extend far beyond those directly bearing upon treatment of the unborn human young.

§29   The general governance of norms varies widely in the degrees in which it is reflective and conscious, rather than unreflective and unaware. Among the varieties of governance it has been the highly reflective, conscious kinds that have been of greatest interest to philosophical investigators.

§30 A major contribution to the understanding of reflective philosophical governance made by the view of norms advanced here is its exposure, under the broad title of the latent aspect of norms, of the richness and variety of the resources available for the governance of norms.

§31 Exposed, in particular, is the authority discernable to philosophical reflection in the latent aspect of norms for features of their manifest aspects. This applies to the manifest aspects of both accepted norms and to candidates for acceptance, including those that in relation to accepted ones are novel and even discrepant.

§32 This exposure is a first big step in the dissolution of the Parmenidean conundrum of how extant norms, in a genuinely legitimating process, can generate norm-results, that is, results in the form of norms that are novel or even discrepant in relation to these same sources.

§§33–34 Of two philosophical tasks in the definition of this legitimating process one is negative and one positive. It is to the positive task, that of elaborating the character of this process, as it in engaged in, that the present essay is primarily directed. The negative task is that of defending the process itself, as elaborated, from the strong attacks of those who strive to show on principle that such a process cannot possibly be legitimating. This latter task beyond the compass of the present paper, having been undertaken in some detail by the present writer in two recent books. One broad metaphysical source of the negative judgment of the legitimating capacity of such a process seems worth brief notice here.

§35 The primary authority that reflection can expose and exploit for the purpose of governance of norms in their manifest aspects lies in the capacity of the norms, in these aspects, to represent the latent aspects in their own particular mode. But to say that this is the primary authority for the governance of norms, in their manifest aspect, is not to say that it is the *only* authority for the governance of norms in any aspect.

§36 Also, to characterize a certain activity with respect to norms as "philosophical" reflection upon and governance of them is not thereby to assign it as a special, proper, and perhaps exclusive function to some group of individuals that may be referred to professionally by this adjective.

The areas in which reflective philosophical governance is called upon are numerous and various, and generally require intimate and penetrating acquaintance with the corresponding numerous and various latent roots upon which norms in these areas depend.

§§37–39 Governance of norms; reflective and nonreflective. The need, in understanding governance, to keep in mind both aspects of norms and the interdependence of these aspects. Crafting norms; dissolving the mystery of ampliative effects. Normative results of ampliative processes.

Parallel characterizations of these processes: "dialectic"; "non-scientific deliberation"; the "pursuit of intimations" (Oakeshott); "reasoned elaboration" of the law (Hart and Sacks); the exploration of "penumbras formed by emanations" (Douglas); "constitutional faith" (Levinson).

§41   Ampliative governance, in both individuals and groups, as the creative formation of the will.

§§42–43   Brief comparison of the view of governance presented here with relevant views of John Dewey.

§§44–48   The authorization or legitimation of governantial results effected through resort to the spirit in philosophic governance is misconceived when it is thought of in a deductive, unilateral mode.

§49   The insufficiency of such a mode of conceiving philosophic governance at many junctures of our lives has been one of the emphases of recent Existential philosophy.

§§50–51   This sound emphasis needs to be supplemented in two respects: (1) by a broad view of the resources available for philosophic governance, and, especially, (2) by a similarly broad view of the communal character of the resources, the process in which they are employed, and their results.

1   Following a rule or, more broadly, acting in accordance with a norm, entails proper identification of the occasions for action and determination of the proper actions. Knowing how to go on in accordance with a rule or norm embraces a capacity to discern both these things.

2   This required discernment varies greatly in difficulty from case to case.

3   One natural and common way of conceiving a norm is in terms of these occasions and responses. The norm so conceived consists in a connection holding between the occasions and responses that is exemplified in the settled application of the norm. For many purposes this aspect of norms, which may be termed their "manifest content," is all that we need to pay attention to.

4   It is also natural on such a view to think of someone who learns the norm as establishing or having established in himself (herself) a corresponding connection. This internalized connection provides the possessor with a template of action according to the norm.

5   A common abstraction in epistemology corresponding to the norm as internal template of action has been the "state-of-affairs," that curious external correlate that is supposed to make our propositions true. The exorcism of these *Doppelgänger*, as J. L. Austin aptly termed them, does not mean that there is nothing external to the proposition (statement, or whatever) in

relation to which the proposition is true or false. It does mean that, contrary to the illusion that this term of art ("state-of-affairs") tends to generate, there is no otherwise easily identifiable object corresponding to this term. Ordinarily the only way we have of referring to what would make the proposition true is the proposition itself.

6   Much of modern rationalist and empiricist thought about norms was fatally faulted by the misidentification of norms with certain manifest, easily encapsulable aspects of them. Thus rationalists, for example, were led to suppose that there could be accessible archetypal norms in the form of "ideas" of them implanted in the human mind, and empiricists to suppose that such archetypes could be skimmed by an attentive mind off cursory experience.[1]

7   Mathematics, and the idea of computation in this domain, seems to present strong, clear, confirming exemplifications of the template conception of norms and of what it is like to follow them. The model is one of translating such a paradigm from the realm of thought, intention, language, or whatever, into the realm of action. The norm, so conceived, provides anyone who has learned it, who understands it, with an immediate grasp of what action according to it is like. Thence, to appropriate some words of Wittgenstein, "comes the idea that the beginning of a series is a visible section of rails invisibly laid to infinity."[2]

8   Wittgenstein's thought-experiments about action guided by rules enables one to see that even in cases in which one would least expect it there is a logical gap between the supposed internal template of action and the action itself. Reflecting on such examples as the "add" rule, measuring lumber, measuring with rulers, construing the gesture of pointing, and so forth, one can come to see that more is involved in following a norm than some simple connection of occasion and response such as can be witnessed and absorbed as a paradigm by the learner.

9   It is not the connection of occasion and response, by itself, that suffices to make this an instance of the universal that is the norm here. There is, as always, a large and complex background of living social practice which, when it is removed, takes from this connection its character as a norm of action. Abstract the connections between occasion and response exemplified in the settled, routine applications of the norm that constitute the manifest aspect of the norm. Abstract this from the latent but no less real aspect of the norm as an expression of some facet or facets of our lives. Then the central normative guiding character of the erstwhile norm is dissipated. Then, as Wittgenstein said about rules, "Every course of action can be made to

[1] [Cf. ch. 8 above.—*Ed.*]

[2] *Philosophical Investigations*, I §218.

accord with the rule" (§201). Recall that curious person made bereft by Wittgenstein's imagination of this aspect of the rule, when he rounds the turn of 1000, produces 1004, 1008, 1012, and so on, instead of our more normal 1002, 1004, 1006, and so on.[1]

10 If in mathematics, that perduring source of Platonism, the defining, guiding power of a rule is dependent upon that aspect of it that extends beyond its manifest content and reflects its integral relations with complexes of practices, customs, pursuits, and even institutions—if this holds for rules in mathematics—how much more must it hold for the broad and deeply entrenched norms of thought and action that are of special concern in philosophical reflection? Once one recognizes the role of the latent aspect of a rule in contributing to its definition in so abstract a domain as mathematics, one is in a better position to recognize this function in all sorts of norms where, though it is vastly more prominent, it has been disregarded in consequence of a strong and widespread epistemological preconception. The general dependency upon ways of living that is easily discerned in many moral, political, and cognitive norms has been regarded as an aspect of them needing to be minimized, if it cannot be totally eliminated, in order to render them as close as possible to those mathematical and logical rules that in this respect seem to be models of utter independence. The plausibility of this way of regarding the latent aspect of norms suffers greatly, if not fatally, from the dissipation of its apparent exemplification in the supposed model cases.

11 Similar glosses may be and have often been made upon other rules or norms that have been for certain philosophical purposes so abstracted from their latent content that they can no long perform their expected guiding function. Strikingly similar in this aspect are many criticisms advanced against Kant's principle of universality in his Categorical Imperative, and, more recently, in Goodman's effective criticism of an abstract rule of inductive projection. In both these and many other cases a major point of the criticism is that embarrassingly many conflicting courses of action "can be made out to accord with the rule."

12 The general point about norms that is expressed here in terms of manifest and latent aspect could be expressed in other ways, some of them perhaps more felicitous though not at present apparent to the writer. The pivotal point, to use traditional philosophical terminology, is an anti-Platonic one. It is that the kind of understanding of norms that is necessary for certain philosophical purposes must encompass the aspect that norms have as components of larger complexes of human life and practice.

---

[1] This point was elaborated by the present writer in *Beyond Deduction* (London: Routledge, 1988), ch. 5.

13 Incorporation into our conception of norms of what has been here called their latent aspect alters this conception in an important way and with it our view of what is entailed in philosophical scrutiny of them. While for certain purposes their latent aspects may be neglected in favor of the manifest ones, for purposes of understanding both permanence and change in norms, and philosophical reflection and judgment concerning them, it makes a vast difference whether one considers only these local, phenomenally prominent, manifest aspects of them, or considers them more broadly as components that at one and the same time are formed by and give form to wider or narrower spheres of our lives.

14 One's view of the landscape that one is exploring under the title of "norms" is radically altered the more clearly that one recognizes that the central objects of one's inspection are not to be identified with propositions to be analyzed, ideas to be dissected, meanings to be clarified, sentences to be scanned. They are essentially aspects of human life, typically of social life. They are concrete ways of doing and thinking, and questions about their value—their validation, justification, legitimacy, and so on—are questions about these processes and the products that are realized in and through them.

15 Conceived in this more fully concrete way, norms are explicitly sociopsychological entities. And they are by no means inert in their aspects as features—and sometimes very basic features—of various spheres of life; they are typically, and always at least to some degree, in dynamic relation with other features of life, including other norms, in consequence of which they are liable to alteration both in respect to the conditions under which they are properly applied and to the character of the responses that are proper to their application. This is a broad feature of norms that a catalogue of the manifest aspects of them—such as seem to have been taken to be exhaustive of them in some forms of ethical naturalism—neglects. This is to say that, in consequence of being live rather than inert objects, norms are always in some degree open, rather than closed with respect to their manifest aspects.[1]

16 Speaking of norms as open (not closed) and as alive (not inert) is a mildly metaphorical way of calling attention to aspects of them that are essential for understanding both stability and change (and stability *in* change) in them, and also for understanding the way in which reflection, philosophical and otherwise, can perform a critical function upon them. Norms are not, either in their referential-applicative or their response aspects, completely defined. There are always possible borderline situations in which there is no settled determination whether a norm is or is not applicable, and there are always possible occasions in which there is no settled determination what the response, if the norm is applied, should be.

---

[1] [Cf. above, chs. 1, 4, 5, 7, 8.—*Ed.*]

17 With respect to this character, as with respect to their character as live or active, there are great variations among norms and among bodies of norms. The body of accepted norms in some limited sphere of life is not a collection of more or less disparate, independent ways of proceeding. Rather the norms are bound together, though with greatly various degrees of tightness: bound together as instruments, vehicles for producing in thought and action what in large spheres of life are counted as *ways* of life; of professions, crafts; modes of cultural enjoyment, modes of ethical and religious cultivation and devotion. Examples of the latter are various Christian, or more narrowly Protestant bodies of norms of belief and conduct, and similarly Muslim systems, be they of Shia or Sunna. In the wide range of scientific pursuits there may be such a large subdomain as that of natural science, or, more narrowly, organic chemistry, or still more narrowly biochemistry, and so on.

18 The more cohesive such bodies of norms are, the more they may be truly said to articulate a way of living, of occupation, and the rest. And this way of living, of devoting one's working life, both embodies norms, is guided by them, and generates further, and also, on occasion, contrary and transcending norms. Without uttering the dreaded "D" word that like a specter of its own sort, has haunted much of Western philosophy during the past century, one can recognize philosophically the reciprocal effects of the formation of life by norms and the continued formation and reformation of norms by life.[1]

19 The four interrelated features of norms just specified—(1) liveness; (2) openness; (3) disposition to cluster in more or less tightly organized Gestalten; and (4) dependence and reciprocal determination in relation to the spheres of life which they inform—all these are implicated in a conception of them that embraces their combined aspects as manifest and latent. The motives and resources of the determination of norms lie in the complex and widely extending combination of both these aspects. And in the understanding of these resources also lie the bases for the kind of critical scrutiny and governance that philosophical understanding can provide for them.

20 The repetition of the word "understanding" in the preceding sentence is intended to emphasize that the basis of sound scrutiny, the basis of evaluative judgment concerning norms lies in the norms themselves. It lies in the character of the norms, that character being very broadly construed to include both their manifest and their latent aspects. The thesis here needs to be unmistaken. An evaluative judgment concerning a norm, for example, a judgment advancing the cause of some particular change in it, is a judgment concerning a feature of the norm itself taken in its combined aspects. One

---

[1] [The "D" word is "dialectic."—*Ed.*]

view of such a judgment that is thus being rejected is the one that distinguishes sharply and absolutely between judgment about what the norm is and judgment about what it should be. If there is any "should be" that applies to the norm, it is not some kind of linguistic or intellectual or emotive topping that is added to the norm, not itself being a feature of it. If it can be rightly said that norms forbidding the practice of euthanasia under any circumstances require revision, this requirement is something to be discovered in the norms themselves, in their wide and complex characters both manifest and latent, and in the role they play in the spheres of individual and social lives to which they apply.[1]

21 What is being advanced here is indeed a version of naturalism; but it is well understood only if its difference from some other versions is recognized, for example, versions that may be called "scientific" or "positivist." These versions typically neglect or disregard the latent aspects of norms, concentrating upon the "hard data" that are represented by the manifest contents. The more complete this concentration is, the more will the views embodying it fail to illuminate how careful, respectful, unprejudiced examination of norms can yield evaluative judgments concerning them. Blinded by this concentration, naturalists of this kind cannot recognize those other aspects of norms that are implicated in the judgment process, any more than their great teacher, Hume, was able to recognize beauty in an circle, because, as he said, Euclid, who "has fully explained all the qualities of the circle ... has not in any proposition said a word of its beauty."[2] Of course, no circle can ever be rightly said to be beautiful if one restricts one's view of qualities to those mentioned in Euclid's *Elements*; and still less can this be said if one moves further in restriction and recognizes only those qualities spoken of in the arithmetization of geometry that we now call "analytic."

22 In the process of scrutinizing, evaluating, and developing programs of governance of norms, philosophical reflection encounters many complex, difficult, enigmatic, and sometimes insuperable difficulties. But there is one perennially engrossing philosophical quandary that in its bearing on philosophic understanding of the evaluation of norms is gratuitous, as it is elsewhere. The quandary is one that has commonly gone by the name of the "Problem of Value," and has been a remarkably similar intellectual twin of another philosophic quandary, namely, the Problem of Induction. In the latter case the Problem has been set as that of devising techniques by which one might derive, and so "justify" general or universal conclusions on the basis of strictly "particular" data; in the former the desiderata are comparable tech-

---

[1] [Cf. *Beyond Deduction*, ch. 7 §§19–27.—*Ed.*]

[2] "The Sceptic," in *Essays: Moral, Political, and Literary*, Eugene F. Miller, ed. (Indianapolis: Liberty Fund, 1987), 165.

niques by which one might justifiably proceed from strictly "factual" premises specifying "what is" to conclusions determining which among contemplated existences would be better or worse. Both quandaries are generated less by understanding than misunderstanding. In the case of the one that is the more germane here, namely that of the evaluation of norms, the primary source is a severe, theoretically guided exclusion of aspects of norms that are essential to evaluation, and hence to the understanding of that procedure. For certain purposes in the study of norms, it has already been observed, concentration upon manifest content is legitimate and desirable. The adjectives "scientific" and "positivist" indicate the character of some of the most important of these purposes. Having, in the pursuit of these purposes, legitimately and desirably abstracted the norm from its latent aspects, one proceeds quite beyond legitimacy and desirability if one supposes that such abstraction must be preserved for all purposes whatever. At this point, having excluded from consideration aspects of norms that are necessary for understanding and carrying out philosophical evaluation of them—having blinded oneself by the misapplication of philosophical principle to these considerations—one has precipitated oneself into a great and irresolvable quandary that, like a giant intellectual black hole, constantly swallows up efforts to understand and participate understandingly in the processes by which evaluation proceeds.[1]

23 The effective conceptual denuding of norms that has been carried on for centuries in Western philosophy will not be redressed by easy measures: by, for example, enriching our conception of norms by adding to their fundamental "primary" qualities secondary, "nonnatural" ones that in some cases accompany the primary ones like a delicate scent detectable only by highly refined academic noses. The needed transformation of our conception is not achieved by superimposing upon the supposed primary and value-free qualities refined valuative ones: qualities which on the philosophical principles at work in the denuding program are destined to seem mystical and ad hoc, the faint mistaken after-images of a grin of a cat long since exterminated. Nor are the defects of conception to be remedied by recourse to some occult intellectual domain from which "sources of normativity" can be imported and conferred upon norms. What is required is a fundamental recasting of conception that recognizes that the formula of "norms-plus" is mistaken at the outset, since what are taken to be elementary norms in such a formula are not norms, but deceptive substitutes for them.[2] As is exemplified in the case of those relatively strict and binding norms that we call "rules," the basis for our capacity to evaluate them, like the basis for their capacity to direct us in

---

[1] Similar effects of this abstract view of norms may be discerned in various discussions of the now much treated Problem of Intentionality.

[2] [Cf. ch. 7.—Ed.]

thought and action, lies so much, indeed coincides so closely, in the wider
and often deep features of them that have been termed "latent," that altogether apart from these features there remain neither entities that may
properly be called "norms" nor a problem about their philosophical
evaluation.

24 A norm, comprising both aspects discriminated here, is part of the fabric
of life, of thought and action of the individual or community that accepts or
follows it. It is in some degree a constitutive feature of this life. Commonly
the occasion for the scrutiny, evaluation, and possible active management of
such entities is apparent dysfunction in their performance. And likewise
commonly the primary clues for proceeding with these activities lie in the
particular character of the dysfunction. For one reason or other the relatively
smooth and automatic responses exemplified in the manifest contents of the
norm falter, or at least appear to falter. To some considerable extent the overt
recipe, or set of recipes, for activity embodied in the manifest content fails,
or at least appears to fail, to articulate successfully the complex of wishes
intentions, interests, values and other settled norms and practices that are the
necessary support and ballast of full and accepted norms. The primary task
of reflective reconstruction in such situations is then to devise means for the
restoration of the articulation between these two components of the norm.
Completion of this task normally entails some significant alteration in both
components.
25 This brief characterization of occasions and responses of scrutiny applies
not only to episodes that issue in judgments and overt activity favoring
change in norms, but also, *mutatis mutandis*, to judgments and activities, both
overt and covert, favoring maintenance instead. And it applies both to the
nonphilosophical as well as to the philosophical forms of these activities.
Without a secure basis of multiform connections between occasions and
responses, human life as we have it would not be possible. And without
some faltering and readjustment of these connections in the past, many of the
secure connections that we now have would not have been developed.
    The ever-present possibilities of disarticulation between manifest and
latent aspects is the analogue in the idiom of norms of open texture in the
idiom of concepts. Furthermore, as is the case with open texture, not only is
this feature in principle not completely eliminable, but its complete elimina-
tion is not something that can be coherently contemplated, or even if contemplated, coherently desired. Just as human life, as we have it, would not be
possible without secure correlations between occasions and responses, so it
would not be possible were these correlations not susceptible to and actually

subjected to disruption.[1] In any large area of life one chooses to examine, the extant norms in general display plainly the effects in generation and molding of earlier disarticulation and disruption. And at least as important, though less obvious, is the effect of the possibility of disarticulation in norms in our normal employment of them. The employment of norms in any form of human life of which we have any trustworthy knowledge, and a fortiori in the forms of civil life that we now have, is never just following, just replicating sanctioned connections between occasions and responses. This is because, for one thing, as the early pages of this chapter have striven to show, there is no such thing as mere replication.[2] What binds together instances of application of a norm as instances of that norm is not their phenomenological similarity either to each other or to some supposed archetypal norm. And for another thing, and more concretely, the infusion of norms in life is always, though in highly variant degrees, a highly holistic process, in which norms are adapted to each other, in both their manifest and in their rich and deep latent aspects, and to the circumstances in which the infusion is called for. In consequence of this, the conduct of life infused by norms is never a matter just of conformance of episodes of overt action or thought to patterns of such represented in them. Though there are great variations in the degree with which different portions of our lives approach this state, they are never, even in the most extreme cases, just this. Always to some degree in following norms we are engaged in producing, not just *re*producing, states of life. We are forming our lives and ourselves, and reciprocally our norms and our ideas of ourselves. We produce a kind of life on the basis of which, for better or for worse, we are able to contemplate further, different kinds of life that, given the norms we now have, attract or repel us in varying degrees, and in the process of committing ourselves to or against, we effect changes—again, for better or worse—in the repertory of norms from which we began and to which we cannot quite return.

26 The latent aspects of the norms of any important institution, cognitive or otherwise, extend widely throughout the societies in which they are supported. This is especially true of those large scale institutions—the physical and the life sciences, medicine, the family, business, government, law, politics, religion, and the rest—with which philosophical scrutiny is mainly concerned. Various specific enterprises of scrutiny may nevertheless be limited in their exploration of the latent aspects of the norms that are the foci of attention; there may be vast areas of latent aspect, the relevance of which may be minimal and negligible. On the other hand there is in principle no limit to the area of latent aspect that in one case or other may require serious consid-

[1] [Cf. chs. 4, 5, 7, 8.—*Ed.*]
[2] [Cf. above, ch. 7.—*Ed.*]

eration. Religious beliefs and practices, for example, may become relevant to controverted issues concerning civil rights, or the levies of services upon citizens made by the state, or taxation, or the practice of medicine.

27 Ancient observers of the heavens developed valuable connections, valuable complexes of manifest norms embodied in the general view that the stars move in circular fashion about the earth. Faced with the observed aberrations of some of these stars, some aberrations minor, some to the extent of retrograde motion, early Greek astronomers were not prepared, and had good reasons not to be prepared, to rest content with the apparent exceptions to what seemed generally sound norms. Commonly in confronting a challenge to some proposed or already accepted norm of thought or action in some enterprise or institution, we appeal as a basis for responding to the challenge to other deeply entrenched and apparently ruling norms of that same enterprise or institution. These astronomical developments illustrate an important feature of the relation between the manifest and the latent aspects of norms. This is that they are complementary rather than contrary to each other. Each is important, indeed quite essential to the other, and to the enterprises, institutions, spheres of life of which they are components.

As the astronomical example also illustrates, the proximate resources of evaluation and determination lie in the accepted ends and practices of the enterprise of which the affected norms are a part. These enterprises and their informing institutions are extremely various: cognitive, technical, economic, religious, legal, political, and so on. In the first instance, then, one appeals to the wider accepted norms of the enterprise and institution. This kind of appeal, in the case of the astronomical example, was at first relatively successful. This because the prospect of "saving the appearances" was primarily calculative rather than cosmological. By the sixteenth century the cosmological ends of astronomy, and the norms expressing these ends, were becoming more prominent, and by the seventeenth, given the calculative equipollence of the two competing world systems, the heliocentric one more and more manifested its superiority. An important aspect of this superiority was the adduction into the resources of evaluation of the less proximate but increasingly influential enterprise of the burgeoning new physical dynamics. Galileo, a key figure in this development, aptly symbolized this latter strong influence, which, in its bearings on astronomy, came into conflict with an other influence symbolized by the prosecutors in Galileo's trial for heresy.[1]

28 The present controversy in the United States over a very extensive cluster of norms concerning the proper treatment of fertilized human egg cells, embryos, and fetuses of various stages of development exemplifies in an

---

[1] [Cf. ch. 5 above.—*Ed.*]

extreme degree the depth and breadth to which the latent aspects of norms may extend. Included among many other items of controversy, is that of surgical operations to terminate unwanted pregnancies; the proper disposition of fetal materials resulting from such operations; the use of male cells of a married man to impregnate a designated woman other than his wife; the rights of such a "surrogate" mother with respect to a resultant child in relation to both the natural father and his wife; in vitro fertilization; the disposition of surplus embryos resulting from this process; and including the custody of frozen embryos that remain in some legal limbo when perhaps the couple who produced them have dissolved their relationship or even no longer survive. Also affected in one way or another are analogues of these matters arising in norms of thought and action concerning the apparent merciful termination of life of the hopelessly ill, enfeebled, possibly also suffering individuals who must now stagger toward the finish line in their particular race in life because no one can clearly see how they can be mercifully helped to cross the line without breaching in a perilous way some of our most deeply held and jealously guarded moral principles.

Interwoven with these more obvious moral, religious, medical, and legal strands of the fabric of our lives are a host of less obvious ones, moral, religious, sociopolitical, economic, and so on. Helpful, for example, in understanding how unsettling some changes already effected and others contemplated may be is an awareness that implicated in the issue about the ruling force of a constitutional right of privacy in the matter of abortion is some deep evaluation about roles of women as wage-earners and pursuers of careers, on the one hand, and as mothers and homemakers on the other, and, of course, the effects of changes made in all these upon the family as a fundamental institution long nourished and protected by religious, legal, and political institutions in American society. In a compressed comment upon Kristen Luker's study of some demographic aspects of the abortion controversy,[1] *Newsweek* wrote: "The abortion opponent believed in the traditional sex roles and saw motherhood as her highest mission in life, while the abortion supporter saw herself more as her husband's equal and viewed the unavailability of birth control and abortion as limiting her competitive chances in the world."[2]

In a great variety of ways, as in the great controversy over slavery in the last century, partisans of both sides of the abortion-rights issue are envisioning and advancing what are at various places and in some important respects contrary visions of what American life should be. An aspect of the width,

---

[1] *Abortion and the Politics of Motherhood* (Berkeley: University of California Press, 1984).

[2] January 14, 1985: 21.

depth, and intensity of the issues involved is that not only are the prominent groups of partisans on each side engaged in working for the resolution of them. Together with them in their efforts is a vast array of social agencies, of which the courts and a variety of religious and political agencies are but the most prominent. Likewise engaged at one sector or other of the task are the institutions of higher learning, other research institutions, the press, and other media of communication. Those who are appalled by the noise and disorder of the entire process, compared, say, to calculative and computative ones, need perhaps to be reminded that these are characteristics of decision procedures endemic and appropriate to a modern democratic society.

29 The general maintenance, change, revision, *etc.*—let the collective term "governance" cover all of these—that is and can be effected by us upon items in our store of accepted norms in various domains differs widely from case to case in the degree to which it is carried out reflectively and consciously, or thoughtlessly and unaware. Of these two kinds of governance, the former, the more reflective and conscious one has been by far of greater interest to philosophical investigators, this being the kind with which, in their concern with broad and deep norms of thought and action, these investigators have been vocationally engaged. Throughout the three and a half centuries since Descartes' *Discourse* on "rightly directing one's Reason and ... seeking Truth in the Sciences," questions of how to think well about philosophical matters have been central in Western philosophy, and the epistemological disputes emerging from attempts to deal with the questions have been extended and intense. What can one say briefly and sensibly about "directing one's reason" that would be helpful in the conduct of philosophical governance? More particularly, how does what has been elaborated above about norms contribute to our understanding of what we are doing when we engage in the philosophical governance of them? Even more particularly, how does it illuminate the kind of governantial results—call them "ampliative" ones—that cannot be validated exclusively by the secure, unproblematic employment of prior accepted norms and which thus represent departures from these norms?

30 A major contribution to the understanding of this governance made by the view of norms advanced here is its exposure, under the broad title of the latent aspect of norms, of the richness and variety of the resources available for this governance. Just as an appreciation of the broader though less prominent aspect of norms is a necessary and valuable component of an understanding of the guiding power of an already accepted norm, it is a similar component of our understanding of the guiding power of a norm that is not yet accepted, including under this heading those that represent more or less serious revisions, excisions or replacements of already accepted ones.

The richness of a norm that extends beyond its manifest aspect includes much more than systematic relations discernible between the manifest content of this norm and the manifest contents of others. Each manifest content itself reflects and expresses a rich supporting latent content comprising habitual modes of thought and action, and, integrally related to these, an amorphous and variously concordant and discordant set of predispositions, learning, preferences, aspirations, ideals, expectations, injunctions, prohibitions, and so on; all of which in a rough, incomplete consensus help to constitute the tissue of life among those who accept and follow them. The manifest contents of norms are expressions of certain aspects of life and thought of the individuals and groups that accept and follow them, of aspects that are tractable to more or less routine sanctioned connections between occasions and responses. From time to time, at various speeds, and in various degrees, and in various places, these aspects of life change. Some accepted manifest contents that hitherto have served well as the routinized expressions of their latent contents no longer do so. And in consequence revisions, even excisions of them, and the development of new contents naturally, and in many cases inevitably, take place.

31 The particular question of the authority of a not yet accepted norm—or the authority of it that is accessible to philosophical reflection—has been a crucial testing point of theories of governance that take the primary source of authority of accepted norms in general to lie in the functions they perform in the lives of individuals and groups that follow them. Integral to the version of this general view advocated here is the principled assimilation of the authority that a not yet accepted norm can display under inspection to the corresponding authority of an already accepted one, that is, the assimilation of the grounds for acceptance a not yet accepted norm may offer to critical judgment, to the grounds that an already accepted norm may offer, should it become the subject of such judgment. This does not entail any depreciation of the practice of *stare decisis* and its widespread analogue practices in various nonlegal lines of endeavor. Before the court convenes, as it were, accepted norms, as accepted, have authority, and often sufficient authority for the circumstances, just because of their position in a corpus of norms already in place. But once trial has begun, once the occasion has arisen for the critical comparison, say, of a hitherto accepted norm and a proposed alternative, the grounds that may be advanced for the new proposition are quite of the same cloth, and subject to the same kind of appraisal, as those that may be offered on behalf of the hitherto accepted one, in support of its continued acceptance, with or without possible alteration. The authority of a not yet accepted norm that is accessible to philosophical reflection lies in its promise to perform the same broad function in the lives of individuals and communities that norms in general perform. And this function, speaking generally and abstractly, lies in the way in which their manifest contents serve as local

exemplifications, local representations of more or less extended spheres individual or communal life. Each norm is an expression of an aspect of a sphere of life to which it belongs; more particularly, it is an expression of an aspect that is tractable to this general mode of expression, namely, that of more or less settled patterns of procedure.

32 From the point of view taken here it is easy to see that a major source of the supposed logical difficulty about how novel norms can be legitimated by already established ones lies in an extremely abstract view of norms themselves. That view substantially identifies norms with one aspect of them, namely, the manifest one. Given this identification, the logical difficulty ensues.[1] On the one hand there are the extant, established norms, a multitude of associated occasions and responses, cut and dried, taken to be just what norms are and need to be treated as by properly scientific, factual view of them. And on the other hand there are novel and even discordant norms, and the conundrum of how the properly sterile original objects can generate and legitimate such offspring. Against this, the message of the present paper is that the legitimating sources of new norms are not the barren sets of coincidences of occasions and responses that the premises of this problem have taken them to be. In their latent aspect norms comprise so rich a background of life and thought that out of established ones, novel and discordant norms are constantly being generated and legitimated. This being so, the problem of new norms is not the sterility of extant norms, but rather, one may say with perhaps pardonable exaggeration, their fecundity. The grand and apparently daunting question of how *any* new norm can be legitimately developed out of older accepted ones is dissolved by recognition of the resources for just this legitimation, in view of which the focus of philosophical inspection of legitimation necessarily alters. Then attention may return to the original question from which the inquiry naturally sprang, and to which the grand tantalizing question represented what seemed to be a necessary, though prolonged diversion. Freed from that diversion, and recognizing that from the sources and bases of norms multiple candidates of various apparent degrees of validity are constantly in the process of generation, one may proceed to investigate how, in situations in which thoughtful choice is possible, the choice may be made.

33 To a further exposition of the resources accessible to philosophical reflection in the governance of norms the remaining pages will be primarily devoted. But before continuing with that positive task it is worth noting that there is also a large negative task with respect to these resources that cannot be undertaken within the limitations of this chapter. This is the task of meeting the response of those who admit freely the existence of what are here viewed as resources of governance but deny on principle their capacity

---

[1] [Cf. above chs. 7, 8.—*Ed.*]

to serve as such when the governance in question is deeply and thoroughly philosophical. What is exposed, the response may run, though matters of historical, sociological, or psychological interest and importance, are nevertheless quite incapable of performing as grounds in philosophical governance. They have not the quality that is required, that is quite indispensable for the support of acts of philosophical criticism and judgment.

34 From the point of view concerning governance that is being elaborated here such a response, though altogether understandable, is an expression of a deeply embedded and widespread philosophical prejudice. To the exposure of this prejudice the present writer has devoted a major portion of one book, and a lesser portion of another.[1] In the latter work some sources of this prejudice were briefly discussed, one of which is worth mention here. Surely one most important of these sources is the presumption that the legitimacy, validation, or authority of any extant or proposed norm that can withstand thorough philosophical scrutiny must derive from some realm utterly outside norms, practices, or human life itself. This presumption may be recognized as, among other things, an intellectual inheritance from early types of social organization in which great dependence for leadership was reposed in priests, prophets, oracles, shamans, and other figures supposed capable of speaking on behalf of some awesome, transcendent realm. Over the centuries of Western philosophical meditation, expressions of the need for some such transcendent authority have varied widely, from the calm Hellenic and cool Gallic ratiocinations of respectively Plato and later Descartes, to the more passioned inner reflections of Augustine and Dostoyevsky ("If God does not exist, then everything is permitted").

Countering and dispelling this philosophical prejudice in its present deductivist-foundationist form entails addressing the claim that resources of governance of norms that are capable of withstanding thorough philosophical scrutiny must, in the end, fundamentally lie outside the realm of norms themselves. The central countering claim that can be mounted against this is that, though from some points of view it may seem that the resources of such governance must be external in this respect, a more thorough and sounder appraisal of the situation is that these resources *neither are nor can be so*. That central counterclaim is itself a presumption, a major premise upon which the elucidation of the internal grounds of philosophical governance here proceeds. Though by itself this elucidation will surely not prevail with someone firmly convinced that the premise is in error, and will therefore seem rather to have begged the chief question that a deductivist-foundational challenge represents in the debates over governance, to others less committed to that view, and those aware of the manifold exposure of the difficulties of

---

[1] *Induction and Justification* and *Beyond Deduction*.

the view over many years in modern philosophy, elaboration of positive aspects of an alternative to it may be of value.

35 Diverging radically from the view of norms and their governance that has been dominant in modern philosophy, the view advanced here finds the grounds of governance of norms in their performance, actual and promissory, in the lives of those who follow them. Reflective, conscious governance of norms, in both philosophical and nonphilosophical forms, normally arises from and is first focused upon the manifest aspect of the norms that are its objects. And the primary authority that reflection can expose and exploit for purposes of governance of norms in their manifest aspects lies in the capacities of these aspects of the norms to represent their latent aspects in this particular mode. This applies, whatever the depth and breadth of the norm may be. It applies to the rule of *modus ponens*, to the Golden Rule, to amendments proposed and amendments made to the United States Constitution, and, of course, to the subsequent juridical and other needed interpretation of such amendments.

But to say that this is the primary authority is not to say that it is the only authority. For, in the process of generating manifest expressions of itself, the latent aspect of a norm is commonly affected. The latent aspect, or some portion of it, may, to speak metaphorically, recognize itself in the manifest aspect, and affected by this recognition come to display features that hitherto were either not present or present in a less explicit way.

It is a task of philosophical reflection, then, as it is engaged in the scrutiny and governance of norms in law, morals, politics, science, mathematics, and so on, to develop a judgment of the capacity of the manifest aspect of norms under inspection to express the settled, the incipient, and the still unawakened capacities that reside in the latent aspects of the norms in question. And with this goes the task of recognizing the capacities of the manifest expressions of these latent aspects to call, as expressions, for alterations as well as maintenance of selected components of the latent aspects that it is their function to express.[1]

36 What has been portrayed here under the title of reflective philosophical governance is by no means an activity and function that can be abstracted and consigned to some special group of intellectual specialists such as those who in Western academic institutions carry on the studies that now fall within the traditional rubric of "Philosophy." The term "philosophical," as it is construed here in application to governance, refers to a very widespread form of activity that neither is nor can be carried on exclusively or primarily by any such group whose proficiency in the art of reflection is thought to

---

[1] [For further examples, cf. above, ch. 5 §6.—*Ed.*]

equip its members to perform this function generally in the vast variety of areas in which it is called for. It is not to be denied that there are typical philosophical interests, skills, and temperaments, although these are capable of great variation. But the areas in which reflective philosophical governance is called upon—from what are called the foundations of mathematics, to physical theory, to psychological theory, and to law, morals, and politics—are so numerous and various as to dispel the Leibnizean dream that somehow the essentials of it all can be encapsulized and taught in some sovereign, universally applicable set of techniques. Philosophical skills can be learned and taught; insights can be cultivated and deepened; narrowness can be dispelled; but not, as Wittgenstein said about learning in another area, "by taking a course" in them; not as one learns computative skills in mathematics or the techniques of prophylaxis in medicine.

In view of the great variety of activities carried on by members of modern societies there is a great diminution in the plausibility of the supposition that the task of reflection philosophical governance of the norms of these activities may be entrusted primarily or exclusively to some select group of Platonic guardians. However plausible such a supposition may have been in times of much less diversity of activities and norms pertaining to these activities, it is no longer plausible to suppose that societies and infrasocietal groups can depend, for critical judgment in the governance of these norms, upon colleges of individuals whose chief expertise is in an abstracted dialectic or in some more modern version of that ancient craft. What plausibility this supposition once had is further dissipated by the discrediting of what were once thought to be the available resources of that craft, for example, the divine archetypes either imprinted originally upon the human mind or, more recently and secularly, in given human quasilinguistic resources available for explication in one or other version of "conceptual analysis."

Much of what has just been said follows closely from the view that has been elaborated concerning the resources of philosophical governance that reside in the latent aspects of norms that are the objects of governance. The general indispensability of these resources implies the general indispensability of wide, deep, and direct acquaintance with them on the part of agents seriously engaged in the activity of governance. To be sure it has been emphasized that these resources extend widely, and sometimes most important elements of the latent aspect of norms may be remote ones. Darwin's theory of evolution drew in important ways from the earlier work of geologists such as Charles Lyell; the influential governance effected by Justice Oliver Wendell Holmes upon features of the United States Constitution displayed influences of a somewhat "inarticulate" (Holmes's word) but deeply engaged philosopher at Columbia University, namely, John Dewey. Hobbes was glaringly wrong, we now recognize, to speak so loftily and disparagingly of the scientific significance of Boyle's experiments with air pumps, in this

respect departing from the attitude toward the Dutch inventors of the telescope taken by the prince of the Italian practitioners of the mechanical
philosophy which Hobbes himself much admired. These and many other
serendipidic infusions of governance are striking to us in part because they
constitute exceptions to the general rule that while ignorance of the broad
latent background of norms does not guarantee misjudgment and misgover-
nance, it increases liability to these sharply, and with them the sometime cost,
when these intrude into grave and important issues, as in the steep cost,
socially and scientifically, to genetic theory and practice in the former Soviet
Union of a philosophic partiality to Lamarckian principles. In general in
reflective philosophical governance there is no substitute for intimate, broad,
deep, and mature understanding of both the manifest and the latent aspects of
the norms under governance. This applies whether the norms in question, for
example, are those clustered about determinism in its application to minute
physical particles or to human action, or, for a further example, whether they
are norms with respect to congressional action respecting "an establishment
of religion" in their application to tax laws or to the respectful display of
religious symbols on state property.

37 Setting out from the exploration of some philosophical aspects of what is
involved in action following norms, as that topic was broached in a distinctive way by Wittgenstein, this paper proceeded to expound the thesis that
understanding of these aspects entails a very considerable reconception of
norms themselves. And this reconception in turn leads to a considerable,
indeed radical, reconception of what it is like to govern, reform, reconstruct,
or otherwise reorder these norms. We engage in these latter activities; we
develop new norms and reform old ones when the ready patterns of activity
that we call "custom," "habit," and the rest, no longer suffice: when for one
reason or another patterns already in place no longer suffice to guide action.
Needing, for one reason or another, new patterns, we proceed, with varying
degrees of awareness of what we are doing, to craft them. In consequence,
the procedure of governance of norms is always in some degree legislative.
"Legislative" is of course a heavy word suggesting as it often does deliberation, decision and enactment. But not all legislating is of this formal and self-
conscious kind. We now recognize that people vote with their feet as well as
with their hands, their larynxes, and other parts of their bodies. And similarly
they "legislate," they develop and install norms in a great variety of ways.
Think, for example, of the variety of ways in which the norms of speech and
writing of the English language in the United States are constantly crafted in
use, in practice, rather than by teaching and doctrine, though the effect of
governance of this latter, more formal kind is also continuous and great.
Expounding on "The Results of Human Action But Not of Human Design,"
F. A. Hayek wrote:

we need merely to consider languages, which today nobody believes to have been "invented" ... in order to see that reason and civilization develop in constant mutual interaction. But what we no longer question with regard to language ... is by no means generally accepted with regard to morals, law, the skills of handicrafts or social institutions.[1]

38 A first step toward understanding the governance of norms is breaking free of the fixation upon the manifest contents of them. Proceeding from this, a further step is comprehending, in the relations between manifest and latent contents, how it is integral to the character of norms that the former aspects serve as expressions of the latter, and, reciprocally, that in their character as expressions of the latter, these manifest aspects help define, they help form the identity of the latent ones that they express. Thus the latent aspects generate and determine the character of manifest ones, which in turn, realizing this character, react upon and help determine the character of the latent ones that, in this determination, contribute to their own definition.

Reflective governance, of which philosophical governance is one broad and variegated species, is one important way in which this mutual determinative process takes place and generates its effects. This mutual determination characterizes, it is integral to, the kind of reflective governance that has been here called "ampliative." Insufficient understanding of it, indeed a resolute and almost complete lack of such understanding, has been for many in modern and contemporary philosophy an effective block to the development of a realistic, illuminating, and practicable conception of ampliative philosophical governance. Understanding of this mutually determinative process is a powerful solvent of the major difficulties that the development of a satisfactory conception of ampliative philosophical governance has long encountered in theory and practice. The broad character of ampliative governance of norms, in its various forms, is that of crafting expressions of broad latent contents in the mode of more or less routine responses that are themselves, as realized in these responses, subject to both stabilizing and mutative effects of these responses.[2] This being so, it is thoroughly inappropriate, if not perverse, to attempt to rationalize such a procedure on the model of the kind of use of norms in which such mutual effects are so far as possible suppressed. The procedure to be understood and rationalized is integrally—not fatally, but blessedly—both legislative and judicial; and the imputed faults for which it

[1] *New Studies in Philosophy, Politics, Economics and the History of Ideas* (Chicago: University of Chicago Press, 1978), 4.

[2] [Cf. above chs. 7, 8.—*Ed.*]

has been condemned by centuries of rationalistic criticism are, rather, fundamental virtues.

Finally, given the richness of resource for governance available in the manifest contents of norms, the development of novel normative effects in the process of governance is a commonplace, requiring for its understanding and criticism no intellectual legerdemain or conjuration. Ampliative effects upon norms are not generated solely by and out of other manifest norms. They arise out of, are supported or rejected by, a rich mass of practice, commitment, aspiration, hopes, expectations, ideals, and other more or less rich and binding attachments. These effects are, in short, generated and validated by more or less broad segment of the life that they express. And that life includes always, in some form, and however obscure, visions of what it might be, might be desired to be, as well as what, at any moment, it is.

39 This last point deserves some emphasis and explication. As was noted earlier, norms, in both their manifest and latent aspects, occur in more or less extended, more or less systematic and coherent clusters. These clusters define in a variety of more or less loose ways, certain broad forms of human activity: for example, types of crafts and other vocational pursuits; various forms of sports and other games; forms of economic practice, of scientific pursuits and pursuits in law, politics, religion, and so on. Peirce began one of his better known papers with a comment that

> every physicist, and every chemist, and, in short, every master in any department of experimental science, has his mind moulded by his life in the laboratory to a degree that is little expected.[1]

What is true of the laboratory is also true of the classroom, as it is true of the cloister, the vicarage, the court, the playing field, the newspaper or television newsroom, the legislature, the sales room, the medical clinic, the machine shop, the farm, and the armory. And what the laboratory scientist—to return to Peirce's example—develops in his scientific work, is not restricted to refined knowledge of fact, skill, and theory, as they are embodied in the presently followed practices of his discipline. Also developing in him, though there are great variations among individuals in this respect, is some sense of what this discipline might become if certain potentialities in it were realized. This sense or vision, with its embedded hopes, aspirations, and dispositions, is most often a very implicit part of one's indoctrination in and assimilation to a certain kind of endeavor. Resident in the individuals engaged in the endeavor, it emerges in times of controversy and indecision in the governance of norms. Commonly it dictates no resolution of the contro-

---

[1] "What Pragmatism Is" (1905), *Collected Papers* 4:272, §111.

versy and indecision, but rather sets some parameters which that resolution must respect. Indistinct as these parameters may be, in so far as they extend they are governing and controlling, and so far as they extend they are genuinely normative in relation to the course of the endeavor at hand.

Thus it is that there is a resource for governance in any considerable human enterprise that, in the fashion of Montesquieu's celebrated title, one might refer to as the "spirit" of the enterprise, or, in more Hegelian idiom, might refer to as its "will." Those indoctrinated in the Cartesian-Lockean identification of thought with consciousness will have some difficulty seeing in these terms more than striking metaphors. It may reduce the difficulty for some of these if they reflect upon the homely, concrete circumstance that we do not hesitate, but rather we insist that there is more to the character of an individual person than a collection of habits, dispositions, and velleities resident in that body. So there is more to any considerable human enterprise than a collection of individual norms.

40 Perhaps sufficient has been said to make clear that the employment of the component of governance discerned here does not render that governance a weak form, or indeed any form at all, of calculative decision procedure. Both the component and the procedure are hard to characterize in a philosophical language much molded by now deeply entrenched modern rationalistic preconceptions. The term "dialectic" has been pulled so many ways from the time of Plato, through Hegel, Marx, and the post-Hegelian idealists, as to render its effect at the present time in defining the procedure more to confuse than clarify. In her valuable exposition of Aristotle's views on practical reason, Martha Nussbaum employs the apt phrase "nonscientific delibera-tion."[1] The phrase by itself is primarily negative in force and in her usage is supplemented positively by what in the present writer's judgment are unfortunate infusions of somewhat raw elements of passion, appetite, love, and mania. In his essay on "Political Education,"[2] Michael Oakeshott used to good effect (and also bad effect) the term "intimations" to refer to the resources in life from which a broad, responsive, tentative judgment of governance may be made. A primary benefit was the emphasis on the broad resources that are the grounds of governantial judgment, and on the proper tentativeness of such judgment. An unfortunate effect was the possibility, all too easily realized, that responsiveness to the intimations implied to many an appeal to intuition in its more cloudy and disreputable forms.

[1] *The Fragility of Goodness* (Cambridge: Cambridge University Press, 1986), ch. 10.

[2] *Rationalism in Politics* (London: Methuen, 1962), 111–36.

An apt term for the kind of procedure referred to here as it appears in a very fundamental way in juridical judgment was introduced into the philosophy of law by Henry M. Hart and Albert M. Sacks. It was the expressed judgment of these authors that the "gradual spread of the obligation of reasoned decision and elaboration [was] one of the major phenomena of contemporary law,"[1] and that the standards of this process, as applied to the Supreme Court, required, among other things, that their reasons supporting decisions exemplify "the maturing of collective thought."[2] In the jurisprudential battlefield laid waste by the oppressing barrages of the legal positivists and those precursors of contemporary Critical Legal Studies, the Legal Realists, this philosophical seedling did not flourish.

A recent and, for a variety of historical reasons much more influential, characterization of the bases of such a process was presented to American legal thought by Justice W. O. Douglas in the Griswold (1965) decision affirming the right of married persons to use contraceptive devices. Speaking for a majority in the Court, Justice Douglas urged as a basis for the above right a more general right, that of privacy, discerned by him as emerging from "penumbras, formed by emanations" from the specific rights enunciated in the Bill of Rights. Eight years later, in the majority opinion in *Roe v. Wade*, Justice Blackmun employed this right as a major basis for affirming the constitutional right of women to terminate their pregnancies under broadly defined circumstance. Important as the matter is, whether or not there is such a right is not central here. If such a right can be developed by reasoned elaboration of the rights specified in the Bill of Rights, as we have them today, surely that elaboration can be delineated in a more sober, less airy and almost perversely figurative way. It has been one of the main objectives of this present essay to increase understanding of the bases and procedures by which more sober, convincing, and thoroughly acceptable elaborations can be made.

In the semantic contest between such terms as "intimations" and "emanations," on the one hand, and "nonscientific deliberation" and "reasoned elaboration" on the other, the latter and similar expressions must not be permitted to mask the optative, connotative, and aspirant elements that are essential components in the latent aspects that are constantly expressing themselves, losing their identities, and finding them in the manifest aspects of our norms. It is equally important that emphasis on these latter elements not

---

[1] Henry M. Hart and Albert M. Sacks, *The Legal Process* (temp. ed. Cambridge, Mass.: 1958), William N. Eskridge Jr. and Philip P. Frickey, eds. (Mineola, N.Y.: The Foundation Press, 1994).

[2] These quotations are taken from G. Edward White, *Patterns of American Legal Thought* (Indianapolis: Bobbs-Merrill, 1978), 144 and note 25.

be permitted to overshadow or even exclude recognition of the deliberative, reasoned aspect of these same processes. Failure to resist this common inclination (an *Idola Theatri* of our time) is a serious defect in Sanford Levinson's stimulating recent book, *Constitutional Faith.*[1] The use of the model of religious faith in the exploration of aspects of constitutional thought and practice is illuminative of some of the aspects of the governance of norms that have just been emphasized here. There is surely, let it be said plainly, an aspect of faith in our proceeding in this governance, which is open to sober inspection, even by those not transfixed by Hegelian dialectic or dazzled by the brilliance of some "Post-Modern" criticism. And further, this aspect of governance may be recognized and assimilated to the reasoned, deliberative aspects of this process without permitting it, like an aggressive young cuckoo, to end by ejecting these latter aspects from their naturally proper nests. Yet, so strong and enduring has been the contrary supposition, that one is tempted to expand the characterization of particular *Idola* from *Theatri* to *Tribus.*

41 "Profundity is the alcohol of the intellect" is one of the many acute epigrams attributed to that analytic philosophic genius of a generation ago, J. L. Austin. Danger of intoxication is one of the lesser hazards of most aspirants to philosophical depth, and should not deter one from the valuable insights conveyed in the comparison of the acceptance of broad constitutional provisions with religious faith, with the correlated conception of "civic religion," and with others of the expressions with which a variety of writers have sought to capture the conative and trusting components of life and thought that infuse a certain spirit and will into the norms by which that life and thought are informed. Millennia of theologians have striven to teach us that the faiths to which we devote ourselves need not be blind. Furthermore, the will of an individual or group need not be, indeed almost never is, a fully conscious articulated will. "To know what one wills," said Hegel, "and even more, what the will which has being in and for itself—i.e. Reason—wills, is the fruit of profound knowledge and insight."[2] On a much less lofty, more homely level, one may observe that an individual or group may not recognize expressions of such a will as their own until that expression has been more fully achieved. Then it is not paradoxical, but even common for an appreciative reaction to be, "Yes, I guess that is the sort of thing actually that I was aiming at, though I could not have said so at the time."

[1] Princeton: Princeton University Press, 1988.

[2] *"was der an und für sich seinde Wille, die Vernunft, will"*; *Elements of the Philosophy of Right*, A. Wood, ed., H. B. Nisbet, tran. (Cambridge: Cambridge University Press, 1991), §301 Remark; tran. emended.

That one could not have said so, in cases like this, is not due merely to a failure of an individual or group to articulate a will already existent but needing only translation in some chosen mode ("to put in words," as the embarrassed student frequently says about what he says he knows). This is one of these frequent, hardly noticed cases in which the agent, say one individual person, in articulating an act of will does not merely report on some previously existent state, but rather in articulating, completes, for the moment, that state. One sits down to write a letter, "knowing" what one wants to say, and little notices, the letter having been written, that prior to the completion of this act, there was nothing whatever in one's mind of which the completed letter could be regarded as a replica. One sits down to write a paper, as the present writer did some time ago, and the product later diverges markedly from anything he could have imagined and foretold. The paper written, reread, and revised repeatedly is and is not the paper that one set out to write: *is not*, for undeniably the present product diverges markedly from anything one could have articulated and recognized as one's own before its actual production; *is*, because the actual production of it is the process through which an act of will of this kind gets to be made.

Analogous comments apply to the formation of the will of groups of individuals including the large groups that form national communities. In the fifty-eight years since *Plessy v. Furgeson*, in response to many influences that help form our national consciousness, including to some considerable extent the constant reformation of resolve entailed in waging a war against the undemocratic Axis Powers, the people of the United States began to form and articulate a resolve against state sponsored and supported racial segregation. As is now well recognized, the most prominent and important agents in formulation and articulation of this resolution were the Federal courts, and in a crucial act of will, the decision of the Supreme Court in *Brown v. Board of Education* (1954). These courts, their legislative, administrative, and other nonofficial opponents and supporters, did not discover the rationale of this act ready-made but implicit in the Bill of Rights of the United States Constitution, nor in some more lofty catalogue of human rights in general. Not spokesmen for some Platonic directive that had somehow escaped even great Plato, and not amanuenses of the one great World Spirit, all these agents were engaged in the formulation and articulation of the will of the national community: a will partly adumbrated in the celebrated Bill of Rights, in the Thirteenth, Fourteenth, and Fifteenth Amendments to the Constitution, and drawing upon, as Lincoln so eloquently said in his First Inaugural Address, "the mystic chords of memory ... all over this broad land ... touched ... by the better angels of our nature."

Those with fresh memories of the articulation of these aspects of the national will, and its further articulation through almost four decades of legislative and administrative expansion and reverberation, need hardly be reminded that the formation and implementation of such an act of communal will is an extremely long process, and not least in the conditions prolonging this particular act were ambiguities, gaps, and imperfections exposed in various forms of it as it slowly established itself as an item of national constitutional policy. Among the imperfections strongly urged by some was the partial displacement and neglect in the elaborating opinion of the kinds of fundamental grounds available in the Fourteenth Amendment in favor of much more contingent and disputable claims about the educational and psychological effects of racial isolation. One of the gaps in the will as articulated in the 1954–55 decisions, still the subject of great debate, is to what extent a constitutional bar to individious racial discrimination entails a similar constitutional sanction, even demand, for the kind of well-intentioned discrimination now widely practiced under the title of "affirmative action."

42 Much of what this paper expounds about the governance of norms was either taught expressly or adumbrated by Dewey in a different idiom in the first half of this century. The primary ambition of the paper has been, not to rehearse old lessons, but to carry what may be called the theory of governance one small step beyond the instrumentalist version elaborated by Dewey. This it has attempted to do mainly by bringing to prominence in the general theory an element that the occasionalist emphasis of Dewey had somewhat, to the detriment of the theory, neglected.

The element in question is, in general, the latent aspect of norms. And it is, more specifically, a feature of this aspect that is more and more important, and finally crucial, as the subjects of governance are of that special broad and deep character that renders them philosophical. A variety of expressions, some borrowed and some not, have been employed to try to capture and expose this crucial feature. The "spirit" or "will" of the enterprise, the individual, the group, or the community seem to assist the process of definition, as do also in some ways such coinage as "constitutional faith," "civic religion," and the rest. Tempting as it is to reach back into the vasty depths of Hegelian metaphysics and exploit that master's distinction between "existence" and "actuality,"[1] experience teaches that this route of explication is usually far more obscuring than clarifying.

As is well known, in treating the role played by intelligence in the reformation of habits, Dewey repeatedly stressed that the authority of acts of governance lies in the capacity of these to meet the needs of the problematic situation in which the governance occurs and to which it ministers. In the view outlined here there is more emphasis on the role of the complex

---

[1] *The Encyclopedia Logic*, G. F. Geraets, W. A. Suchting, and H. S. Harris, trans., (Indianapolis: Hackett, 1991), §6 Remark.

latent aspect of norms, extending far beyond the immediate situation yet deeply implicated in defining the needs of the situation and thereby determining the authority of steps taken to meet it. It is understandable that, breaking away from the grand holistic idealism of Hegel and the great remove to which it seemed to put any point of definitive decision in governance, Dewey wished to emphasize the propriety of piecemeal governance that does not pretend to absolute finality and incorrigibility. The present view does not so much deny the role of the needs of the situation, as, rather, expand the boundaries of these needs, emphasizing that definition of these requires sensitivity to the latent aspect of the norms one is engaged with, however vague, incomplete, and discordant that aspect may be.

A wise commentator on the educational process once defined education as what you have left after you have forgotten all you have learned. This witticism obliquely refers to an aspect of our education, our culturation, training, and formation, which Oakeshott strove to call attention to in the distinction he drew between "technical" and "practical" knowledge.[1] An individual engaged in political activity directed to the governance of norms, a legislator, a judge, a teacher, a scientist, a member of the clergy—all these speak and act legitimately and with authority in the governance of norms when they do so, not in their capacities as individuals, but as spokesmen for, as articulators of, the spirit or will of the enterprise, the facet of life that they represent. This spirit or will is constantly aborning and dying. There is nothing mystical about it. We are constantly engaged with it: in the family, the faculty meeting, the church council, in the political party, at the ballot box, as well as in those greater, sometimes triumphant, sometimes tragic cases as when the people of the United States, after travail on the subject reaching back into the preceding century, finally did make up their mind, in a welter of blood and iron, about slavery. Cannon and bayonets have been and remain methods of the determination of the will, though the rising costs of their employment, especially when the cannon takes the form of multiple-head, multiple-directed nuclear armed intercontinental missiles, argue for extreme economy in if not total abstinence from their use.

The location of the formation and articulation of all these and sundry other multiform activities of governance, if understood, annihilates the now forlorn hope that somehow, somewhere, a magic philosophical formula will be devised that will enable serious philosophical minds to pierce, once and for all, the fog of indecision that attends ampliative governance when it is engaged with norms that broadly and deeply give form to our lives and thought. The agitation, doubt, indecision, controversy, *etc.*, are not ailments suffered, not symptoms of disease, but normally signs of health. The idea that

---

[1] "Rationalism in Politics," in *Rationalism in Politics*, 1–36.

a fully healthy individual or community would be free of these processes and activities is as fatuous as the supposition of Midas that, once given his magic touch, he would be supremely, happily rich.

43 A second, much lesser contrast between the view of governance conveyed in Dewey's writings and that outlined here is that the present view emphasizes more pronouncedly than Dewey the continuity of reflective governance (be that governance philosophical or not) with unreflective processes constantly going on, processes that are integral themselves to norms, to our very activities in following them. The continuity of these two kinds of process was elaborated by the present writer at various places in *Beyond Deduction*,[1] as well as in an earlier chapter.[2] The central contention on this point is that *reflective* governance is a continuation of governance in general, a process that we engage in constantly and necessarily while following norms. It is a continuation at a high level of awareness of this general, broader process, of which at most times we are as little aware as Molliere's Bourgeois Gentleman was aware that he was speaking prose. However, it bears saying that what difference of emphasis there may be on the particular point between the view of reflective governance outlined here and Dewey's views as they apply to the same subject is extremely minor in relation to the greater confluence of view concerning what in the idiom of this paper would be termed "the naturalization of governance," or what Dewey would no doubt have preferred to speak of more generally as "the naturalization of intelligence."

44 It is easy for one who has grasped the determinative role in philosophic governance of what has here been termed the "spirit of the enterprise," to be led by long habituation with deductive methods to conceive this determination in a broadly deductive, hence unilateral mode. Recognizing that commonly in cases of philosophic governance there are competing candidates for recognition as the determinative spirit, such a person may reason that proper employment in governance of any candidate implies that its claim to be superior to the others must be capable of being determined independently of any consideration of appraisal of its determinative effects. That is to say, the determination of norms effected properly by the "spirit" must be altogether unilateral with respect to these norms, must be determinative altogether *for* them, in no degree *by* them.

45 This is fatally wrong: fatally, that is, for any adequate understanding of philosophic governance. For the superiority of any reading of the spirit, in such a case, is itself determined in part by its relations with the norms under governance. Apart from these, apart from their relative capacities to compose

---

[1] Cf. 209–13, 223–27.
[2] [Ch. 4 above.—*Ed.*]

the conflict among them that has generated the need for governance, there is no possible determination of better and worse. Superiority here is something that often can only be guessed at and can be determined with assurance only by the way in which one or another competitor succeeds in effecting a resolution of the conflict that originally gave rise to the governing activity. Essential to understanding governance as it occurs at this crucial philosophical point is the avoidance of the seemingly strong temptation to treat the process as a rarified form of the foundational cum deductivist model.

46 For what is needed in a case of governance that is responding to conflict between hitherto accepted readings of the spirit of the enterprise, is not some increasingly forceful appeal to one or more parties of that conflict. It is rather some new reading, some new version, some new entrant into the arena that is capable in some substantial degree of composing the hitherto apparently irrepressible conflict. A new version of the spirit establishes its credentials, not because of what sanctions it can offer that are independent of the determinative effects it may have upon the competing versions and the logical force it can exert over these competitors, but rather through its composing effect upon the competitors, upon the versions of "constitutional faith" that each represents.

47 Given the richness of the resources for philosophic governance emphasized in this paper, given all the ways in which these resources limit the indeterminacy between occasion and results in these governantial processes, there remain in the process ineradicable elements of indeterminacy. The typical occasions of philosophical governance are those in which for one reason or other accepted, ready-to-hand norms are insufficient to guide decision and action. Aspirant governors trained in and committed to deductivist procedure will continue to search and fail to discover occult, recondite norms that will enable them to avoid the disagreeable indeterminacy. Here philosophic minds need to learn the merit of the common practice of learning to live with, and then learning to appreciate the absolute indispensability to reflective human life of this indeterminacy. For it is out of occasions of such indeterminacy, out of the frustration, indecision and painful travail in them, that new norms, superseding forms of life, are developed. *Solvitur ambulando.*

48 Of course, this does not mean that on these occasions reflective guidance of the norms concerned can make no contribution to the reduction of the indeterminacy and the attendant indecision: that the norms in question must retire, as it were, to the sidelines, until somehow, from the melee of unrelated activity new norms emerge, fully armed, like the fabled Athena, with an immediate sanction and sure direction to the contexts of appropriate application. For typically a major indispensable source of new norms is norm-influenced action itself. In it norms are crafted and refined; not given *to* activity, but generated *by* it, as the Sabbath, we are enjoined to remember, was made for man, not man for the Sabbath.

49 During the latter half of the present century the Existentialist philosophers more than members of any other single movement have emphasized the incompleteness of traditional rationalistic methods, using accepted norms, to provide guidance to thought and action at many junctures in our lives. The particular way in which the Existentialists elaborated this point has historical roots extending back at least as far as Hegel.

50 This sound view of the indeterminacy of traditional recursive methods in effecting governance of norms needs to be supplemented with a view of the resources available for governance beyond the canon of strictly applicative methods. These acts need not always be, if they ever are, the expressions of some kind of individual pure will, inclination, or velleity. Both individuals and communities may be condemned to freedom; they are not in governance condemned to blindness. Further, in its application to governance of a philosophic kind this view very greatly needs to be supplemented by emphasis upon the metaindividual, communal character of the norms concerned and the similar character of the acts and results of such governance.

51 By what authority does any individual or group speak or act in philosophic governance? Governance being the kind of procedure that has been portrayed here, one speaks with authority of reflective governance—the results of one's reflective governance have authority—only to the extent that these results represent some plausible reading of the spirit of the group, the enterprise, and so on, of which the norms are constitutive elements: to the extent to which the results can be shown to be more or less legitimate expressions of that spirit. It was emphasized earlier that legitimate steps in the governance of norms arise from the norms themselves: the norms, not in their truncated abstract manifest form as supposed templates of thought and action; but these more fully with their rich sustaining latent aspects and—now more important—as the constantly continuing sources of the most general, less specific aspects of the totality referred to as the "spirit."[1] To the extent that rival proposals of governantial results are indistinguishable in the force of their claims to be legitimate expressions of that spirit, they are indistinguishable in the force of the authority that each can claim in philosophical reflection. And to the extent that one proposal is distinguishable as superior in this

---

[1] It may be helpful to some readers for me to disclaim explicitly any interpretation of the term "spirit" employed in the final pages of this essay, as referring to some brooding, etherial, more or less transient state of mind (or, linguistically, contingent state of discourse) in the community or enterprise to which it is applied. The roots of the spirit, as referred to here, embrace much in the existential setting of life and thought in the community, without which thought about norms, about ways of life, would not be possible. This fuller aspect of the spirit, though not under this name, was emphasized by me in a variety of writings, including [chs. 1 and 5 above—*Ed.*] and *Beyond Deduction*, esp. 96–97.

respect, that one is superior in authority. Thus, when based upon reflection upon the norms concerned in any act of governance, one speaks or acts in the governance of them, in the furtherance of change or in maintenance against change, one speaks legitimately not as an individual presuming, as Hegel ironically put it, to tell the world "how it ought to be, but is not,"[1] but as a spokesman of some aspect of that world, projecting into the interstices and conflicts of given norms what, consonantly with the spirit which they embody, they may be expected to manifest both in the way of maintenance and in the way of change. One speaks legitimately for the spirit, not for oneself or for any contingent collection of individuals, only to the extent that oneself, or those individuals, are already adherent to the spirits now under elaboration in the governance. Both individuals and communities are enduringly engaged, sometimes intensely and sometimes much less, in the constant elaboration of the various components of spirit, and hence in the elaboration of their identities and the various norms of thought and action that are components of these identities. This process permeates, and also draws upon, all the important aspects of their lives. It embraces elements of ambition, faith, hope, and love, along with elements of lethargy, diffidence, despair, distaste, and rejection. However formless and vague the instinct, both individuals and communities in moments of reflective governance share the aspiration that at later times they can look back with equanimity upon those acts of governance, reflective or otherwise, that were instrumental in the process of moving from where they were once to where they are now, that they can view those acts with a minimum of embarrassment, regret, and shame, and a maximum of well-founded satisfaction and pride.[2]

---

[1] *The Encyclopedia Logic*, §6 Remark.

[2] I'm very pleased to have the opportunity to thank publicly Ken Westphal for the great help he has been in encouraging my work on this chapter.

Bibliography

I. Writings of Frederick L. Will.

1940a. "Verifiability and the External World." *Philosophy of Science* 7, no. 2: 182–91.

1940b. "Internal Relations and the Principle of Identity." *The Philosophical Review* 49, no. 5: 497–514.

1942a. "Democracy and the Managerial Revolution." *Journal of Social Philosophy and Jurisprudence* 7, no. 2: 172–80.

1942b. "Is there a Problem of Induction?." *The Journal of Philosophy* 39, no. 19: 503–13. Rpt. in *Belief, Knowledge, and Truth*, R. Ammerman & M. Singer, eds. New York: Scribner's, 1970, 344–52.

1947. "The Contrary-to-Fact Conditional." *Mind* 56, no. 223: 236–49.

1948a. "Will the Future Be Like the Past?." *The Philosophical Review* 56, no. 224: 231–47. Rpt. in *Logic and Language*, 2nd Series. A. Flew, ed. Oxford: Blackwell, 1953; *A Modern Introduction to Philosophy*, P. Edwards and A. Pap, eds. Glencoe, Ill.: Free Press, 1957; *Philosophic Problems*, M. Mandelbaum, F. Gramlich, and A. Anderson, eds. New York, Macmillan, 1957. German tran. in *Philosophie und normale Sprache*, E. von Savigny, ed. Freiburg: Alber, 1969; Italian tran. in *Induzione e uniformita del mundo*, A. Meotti, ed. Milan: Editioni Di Communita, 1978.

1948b. "Donald Williams' Theory of Induction." *The Philosophical Review* 57, no. 3: 231–47.

1948c. "Values, Objectivity, and Democracy." In *Essays In Political Theory*, M. Konvitz and A. Murphy, eds. Ithaca: Cornell University Press, 257–78.

1948d. "Generalization and Evidence." In *Philosophical Analysis*, M. Black, ed. Ithaca, NY: Cornell University Press, 257–78.

1950. "Skepticism and the Future." *Philosophy of Science* 17, no. 3: 336–46.

1951. "Relativism and Experimental Inference." *Philosophy of Science* 18, no. 2: 155–69.

1954. "Kneale's Theories of Probability and Induction." *The Philosophical Review* 63, no. 1: 19–42.

1955. "The Justification of Theories." *The Philosophical Review* 64, no. 3: 370–88.

1959. "Justification and Induction." *The Philosophical Review* 68, no. 3: 359–72.

1963. "Language, Usage, and Judgment." *The Antioch Review* 23, no. 3: 273–90.

1964. "Intention, Error, and Responsibility." *The Journal of Philosophy* 61, no. 5: 171–79.

1965. "The Preferability of Probable Beliefs." *The Journal of Philosophy* 62, no. 3: 57–63. Italian tran. in *Edizioni Di Communita*, Milan.

1966. "Consequences and Confirmation." *The Philosophical Review* 75, no. 1: 34–58.

1969. "Thoughts and Things." *Proceedings and Addresses of the American Philosophical Association* 42 (1968–69): 51–69.

1972. "Philosophy, Institutions, and Law." *Modern Age* 16, no. 4: 279–86.

1974. *Induction and Justification: An Investigation of Cartesian Procedure In the Philosophy of Knowledge*. Ithaca, N.Y.: Cornell University Press.

1976. "The Future Revisited." *Philosophical Studies* 30, no. 2: 111–14.

1977. "Truth and Correspondence." *The Philosophical Forum* 9, no. 1: 60–77.

1979. "The Concern About Truth." In *The Bertrand Russell Memorial Volume*, G. Roberts, ed. London: George Allen and Unwin, New York, Humanities Press, 264–84.

1981a. "The Rational Governance of Practice." *The American Philosophical Quarterly* 18, no. 3: 191–201. Rpt. in *Hermeneutics and Praxis*, R. Hollinger, ed. Notre Dame, In.: University of Notre Dame Press, 1985, 192–213.

1981b. "Reason, Social Practice, and Scientific Realism." *Philosophy of Science* 48, no. 1: 1–18. Rpt. in *Hermeneutics and Praxis*, 122–42.

1983. "Reason and Tradition." *Modern Age* 27, no. 2: 171–179. Rpt. in *The Journal of Aesthetic Education* 17, no. 4 (1983): 99–105.

1985a. "Rules and Subsumption: Mutative Aspects of Logical Processes." *The American Philosophical Quarterly* 22, no. 2: 143–151.

1985b. "Pragmatic Rationality." *Philosophical Investigations* 8, no. 2: 120–142. German tr. in *Die eine Vernunft und die vielen Rationalitäten*, M. Kettner and K.-O. Apel, eds. Frankfurt am Main: Suhrkamp, 1996, 296–317.

1988. *Beyond Deduction: Ampliative Aspects of Philosophical Reflection.* London: Routledge.

1989. "Response to Fukuyama." *The National Interest* 17: 99–100.

1993. "Philosophic Governance of Norms." *Jahrbuch für Recht und Ethik/ Annual Review of Law and Ethics* I: 329–61.

1996. *Pragmatism and Realism.* K. R. Westphal, ed. Lanham, Md.: Rowman and Littlefield.

II. Works Cited.

Austin, John L. 1950. "Truth." *Proceedings of the Aristotelian Society*, sup. vol. 24: 111–28. Rpt. in Pitcher, 1964, 18–31; and in Nagel and Brandt, 1963, 166–76.

Austin, John L. 1946. "Other Minds." In Flew, 1965, 342–80.

Blandshard, Brand. 1961, *Reason and Goodness.* London: George Allen and Unwin.

Bradley, Francis H. 1893. *Appearance and Reality.* Oxford: Clarendon Press.

Carnap, Rudolf. 1950/1956, "Empiricism, Semantics, and Ontology." *Revue International de Philosophie* 4 (1950): 20–40. Revised ed. in *Meaning and Necessity.* Chicago: University of Chicago Press, 1956, 205–221.

Carnap, Rudolf. 1952. *The Continuum of Inductive Methods.* Chicago: University of Chicago Press.

Carnap, Rudolf. 1963. "Replies and Systematic Expositions." In *The Philosophy of Rudolf Carnap*, P. A. Schilpp, ed. Library of Living Philosophers, 859–1013.

Carroll, Lewis. 1895. "What the Tortoise Said to Achilles." *Mind* N.S. 4: 278–80.

Descartes, René. 1911. *The Philosophical Works of Descartes.* Trans. E. S. Haldane and G. R. T. Ross. Cambridge: Cambridge University Press, 2d ed. 1967.

Descartes, René. 1958. *Descartes' Philosophical Writings.* Ed. and tran. N. K. Smith. New York: Modern Library.

Dewey, John. 1896. "The Reflex Arc Concept In Psychology." *Psychological Review* 3. Rpt. in *John Dewey: The Early Works.* Carbondale and Edwardsville: Southern Illinois University Press, 1972, vol. 5, 96–109.

Dewey, John. 1922. *Human Nature and Conduct.* New York: Holt.

Dewey, John. 1929. *The Quest for Certainty*. New York: Minton Bach.

Dewey, John. 1941. "Propositions, Warranted Assertibility, and Truth." *Journal of Philosophy* 38. Excerpted in Nagel and Brandt, 1963, 152–60.

Dewey, John. 1939. "Replies." In *The Philosophy of John Dewey*. P. A. Schilpp, ed. Evanston and Chicago: Northwestern University Press, 517–608.

Ducasse, Curt J. 1951. *Nature, Mind, and Death*. La Salle, Il.: Open Court.

Dworkin, Ronald. 1981. "Dissent on Douglas." *The New York Review of Books* (February 19): 3–8.

Flew, Anthony, ed.. 1965. *Logic and Language: First and Second Series*. New York: Anchor.

Foote, Shelby. 1968. *The Civil War*, vol. 1. New York: Random House.

Galileo, Galelei. 1989. *Sidereal Messenger*. Tran. A. van Helden. Chicago: University of Chicago Press.

Gellner, Ernest. 1962. "Concepts and Society." Rpt. in *Rationality*, B. R. Wilson, ed. Oxford: Blackwell, 1970, 18–49.

Goodman, Nelson. 1978. *Ways of World-Making*. Indianapolis: Hackett.

Hart, Henry M., and Albert M. Sacks. 1958. *The Legal Process*. W. N. Eskridge Jr. and P. P. Frickey, eds. Mineola, N.Y.: The Foundation Press, 1994.

Hayek, F. A. 1978. *New Studies In Philosophy, Politics, Economics and the History of Ideas*. Chicago: University of Chicago Press.

Hegel, G. W. F. 1807. *The Phenomenology of Spirit*. Tran. A. V. Miller. Oxford: Clarendon, 1977.

Hegel, G. W. F. 1821. *Elements of the Philosophy of Right*. Tran. H. B. Nisbet. A. Wood, ed. Cambridge: Cambridge Univeristy Press, 1991.

Hegel, G.W.F. 1830a. *Enzyklopädie der philosophischen Wissenschaften* I. In *Werke In Zwanzig Bänden*. E. Moldenhauer and K. M. Michel, eds. Frankfurt am Main: Suhrkamp, 1970, vol. 8.

Hegel, G. W. F. 1830b. *The Encyclopedia Logic*. Trans. G. F. Geraets, W. A. Suchting, and H. S. Harris. Indianapolis: Hackett, 1991.

Hegel, G. W. F. 1953. *Reason In History*. Tran. R. S. Hartman. Indianpolis: Bobbs-Merrill.

Holmes, Oliver Wendel. 1920. "Holdsworth's English Law." In *Collected Legal Papers*. New York: Harcourt, Brace and Co., 285–90.

Hume, David. 1739–1740. *A Treatise of Human Nature*. L. A. Selby-Bigge, ed. Oxford: Clarendon, 1888.

Hume, David. 1936. *Enquiries Concerning the Human Understanding and Concerning the Principles of Morals.* L. A. Selby-Bigge, ed. Oxford: Clarendon Press.

Hume, David. 1987. "The Sceptic." In *Essays: Moral, Political, and Literary.* E. F. Miller, ed. Indianapolis: Liberty Fund.

Janik, Allan, and Stephen Toulmin. 1973. *Wittgenstein's Vienna.* New York: Simon and Schuster.

Junk, Robert. 1958. *Brighter than a Thousand Suns.* Tran. J. Cleugh. New York: Harcourt, Brace and World.

Kripke, Saul A. 1982. *Wittgenstein on Rules and Private Language.* Oxford: Blackwell.

Kuhn, Thomas S. 1962. *The Structure of Scientific Revolutions.* Chicago: University of Chicago Press.

Lakatos, Imre. 1963–64. "Proofs and Refutations." *British Journal for the Philosophy of Science* 14. Rpt. Cambridge: Cambridge University Press, 1976.

Leibniz, G. W. 1705/1765. *New Essays on Human Understanding.* Trans. P. Remnant and J. Bennett. Cambridge: Cambridge University Press, 1981.

Levi, E. H. 1948. *Introduction to Legal Reasoning.* Chicago: University of Chicago Press.

Levinson, Sanford. 1988. *Constitutional Faith.* Princeton: Princeton University Press.

Lewis, Clarence I. 1929. *Mind and the World Order.* New York: Dover, 2d rev. ed. 1956.

Locke, John. 1690. *Essay Concerning Human Understanding.* A. C. Fraser, ed. New York: Dover, 1959.

Luker, Kristen. 1984. *Abortion and the Politics of Motherhood.* Berkeley: University of California Press.

Meyerson, Émile. 1908. *Identity and Reality.* Tran. K. Loewenberg. New York: Dover, 1962.

Mill, John S. 1843. *A System of Logic,* 2 vols. London.

Murphy, Arthur E. 1964. *The Theory of Practical Reason.* La Salle, Il.: Open Court.

Nagel, Ernest, and Richard B. Brandt, eds. 1963. *Meaning and Knowledge.* New York: Harcourt, Brace and World.

Newton, Sir Isaac. 1687. *The Mathematical Principles of Natural Philosophy (Principia).* Tran. A. Motte, revised F. Cajori. Berkeley: University of California, Press, 1934.

Newton, Sir Isaac. 1704. *Optics.* New York: Dover, 1952.

Nowell-Smith, P. H. 1954. *Ethics*. Harmondsworth: Penguin.

Nozick, Robert. 1981. *Philosophical Explanations*. Cambridge, Mass.: Harvard University Press.

Nussbaum, Martha. 1986. *The Fragility of Goodness*. Cambridge: Cambridge University Press.

Oakeshott, Michael. 1962. *Rationalism In Politics*. London: Methuen.

Orwell, George. 1949. *Nineteen Eighty Four*. New York: Harcourt, Brace and Co.

Peirce, Charles S. 1931–1935, 1958. *Collected Papers*. C. Hartshorne, P. Weiss, and A. Burks, eds. Cambridge, Mass.: Harvard Univeristy Press.

Pitcher, George, ed. 1964. *Truth*. Englewood Cliffs, N.J.: Prentice-Hall.

Plato. 1961. *The Collected Dialogues of Plato*. E. Hamilton and H. Cairns, eds. Princeton: Princeton University Press.

Quine, W. V. O. 1960. *Word and Object*. Cambridge, Mass.: MIT Press.

Quine, W. V. O. 1969. *Ontological Relativity*. New York: Columbia University Press.

Quine, W. V. O. 1978. "Review of Goodman, *Ways of World-Making*," *New York Review of Books* 25, no. 18 (November 23): 25.

Raphael, D. D. 1975. "The Standard of Morals" and "Appendix" to "The Standard of Morals." *Proceedings of the Aristotelian Society* 75: 1–12, 12A–12E.

Rorty, Richard. 1972. "The World Well Lost." *Journal of Philosophy* 69: 649–65.

Royce, Josiah. 1885. *The Religious Aspect of Philosophy*. Boston: Houghton, Mifflin.

Russell, Bertrand. 1912. *The Problems of Philosophy*. New York: Oxford University Press.

Russell, Bertrand. 1921. *The Analysis of Mind*. London: Allen and Unwin, New York: Macmillan.

Russell, Bertrand. 1923. "Dr. Schiller's Analysis of *The Analysis of Mind*." *Journal of Philosophy* 19: 645–51.

Ryle, Gilbert. 1949. *The Concept of Mind*. New York: Harper and Row.

Sartre, Jean Paul. 1936–1937. *The Transcendence of the Ego*. Trans. F. Williams and R. Kirkpatrick. New York: Farrar, Straus and Giroux, 1957.

Shapere, Dudley. 1969. "Notes toward a Post-Positivistic Interpretation of Science." In *The Legacy of Logical Positivism*, P. Achinstein and S. F. Barker, eds. Baltimore: Johns Hopkins University Press, 115–60.

Shapere, Dudley. 1975. "Copernicism as a Scientific Revolution." In *Copernicus*, A. Beer and K. A. Strand, eds. *Vistas In Astronomy* 17: 97–104.

Shwayder, David S. 1961. *Modes of Referring and the Problem of Universals.* University of California Publications in Philosophy 35.

Skinner, Quinton. 1978. "The Flight from Positivism." *New York Review of Books* (June 15): 26–28.

Smith, Adam. 1776. *The Wealth of Nations.* New York: Random House, 1937.

Smith, Norman Kemp. 1952. *New Studies In the Philosophy of Descartes.* London: Macmillan.

Steveson, Charles L. 1943. *Ethics and Language.* New Haven: Yale University Press.

Strawson, Peter. 1949. "Truth." *Analysis* 9. Excerpted in Nagel and Brandt, 1963, 160–66.

Stroud, Barry. 1965. "Wittgenstein and Logical Necessity." *The Philosophical Review* 74: 504–518. Rpt. in *Wittgenstein: The Philosophical Investigations,* G. Pitcher, ed. Notre Dame, Ind.: Notre Dame University Press, 1966, 477–96.

Toulmin, Stephen. 1974. *Human Understanding,* vol. I. Princeton: Princeton University Press.

Tuchman, Barbara. 1966. *The Proud Tower.* New York: Macmillan.

Urmson, J. O. 1975. "A Defense of Intuitionism." *Proceedings of the Aristotelian Society* 75: 111–19.

Waismann, Frederick. 1945. "Verifiability." In Flew, 1965, 122–51.

Wechsler, Herbert. 1961. *Principles, Politics and Fundamental Law.* Cambridge, Mass.: Harvard University Press.

White, G. Edward and J. Harvie Wilkinson, III. 1977. "Constitutional Protection for Personal Lifestyles." *Cornell Law Review* 62, no. 3. Rpt. in White, 1978, 308–81.

White, G. Edward. 1978. *Patterns of American Legal Thought.* Charlottesville: Michie, Indianapolis: Bobbs-Merrill.

Wittgenstein, Ludwig. 1921. *Tractatus Logico-Philosophicus.* Trans. D. F. Pears and B. F. McGuinness. London: Routledge and Kegan Paul, 1960.

Wittgenstein, Ludwig. 1953. *Philosophical Investigations.* Tran. G. E. M. Anscombe. London: Macmillan.

Wittgenstein, Ludwig. 1956. *Remarks on the Foundations of Mathematics.* G. H. von Wright, R. Rhees, eds. Ed. and tran. G. E. M. Anscombe. Cambridge, Mass.: MIT Press.

Index

abortion, 107, 145, 173
Adler, Mortimer, 116
affirmative action, 187
argument, 28, 108, 137–39, 147, 153
Augustine, 177
Austin, J. L., 10, 11, 13, 14, 26, 46, 47, 163, 185
Axis Powers, 186

Bacon, Francis, 66, 142
Bergson, Henri, 69
Berkeley, George, 6, 30, 43, 44, 109, 120, 173
Bierce, Ambrose, 119
Blackmun, Justice Harry, 184
Blandshard, Brand, 58
Boyle, Robert, 98, 179
Bradley, Francis, 15, 28
Brandt, Richard, 40, 42, 46
Burgess, Gilett, 12

Carroll, Lewis 26, 128
Cassio, 45, 47, 48, 60
cat, 10, 11, 25, 27, 28, 32, 45, 46, 51–56, 169
coherence, 15, 25, 41, 43, 51, 91, 94–96, 141
coherence illusion, 91, 94–96, 141
Columbus, Christopher 99
concept, 9, 11, 13, 16, 21, 24, 40, 59, 69, 82, 145
conceptual scheme, 29, 35
convention, 48
conventionalism, 132
court, 58, 59, 64, 76, 94, 107, 114, 118, 134, 135, 150, 152, 153, 175, 182, 184, 186
    judge, 72, 114, 135, 137, 150, 151, 153, 188
    juridical judgment, 76, 151, 184
custom, 35, 67, 83, 111, 113–15, 145, 146, 148, 180
    great guide of life, 35, 67, 146, 148

decision procedure, 59, 156, 183
definition, 1, 11, 21, 24, 29, 42, 124, 129, 148, 151, 159, 162, 165, 181, 187, 188
    ostensive, 24
Democritus, 48, 57

200

Descartes, René, 3–6, 14, 15, 17, 23, 38, 43, 48, 50, 51, 55, 58, 59, 65–67, 86, 107, 108–12, 148, 174, 177
 Cartesianism, 3, 6, 15, 23, 25, 41, 67, 83, 103, 106, 107, 111, 122, 183
 cogito, 3, 86
Desdemona, 45, 47, 48, 52, 53, 60
Dewey, John, 2, 28, 29, 36, 42, 45, 67, 69, 163, 179, 187–89
dialectic, 163, 167, 179, 183, 185
discrimination, racial, 118, 187
Doppelgänger, 26, 46, 163
Dostoyevsky, 177
doubt, 5, 19, 32, 40, 47, 54, 61, 68, 77, 80, 82, 83, 103, 111, 113, 146, 188, 189
Douglas, Justice William O. 152, 153, 163, 184
Dworkin, Ronald, 152, 153

education, 72, 92, 116, 118, 183, 186, 188
emotivism, 154
enculturation, 72
Ernst, Philip, 9
Euclid, 168
euthanasia, 168
evaluation, problem of, 161
existential situation, 92, 95, 96, 131
existentialism, 155, 191
exploration, 22, 35, 38, 56, 97–99, 141, 163, 171, 180, 185

Fermi, Enrico, 102
Fisk, Milton, 31
formalizability, 138
formula, 45, 98, 123, 145, 146, 148, 155, 169, 188

foundational, 86, 122, 123, 177, 190
framework, 15
Franklin, Benjamin, 118
Freud, Sigmund, 57

Galileo, Galelei, 17, 50, 55, 99, 100, 172
Gellner, Ernest, 65
Gilbert, William, 50
Golden Rule, 178
goldfinch, 10, 11, 13
Goodman, Nelson, 103, 165
governance, 63–68, 70–77, 79–83, 89–97, 99–104, 106, 110, 149, 157, 159, 161, 162, 163, 167, 168, 174–83, 185, 187–92
 in practice, 71
 of practice, 63–67, 71, 80, 93, 104
 rational, 63, 64, 66–68, 70, 72–75, 77, 80–83, 92, 95, 110
guitar, 12–13

habit, 48, 147, 180
Hahn, Otto, 102
Hamlet, 83
Hart, Henry M. 163, 184
Hayek, F. A., 180
Hegel, G. W. F., 7, 21, 31, 32, 43, 67, 76, 77, 81, 82, 144, 149, 183, 185, 188, 191, 192
Heraclitus, 78
Hobbes, Thomas, 6, 7, 17, 50, 98, 108, 179, 180
Holmes, Oliver Wendel, 83, 179
Hume, David, 7, 17, 18, 23, 35, 43, 48, 57, 59, 66, 67, 109, 133, 142, 146, 148, 149, 151, 152, 168

Hutchins, Robert M. 116

indeterminacy, 75, 145, 149, 151, 190, 191
induction, 6, 18, 19, 65–67, 87, 93, 142, 148, 155, 168, 177
    inductive projection, 165
intentionality, problem of, 169

James, William, 1, 21, 38, 98, 120
Jefferson, Thomas, 118
judgment, 15, 22, 34, 41, 44–48, 51–54, 60, 63, 75–77, 82, 91, 94, 112, 114, 115, 121, 133, 135, 151, 153–56, 161, 162, 166–68, 175, 177, 178, 179, 183, 184
    evaluative, 161, 167
    juridical, 76, 151, 184
Jupiter, 37, 99, 100

Kant, Immanuel, 17, 25, 28, 41, 43, 49, 78, 88, 148, 165
    categorical imperative, 165
    Critique of Pure Reason, 44
    dogmatic slumber, 14
    thing–in–itself, 30, 31, 88
Kelvin, Lord, 145
Kepler, Johannes, 100
Kitty Hawk, 90
Kripke, Saul, 130
Kuhn, Thomas, 71, 87, 138, 148

Lakatos, Imre 146, 147
Langford, C. H. 17
language
    ideal, 23
    private, 67, 130, 131
law, 36, 64, 72, 75–79, 82, 83, 107, 108, 114, 117, 125, 134, 137, 145, 146, 150–54, 163, 171, 178, 179, 181, 182, 184
    constitutional, 77, 134, 145, 146, 151
    Bill of Rights, 152, 184, 186
    Critical Legal Studies, 184
    equal protection clause, 135, 145, 146, 150, 151
    legal realism, 149, 151–54
    legal system, 72
    natural, 79
    Supreme Court decisions (USA), 145-46
        Brown v Board of Education, 186
        Griswold, 184
        Plessy v Furgeson, 186
        Roe v Wade, 184
learning, 69–71, 78, 79, 97, 100, 102, 116, 124, 174, 175, 179, 190
Lehman, Warren, 153
Leibniz, G. W., 6, 10, 13, 43, 110
Levi, E. H. 150
Levinson, Sanford, 163, 185
Lewis, C. I., 26, 87, 128, 141
Lincoln, Abraham, 42, 117, 186
Locke, John, 10, 23, 43, 48, 50, 51, 66, 109, 148
logic. See also symbolic system
    of discovery, 144
    logical necessity, 67, 130–32, 149, 160
    logical positivism, 56, 67
    logistic, 53, 126, 130, 132, 134
    modus ponens, 133, 178
Luker, Kristen, 173

map, 31, 32

Marshall, John, 134
Marx, Karl, 62, 109, 121, 149, 183
mathematics, 164*f. See also* rule
   arithmetic, 55, 138
   calculus, 140
   geometry, 18, 168
mechanical, 116, 145, 180
Meitner, Lise, 102
Mendel, Gregor, 98
Meyerson, Émile, 50
Mill, J. S., 127, 142
Molliere, 189
Montesquieu, 183
Murphy, Arthur, 45, 58, 110

Nagel, Ernest, 40, 42, 46
naturalism, 161, 166, 168
navigation, 99
Newton, Sir Isaac, 50, 56, 87, 100, 101
norms, 36, 105, 110, 114, 159–85, 187–92
     liveness of, 160, 167
     manifest and latent aspects, 160–63, 165–71, 174–76, 178–79, 181–82, 187, 188
     openness of, 160, 167. *See also* open texture
     template view of, 160
Nowell-Smith, P. H., 58
Nozick, Robert, 133
Nussbaum, Martha, 183

Oakeshott, Michael, 163, 183, 188
occasionalism, 187
occasions and responses, 69, 160, 163, 170, 171, 175, 176
open texture, 10, 11, 129–30, 170
Oswald, Lee Harvey, 32
Othello, 47, 53, 60

ought, should be, is/ought, 1, 15, 38, 41, 49, 51, 58, 76–77, 116, 127, 133–34, 155, 166, 168, 173, 192

Pascal, Blaise, 75
Peirce, Charles Saunders, 1, 21, 32, 38, 67, 81, 82, 89, 106, 107, 118–20, 142, 182
Pitcher, George, 40, 46, 132
Plato, 10, 51, 59, 76, 78, 177, 183, 186
post-modernism, 185
practice, 13, 14, 23, 26, 27, 36, 38, 42, 43, 54, 55, 58, 61, 63–75, 77–81, 85, 87, 88, 90–95, 97, 98, 102–04, 106, 107, 112, 113, 115, 121–25, 127–29, 134, 135, 139–41, 143, 149–52, 154, 157, 160, 164, 165, 168, 172, 175, 180–82, 185, 190
pragmatic theory, 43
proposition, 26, 45, 46, 96, 163, 164, 168, 175
Protagoras, 25
puzzle-solving, 138, 139, 142

qualities, primary and secondary, 48
Quine, W. V. O., 70, 87, 103, 141

Ramsey, Frank P. 26, 46
Raphael, D. D., 154–56
Rawls, John, 155
reactive effects, 127, 132, 133
realism, 9, 30, 31, 85, 88, 90, 95, 120, 143, 149, 151–54, 156
reason, 1, 12, 16, 24, 34, 41–44, 49, 51, 56, 58, 63–68, 76, 79–83, 85, 90, 93, 98, 103, 105–13, 115, 116, 119, 124, 129, 133, 137, 139, 144, 148, 151, 152, 170, 174, 180, 181, 183, 185, 189, 190

reflection, 3, 14, 17, 50, 56, 80, 81, 93, 103, 109, 133, 135, 156, 162, 165, 166, 168, 175, 176, 178, 179, 191, 192
reflective reconstruction, 161, 170
reflex, 69, 124
relativist illusion, 91, 94
Religion
    Catholic, 72, 109, 128
    civic, 185, 187
    Muslim, 167
    Protestant, 72, 94, 109, 167
replication, 126, 171
revolution, 41, 43, 86, 101
Rorty, Richard, 30, 31, 62, 103
routine action, 123
Royce, Josiah, 28, 52
rule, 75, 86, 123, 125–33, 138, 150, 155, 163–65, 178, 180
rules of application, 11, 129
Russell, Bertrand, 28, 41, 43, 47, 48, 59, 60
Ryle, Gilbert, 59

Sartre, Jean Paul, 59
science, 22, 28, 29, 36, 38, 45, 51, 56, 59, 63, 71, 73, 75, 86–88, 91–93, 97, 98, 102–04, 107, 110, 116, 133, 134, 143, 144, 147, 148, 149, 151, 167, 178, 182
    atomic physics, 102
    chemistry, 102, 182
    electron, 28, 56
    phlogiston, 59
scientific agnosticism, 148
scientific realism, 85*ff.*
scientific revolution, 101
seeing as, 67
semantic atomism, 22–24

senate, university, 129
Shapere, Dudley, 56, 100, 101
Shwayder, David, 56, 62, 157
Skinner, Quentin, 89
Smith, Adam, 110
Smith, Norman Kemp, 4, 108
Socrates, 76, 133
soldier, 69, 70
Spinoza, Baruch, 6
Strassmann, Fritz, 102
Strawson, Peter F., 26, 46, 47, 61
Stroud, Barry, 132
subsumption, problematic, 125
subsumption, routine, 124, 126, 127
symbolic system 36, 93, 123–26, 130, 133, 140, 141

Tarski, Alfred, 146
technology, 98, 143
terms
    distinction between observational and theoretical, 22, 24, 25
    empirical 11
Thales, 48
Toulmin, Stephen, 39, 65
tradition, 1, 49, 50, 57, 65–67, 79, 100, 105–07, 109, 111–19, 131
truth. *See also* coherence
    concern about, 27, 39, 40, 47–51, 60–62
    correspondence, 15, 21–30, 32–38, 41, 43, 45–47, 51, 52
    problem of, 39, 49, 50, 54, 61

Urmson, J. O., 154–56

value, problem of, 168
verification, 1, 6, 14, 15, 24

Waismann, Friedrich, 10–12, 39
warrant, 121–25, 127
wax, 48, 112
Webster, Daniel, 12
Wechsler, Herbert, 83

White, G. Edward, 53, 107, 184
Wittgenstein, Ludwig, 7, 10, 11, 31, 37,
    39, 58, 59, 67, 112, 130–32, 149,
    159, 160, 164, 165, 179, 180

About the Author

Frederick L. Will was born on May 8, 1909 in Swissvale, Pa. He received his A.B. from Thiel College (Oxford) in 1929, his M.A. from The Ohio State University in 1931, and his Ph.D. from Cornell University in 1937. He was made D. Litt. by Thiel College in 1965. He taught at the University of Illinois in Urbana-Champaign from 1938 to 1977, when he became Emeritus Professor of Philosophy. He was a John Simon Guggenheim Memorial Fellow in 1945-46 and a Senior Research Fulbright Scholar at Oxford in 1961. He held visiting positions as Professor of Philosophy at Cornell University in 1955 and 1964-65, and at the University of California at Irvine in 1978. He has previously published two books, *Induction and Justification* (Ithaca, N.Y.: Cornell University Press, 1974) and *Beyond Deduction* (London: Routledge, 1988), and numerous articles which are listed above in the bibliography.